HAWAI'I'S BEST

PŪPŪ & POTLUCK

HAWAI'I'S BEST

PŪPŪ & POTLUCK

JEAN WATANABE HEE

MUTUAL PUBLISHING

Library of Congress Catalog Card Number: 2004100628

First Printing, May 2004
Second Printing, October 2004
Third Printing, February 2006
Fourth Printing, April 2007
Fifth Printing, May 2009
Sixth Printing, September 2010
Seventh Printing, June 2011
Eighth Printing, March 2012
Ninth Printing, April 2014
Tenth Printing, February 2016
Photography by Ray Wong

Art direction by Jane Hopkins with Sistenda Yim
Design by Sistenda Yim

Mutual Publishing, LLC
1215 Center Street, Suite 210
Honolulu, Hawai'i 96816
Ph: (808) 732-1709
Fax: (808) 734-4094
email: info@mutualpublishing.com
www.mutualpublishing.com

Printed in South Korea

Dedication

To Cheryl and Jennifer. We are so proud of you. Thank you for being who you are and for your total love and support.

And, To Popo Hee. Thank you for your dedication, love and support to all of us. You are the pillar of our family.

Acknowledgments

I want to thank my husband, Don, for all he has done for me in putting this cookbook together. Without his help and support it would have been very difficult for me. Thank you for your patience. Thank you for your assistance on the computer. I also appreciate your taste-testing the recipes and giving me your honest opinion.

To my friends and family who contributed their best recipes and who were also recipe tasters, I thank you for your support and help.

Table of Contents

Introduction   x
Poke Dishes
  'Ahi Limu Poke   2
  Aku Poke   3
  Imitation Crab Poke   3
  Ono Poke   4
  Ono Shrimp Poke   5
  Poke   6
  Seared 'Ahi Poke   7
  Shoyu Poke   8
  Tofu Poke   8
  Tako Poke   9
Dips & Spreads
  Artichoke and Crab Dip   11
  Caviar Spread   12
  Clam Dip   13
  Curry Mango Cream Cheese Spread   14
  Guacamole   15
  Hot Crab Dip   16
  Kamaboko-Crab Dip   16
  7-Layer Dip   17
  Spicy Hot Bean Dip   18
  Spinach Dip   19
  Vela-Bailey Almost Homemade Salsa   20
  Vienna Sausage Spread   21
Sushi Bar
  Vinegar Sauce for Sushi   23
  California Inside Out Sushi   24
  Easy Cone (Inari) Sushi   25
  Hawaiian-Style California Rolls   26
  Layered Sushi   27
  Maki Sushi   28

Ono Broiled Sushi 30

Shinko Maki 31

Spam® Musubi 32

Spicy Tuna 33

Temaki Roll 34

Somen or Soba Sushi 35

Pūpū—Meat

Barbecue Sticks 37

Easy Spareribs 38

Fried Ginger Pork 39

Gyoza (Pot Stickers) 40

Kalbi 41

Lumpia 42

Mini Laulau Pūpū 43

Manapua 44

Peppered Steak 46

Pipikaula (Beef Jerky, Hawaiian-Style) 47

Pork Adobo Pūpū 48

Pūpū-Style Spareribs 49

Shish Kabob 50

Siu Mai 51

Spam® Won Ton 52

Spam® Won Ton with Green Chilies 53

Spring Rolls 54

Stuffed Fried Lotus Root 55

Won Ton 56

Taco Won Ton 57

Teriyaki Meatballs 58

Pūpū—Chicken

Buffalo Wings 60

Easy Macnut Chicken Drummettes 61

Fried Chicken Drummettes 62

Garlic Chicken 63

Oven-Barbecued Chicken Wings 64

Parmesan Chicken Pūpū 65
Sesame Seed Chicken 66
Sweet-Sour Chicken Wings 67
Tasty Chicken Pūpū 68
Yaki Tori Sticks 69

Pūpū—Seafood

Clams and Ground Pork Pūpū 71
Cocktail Shrimp 72
Crab Cakes 73
Crab-Stuffed Mushrooms 74
Deep-Fried Oysters 75
Easy Shrimp Skewers 75
Fishcake and Spam® Pūpū 76
Furikake Seared 'Ahi 77
Namako (or Konnyaku) Pūpū 77
Lomi Salmon on Skewers 78
Mimi's Shrimp 79
Octopus (Tako) Pūpū with Miso Sauce 80
Oyster Bacon Wrap 81
Oyster Rolls 82
Salt and Pepper Shrimp 83
Shrimp Lumpia 84
Bacon-Wrapped Shrimp 85
Seared 'Ahi 86
Shrimp Tempura 87
Shrimp Toast 88
Squid Pūpū (Fried Calamari) 89

Pūpū—Variety

Aburage Pūpū 91
Boiled Peanuts, Chinese-Style 92
Chili Burrito Rolls 93
Deviled Eggs 94
Evie's Local-Style Party Mix 95

Furikake Arare Popcorn   96

Microwave Boiled Peanuts   96

Green Onion Pretzels   97

Lavosh   98

Onion Rings   99

Potato Skin with Imitation Crab Filling   100

Ogo Kim Chee   101

Sesame Pancake Croquettes Pimetees Snack   102

Spicy Edamame (Soybeans)   103

Spinach Rolls   104

Veggie Pizza   105

Warabi Appetizer   106

Potluck

Crispy Gau Gee   108

Chili   109

California Pan Sushi   110

Gon Lo Mein   111

Korean Chicken Wings   112

Lasagne   113

Mochiko Chicken   114

Mun Doo   115

Potato and Macaroni Salad   116

Seafood Salad   117

Shrimp and Kamaboko Tempura   118

Somen Salad   119

Warabi Sushi Rice   120

Taegu Ocean Salad Linguine   121

Stuffed Aburage with Somen   122

Glossary   123

Index   125

Introduction

This cookbook project started out with pūpū, soups and salads in mind. After completing *Hawai'i's Best Desserts* and *Hawai'i's Best Local Dishes,* I now wanted a cookbook in my kitchen that had local pūpū, soup and salad recipes in it. I started gathering my favorite recipes in all three areas. As I began gathering my recipes, I had to remember which cookbook or which recipe file I needed to go to, for example, to find my favorite spinach dip or best dressing for my Chinese chicken salad. At the same time I was cross-referencing and comparing recipes as well.

I soon found myself concentrating only on pūpū recipes trying to organize myself. The list of pūpū grew and I was busy testing them all and writing them so they could be easily followed. My daughter, Cheryl, encouraged me to work only on a pūpū cookbook which she could immediately refer to whenever she needed a favorite recipe. Then, while I was in Maui, Glynnis Ooka also encouraged me to publish a local pūpū cookbook. She felt there was a need for one. Other friends had similar advice. So I put my soup and salad recipes on hold for a later project and focused on pūpū.

The taste is local! I have a section on poke, just a sample of the many varieties of poke that are being created in the market. Instead of buying poke already seasoned, get a pound or two of 'ahi cubes sold unseasoned. Use a poke recipe and adjust it perfectly to your taste. (I have tried fresh, frozen 'ahi cubes with terrific results.)

The sushi section has some fabulous recipes. Be sure to try the "California Inside Out Sushi" and the "Spicy Tuna" sushi. And, of course, the traditional "Maki Sushi." I tried to make it easy and simple to follow. It does take some practice to roll a sushi, but the results will be worth it.

From "Vienna Sausage Spread" to "Caviar Spread," there is a wide choice to choose from. Artichoke hearts are the "in" thing now with young adults. A favorite is the "Artichoke and Crab Dip." Also very popular are hot and spicy pūpū like the "Spicy Hot Bean Dip."

I added a potluck section because pūpū and potluck really go together in Hawaiʻi. One of our best forms of entertainment is to get together at each other's homes, at the beach, tailgating at the stadium, or at the soccer field after a game. Everyone brings something. We love our "heavy pūpū" type of party. And how we love our mixed ethnic dishes! How about Korean chicken wings or kalbi, sushi, poke, won ton and some noodles on the side?

Poke Dishes

ʻAhi Limu Poke

yield: 4-6 appetizer servings

* *

1 pound ʻahi, cut into bite-size pieces
1/4 cup green onion, finely chopped
1 small Maui onion, finely sliced
1/2 cup limu, roughly chopped
1/2 teaspoon sesame oil, adjust to taste
Hawaiian salt, to taste
chili pepper water, to taste or use chili pepper seeds
1/2 teaspoon kukui nut (ʻinamona), to taste

Combine all ingredients and mix well. Adjust seasonings. Refrigerate.

Chili Pepper Water

1 quart water
2 tablespoons Hawaiian salt
2 to 3 dry Hawaiian chili peppers

Boil water. Add salt and stir to dissolve. Remove from heat and let stand until cool. Rinse peppers and place in glass jar. Add salt water. Let stand for one day. Store in refrigerator. (Serve with lomi salmon, poke and stew.)

Aku Poke

yield: 4-6 appetizer servings

* *

1 pound aku, cut in 3/4-inch squares
1 teaspoon Hawaiian salt
1 teaspoon shoyu
1 tablespoon water
1 teaspoon sesame oil (begin with less, adjust to taste)
1/4 cup raw limu, chopped

Combine all ingredients; toss lightly. Refrigerate for at least
1 hour before serving.

Imitation Crab Poke

yield: 10-12 appetizer servings

* *

1 pound imitation crab sticks, cut diagonally into 1/2 to 1 inch
    slices
2 to 3 tablespoons shoyu
1 tablespoon water
1/2 teaspoon sesame oil
1/4 teaspoon pepper
pinch sugar
1/2 small onion, thinly sliced
1 small cucumber, seeded and thinly sliced (optional)

Combine all ingredients (except imitation crab); mix well.
Add imitation crab and toss gently. Refrigerate until ready to
serve.

Ono Poke

yield: 2-4 appetizer servings

* *

1/2 pound aku, 'ahi or marlin
1/2 teaspoon 'inamona
1/4 teaspoon sesame oil
2 pinches Hawaiian salt
1/2 ball fresh limu kohu, thinly sliced
splash of chili pepper water or seeds of Hawaiian chili
    pepper

Cut fish in cubes 1/2-inch to 1-inch. Mix 'inamona, sesame oil and Hawaiian salt. Lomi into the diced fish. Place limu kohu over fish cubes. Add splash of chili water or Hawaiian chili pepper seeds (adjust to taste). Mix together. Refrigerate until ready to serve.

Note: See recipe for "Chili Pepper Water" on page 2.

Ono Shrimp Poke

yield: 4-6 appetizer servings

* *

1 pound shrimp
1/2 teaspoon 'inamona
1/4 teaspoon sesame oil
2 pinches Hawaiian salt
1 tablespoon green onion, finely chopped
seeds of small Hawaiian chili pepper

Clean and devein shrimp; cut into bite-size pieces. Place shrimp in boiling water for about 5 seconds, or until color changes. Drain and cool. Mix rest of ingredients and lomi into the shrimp. Add chili pepper seeds to taste. Chill.

Poke

yield: 6-8 appetizer servings

* *

2 pounds aku, 'ahi or tako
1/4 cup limu, coarsely chopped
1 clove garlic, minced
1/2 cup green onion, finely chopped
1 teaspoon sesame seeds
1 tablespoon oyster sauce
1 tablespoon shoyu
2 teaspoons sesame seed oil
1 teaspoon Hawaiian salt, adjust to taste
1 small Hawaiian chili pepper, seeded and minced

Combine all ingredients and toss gently. Adjust any of the seasonings to your taste. Chill before serving.

Seared 'Ahi Poke

yield: 4-6 appetizer servings

* *

1 pound 'ahi, cut in bite-size pieces
1 tablespoon fresh ginger, grated
1 tablespoon peanut oil

Combine 'ahi, ginger and peanut oil. Mix together. Heat non-stick pan until very hot. Add 'ahi and stir-fry until charred. Remove from heat and cool. 'Ahi should still be red in the middle.

2 tablespoons shoyu
2 tablespoons oyster sauce
1/2 tablespoon sesame oil
1 Maui onion, sliced
1 firm tomato, chopped
1 stalk green onion, chopped
3 tablespoons limu, chopped
Hawaiian salt, to taste
pepper, to taste
1 tablespoon 'inamona (optional)

Mix together shoyu, oyster sauce and sesame oil; set aside. When 'ahi is cooled, drain if necessary and add shoyu mixture and all other ingredients; toss together. Season with salt and pepper. Refrigerate.

Shoyu Poke

yield: 4-6 appetizer servings

* *

1 pound aku, cut in bit-size pieces
1/4 cup green onion, chopped
1/2 teaspoon roasted sesame seeds
1/4 cup shoyu
1 teaspoon fresh ginger, grated
1/2 teaspoon 'inamona
1 Hawaiian chili pepper, seeded and minced

Combine all ingredients and mix well. Chill before serving.

Tofu Poke

yield: 6-8 appetizer servings

* *

1 block firm tofu (20-oz.), drained and cut into 1" cubes
1/4 cup limu, coarsely chopped
2 tablespoons green onion, chopped
2 teaspoons roasted sesame seeds
1/2" fresh ginger, grated
1 small chili pepper, seeded and chopped, adjust to taste
1/4 cup shoyu
1 tablespoon sesame oil

Place tofu cubes in mixing bowl. Add limu, green onion, sesame seeds, ginger and chili pepper to tofu and toss lightly. Mix shoyu and sesame oil. Pour over tofu cubes. Toss lightly. Place in serving bowl and chill before serving.

Tako Poke

yield: 4-6 appetizer servings

* *

1 to 2 pounds tako, cooked and thinly sliced in diagonal
   pieces
1/2 to 1 cup limu (limu or limu and kohu combination),
   chopped
2 pinches Hawaiian salt, adjust to taste
2 to 3 pinches 'inamona
dash chili pepper water, to taste
1/4 cup green onion, chopped
1/2 teaspoon sesame oil or 2 pinches roasted sesame seeds

Mix tako and rest of ingredients and adjust seasoning to
your taste.

Dips & Spreads

Artichoke and Crab Dip

yield: 6-8 servings

* *

1 can artichoke hearts, water-packed (14-oz.)
2 cans crab meat (6-oz. each), drained
2 cups mayonnaise
1/2 cup grated Parmesan cheese
1/2 cup Maui onion, thin slivers
1/4 teaspoon Tabasco® sauce
1 teaspoon parsley flakes
garlic salt, to taste
paprika for sprinkling

Drain and coarsely chop artichoke hearts. Mix all ingredients together (except paprika). Place in 9-inch square pan or ovenround dish. Sprinkle with paprika. Cover and bake at 350°F for 30 to 40 minutes. Uncover and broil 10 minutes before serving or until top is brown. Serve hot with crackers or bread.

Variation: Substitute water-packed artichoke hearts with 2 jars marinated artichoke hearts (6.5-oz.each). Substitute crab meat with imitation crab.

Note: Evelyn Shiraki, my neighbor and a great cook, shared this great dip which is very popular with young adults.

Caviar Spread

yield: about 20 appetizer servings

* *

2 packages cream cheese (8-oz. each), softened
1/2 cup onion, finely chopped
1/2 cup mayonnaise
2 teaspoons lemon juice (about 1 lemon)
1/2 teaspoon cayenne pepper
2 jars Romanoff® black caviar (3.5-oz. each)

Combine first five ingredients. Spoon out cream cheese mixture and form a dome-shaped mound on serving platter. Refrigerate for 30 to 45 minutes until firm. Smooth caviar onto cream cheese mound with small spatula and cover completely. (Soak excess liquid from caviar with paper towel.) Refrigerate. Serve with crackers of your choice (i.e. Carr's® Table Water® Crackers).

Note: This caviar spread is kind of expensive but it makes a very elegant and delicious spread for a very special occasion. If desired, low-fat cream cheese and mayonnaise may be substituted. You can cut the recipe in half for less servings. Wonderful with a glass of wine!

Suggestion: To remove last remaining caviar from jars, rinse out jars with water and strain remaining caviar.

Clam Dip
yield: 1-1/2 cups

* *

1 package cream cheese (8-oz.)
1 can minced clams (7.5-oz.); drained, reserve clam juice
1 tablespoon onion, finely minced
1 heaping tablespoon mayonnaise
1 teaspoon lemon juice
salt and pepper to taste
Worcestershire sauce, to taste (optional)

Leave cream cheese at room temperature to soften. Blend cream cheese, mayonnaise and enough clam juice for good dipping consistency. Add rest of ingredients. Chill. Serve with potato chips.

Note: Family and friends have been using this favorite dip ever since we got this recipe from Jean Tanimoto about 30 years ago!

Curry Mango
Cream Cheese Spread

yield: 10-12 servings

* *

2 packages cream cheese (8-oz. each), softened
1-1/2 teaspoons curry powder
1/2 teaspoon dry mustard powder
1/2 cup mango chutney (Major Grey's Chutney brand
    recommended)
2 teaspoons green onion, chopped (green part only), optional
1/4 cup sliced toasted almonds
1 box crackers (e.g, Carr's® water crackers, Ritz® crackers)

Place cream cheese in large bowl to soften; set aside. Mix together curry powder and dry mustard. Mix in mango chutney. Add to softened cream cheese; mix together thoroughly.

In medium-size plastic container with lid, sprinkle almonds and green onions on bottom of container. Spread curry cream cheese mixture over green onions and almonds. Cover with lid and refrigerate for at least one hour. Use butter knife to loosen mold from around the sides of container. Place serving plate on top of container and turn over. Serve with crackers.

Note: This is one of those spreads that are such great hits at parties and passed on from friend to friend. It not only tastes great but also displays nicely. Thank you to Faye Lynn Au for sharing this recipe. This spread is also great with Tandoori Chicken.

Guacamole

yield: about 1 cup

* *

1 large ripe avocado, peeled and pitted
1/2 cup onion, finely chopped (adjust to taste)
1/2 tomato, seeded and diced
1 teaspoon lemon juice
1 tablespoon mayonnaise
1/2 teaspoon salt
1/2 teaspoon chili powder
1 teaspoon Worcestershire sauce
Tabasco® sauce, to taste

Mash avocados to a coarse texture. Add rest of ingredients and mix thoroughly. Cover and refrigerate 30 to 60 minutes before serving.

Note: When covering guacamole, place plastic wrap directly on dip to keep color fresh. Mix just before serving.

Hot Crab Dip

yield: 6-8 servings

* *

8 ounces imitation crab sticks
2 cups sharp Kraft® Cheddar cheese, shredded
1/2 onion, finely chopped
1/4 cup parsley, minced
2 cups mayonnaise
pepper to taste

Cut crab sticks in fourths; shred coarsely. Squeeze out excess water. Combine all ingredients and mix well. Pour mixture into casserole dish. Bake at 350°F for 20 to 25 minutes. Serve hot with warm French bread or crackers.

Note: My sister-in-law, Evie, made this for a gathering of relatives, and it was gone in no time.

Kamaboko-Crab Dip

yield: 3-1/2 cups

* *

1 block kamaboko (6-oz.), minced
8 ounces imitation crab, shredded
1/4 cup green onion, minced
1 cup sour cream
1 cup mayonnaise
garlic salt and pepper to taste

Mix all ingredients. Cover and refrigerate for 30 minutes. Serve with vegetables or crackers.

7-Layer Dip
yield: 12-15 servings

* *

1 can refried beans (12- to 16-oz.)
1 carton sour cream (8-oz.)
1 carton avocado dip (8-oz.)
1 cup or more Cheddar cheese
1 can mild chili salsa (7-oz.)
1 can olives (5-oz.), sliced
1 large tomato, diced

Layer ingredients in order listed in 9 x 13-inch pan or in 2 smaller serving dishes. Cover with plastic wrap and refrigerate. Serve with crackers or tortilla chips.

Note: This is another favorite that's been around for a long time!

Spicy Hot Bean Dip

yield: 9x13 inch pan

* *

1 package cream cheese (8-oz.), softened
1 can Spicy Jalapeno Refried Beans (16-oz.)
1 can Pickled Jalapeno Nacho Slices (7-oz.), finely minced
1 cup Monterey Jack cheese, shredded
1 cup Cheddar cheese, shredded
1 container sour cream (8-oz.), for garnish
1/4 cup onion, chopped

Spread softened cream cheese evenly in 9 x 13-inch pan. Layer with refried beans, jalapeno peppers and cheeses. Bake at 425°F until hot and bubbly throughout, about 15 minutes. Remove from oven. Garnish with desired amount of sour cream and onions. Serve with Fritos® and tortilla chips.

Note: If you like spicy, you'll love this! My neighbor, Darin Mijo, gave this a thumbs-up!

Spinach Dip

yield: 4-1/2 cups

* *

2 boxes frozen chopped spinach (10-oz. each), thaw and
   squeeze dry
1 container sour cream (16-oz.)
1 cup mayonnaise
1 envelope Lipton® Onion Soup and Dip Mix
1 can minced clams (6.5-oz.), drained
1 can water chestnuts (8-oz.), drained and finely chopped
2 stalks green onion, minced (optional)

Mix all ingredients well; chill. Serve with crackers, cottage bread or vegetables.

Suggestion: Carve out center of round loaf of French bread. Cube excess bread to use as "dippers." Pour spinach dip into the center of bread. Bread can eventually be torn apart and eaten.

Note: What makes this the best spinach dip is the minced clams added to it. I love this with Ritz® crackers!

Vela-Bailey Almost Homemade Salsa

yield: 3 cups

* *

1 jar Picante brand medium hot salsa (16-oz.)
1 large tomato, quartered
1/2 cup green onion or round onion, chopped
1 cup Chinese parsley, chopped
3 cloves garlic, finely chopped

Blend all ingredients in food processor or blender. Serve with corn tortilla chips.

Note: Cecilia Vela-Bailey says that if you like your salsa flaming on your tongue, add some fresh hot pepper. Cecilia created this fantastic salsa 24 years ago and whenever she serves it, she is always asked for the recipe.

I was her daughter, Nicole's, kindergarten teacher at Aikahi Elementary School many years ago and this salsa was always a sold out hit at Aikahi's Fun Fair fundraiser every year.

Vienna Sausage Spread

yield: 1/2 cups

* *

1 can Vienna sausage (5-oz.), drained
1 tablespoon mayonnaise
2 teaspoons pickle relish
1/2 teaspoon green onion, minced
pepper, to taste
1/2 teaspoon onion, minced (optional)

Crush Vienna sausage with a fork. Add rest of ingredients and mix. Serve with crackers.

Note: This is for you old-timers who love Vienna sausage and remember eating deviled meat spreads out of a can.

Sushi Bar

Vinegar Sauce for Sushi

yield: 1-1/2 cups

* *

1 cup rice vinegar
1-1/4 cups sugar
2 tablespoons salt
3-4 dried shrimps, coarsely chopped
1 inch piece fresh ginger, crushed

Place ingredients in bowl. Mix and pour into jar. Cover tightly and shake to mix thoroughly. Set aside for sugar to dissolve. Strain before using. Use about 1/4 cup vinegar sauce for each cup of rice. Adjust to your taste.

Note: This is my mother's old recipe which we've been using when we make our traditional New Year's norimaki sushi. Any leftover vinegar sauce can be kept and used whenever needed. Vinegar sauce can also be used for cucumber namasu, to marinate carrot strips for sushi center filling, and to marinate minced onion and celery in potato and macaroni salads.

California Inside Out Sushi

yield: 10 rolls

* *

4-1/2 cups rice
1 teaspoon salt
1 cup "Vinegar Sauce for Sushi" (see recipe on page 23)
1 package imitation crab sticks (10-oz.)
1 to 2 Japanese cucumbers, peeled and seeded
1 to 2 firm ripe avocados, cut in slices
10 sheets sushi nori
white roasted sesame seeds for sprinkling

Sesame Sauce:

1/2 cup mayonnaise
2 teaspoons honey
2 teaspoons roasted sesame seeds
1/2 teaspoon sesame oil

Rinse and cook rice. Prepare sushi mat by covering one side with a plastic wrap. Overlap in back of mat and secure with tape.

Separate crab sticks in halves or thirds lengthwise. Slice cucumbers lengthwise into 10 8-inch long strips.

Remove cooked rice into large pan, sprinkle salt over and gently toss rice. Add 3/4 cup of the sushi vinegar sauce a little at a time, turning rice over gently to mix. (Reserve 1/4 cup of the sushi vinegar sauce to wet hands for handling rice.)

Place nori sheet on sushi mat as a guide to find the borders for the sushi rice. Remove nori sheet and place 1-1/3 cups of sushi rice directly on plastic wrap. Spread sushi rice evenly staying within the borders noted. Place nori sheet over rice and press lightly. About 2 inches from edge nearest to you, spread desired amount of sesame sauce in a row. Place avocado slices, crab strip and cucumber strip on top of the sesame sauce and roll. Roll like a jelly roll until rice completely surrounds nori. Squeeze gently. Remove mat and roll sushi roll in small pan sprinkled with white roasted sesame seeds. Place seam side down on waxed paper. Cut each roll into 8 pieces.

Easy Cone (Inari) Sushi

yield: 32 sushi

* *

2 cups rice
1/2 package powdered sushi mix (half of Ajishima®
    Powdered Sushi Mix package (2.65-oz.)
4 packages fully cooked and seasoned bean curd (e.g.
    Inari Sushi-No-Moto, rectangle type, 3.8-oz., 8 pieces
    per package)
2 to 3 dried shiitake mushrooms, soaked and finely chopped
1/3 cup carrot, finely chopped
1/3 cup green beans, thinly sliced
2 tablespoons shoyu
4 tablespoons water
2 tablespoons honey

Rinse and cook rice. While rice is cooking, cook mushrooms, carrot and beans in shoyu, water and honey for 15 minutes or until tender; drain.

Remove inner bag of seasoned bean curd (aburage) and place in warm water for 2 to 3 minutes. Open bag and drain bean curd.

Mix hot rice with about half package of the powdered sushi mix (adjust to taste). Fold vegetables into rice. Squeeze drained aburage to remove any excess liquid and loosely pack aburage with rice.

Note: Fast and easy because you're using ready-made seasoned aburage and instant powdered sushi mix. It's tasty and just the right size, too. A great pūpū dish suggested by Sayoko Watanabe, who can whip up a batch in no time.

Hawaiian-Style California Rolls
yield: 6 rolls

* *

2-1/4 cups rice
1/2 cup "Vinegar Sauce for Sushi" (see recipe on page 23)
6 ounces fresh 'ahi
1 teaspoon chili pepper water or chili pepper seeds (optional)
1 tablespoon shoyu
6 imitation crab sticks, cut lengthwise into halves or thirds
1 firm ripe avocado
1 lemon
1 Japanese cucumber, seeded and cut into 6 strips 8 inches
    long
1 tablespoon wasabi paste
1/2 cup mayonnaise mixed with 1 tablespoon furikake
6 nori sushi sheets

Rinse and cook rice. While rice is cooking, cut 'ahi into small cubes and marinate in chili pepper water and shoyu. Cut avocado lengthwise in slices and sprinkle with lemon juice. Prepare rest of ingredients.

Reserve 2 tablespoons of sushi vinegar sauce for wetting hands while making sushi. Add remainder of sushi vinegar sauce a little at a time to rice; toss gently to mix. Adjust amount of vinegar sauce to taste.

Place one sheet of nori on bamboo sushi mat. Spread a heaping cup of rice evenly onto bottom half of the sheet. In the middle of the rice, smear a bit of wasabi paste and desired amount of mayonnaise with furikake horizontally in a line. On top of that, place avocado, 'ahi, cucumber and imitation crab. Roll filled nori sheet halfway, then tuck gently backward, lifting mat. Finish rolling, while squeezing gently. Cut each roll into 8 pieces.

Variation: For crispy panko sushi, heat oil in large pan. Roll sushi rolls in flour, dip in egg wash then roll in panko bread crumbs. Fry sushi rolls, turning until golden brown on all sides. Drain on paper towel and slice into 8 slices.

Layered Sushi

yield: about 24 pieces

* *

4 cups rice
1 package shiofuke konbu (1.4-oz.), shake off excess salt
1/3 cup furikake nori
3/4 cup takuwan, diced

Rinse and cook rice. Line 9 x 13-inch pan with waxed paper; spread shiofuk konbu and furikake nori evenly on bottom. Spread half of hot rice in pan over the konbu and nori mixture. Pack down slightly. Spread diced takuwan over rice and cover with remaining half of rice. Press down so that layers will stick together and hold its shape when cut. When rice is cool (about an hour) invert pan over a tray. Remove waxed paper. Cut sushi into 2-inch squares.

Variation: Place half of hot rice directly in pan. (Not necessary to line with waxed paper.) Press down with spatula. Sprinkle 1/4 cup shiofuke konbu and furikake nori evenly over rice. Add takuwan and other pickled Japanese vegetables such as sambai zuke, finely chopped. Cover with remaining half of rice. Sprinkle lightly with additional furikake nori and 2 eggs (fried and slivered) or 1/2 block kamaboko (slivered). Press down. When rice is cool, cut into 2-inch squares.

Other Suggestions: For the middle layer, use 2 cans tuna (drained, heated and seasoned with 2 tablespoons shoyu, 2 tablespoons sugar and 2 teaspoons mirin). Or use 2 cans unagi, heated and mashed.

Note: Layered sushi is tasty, very simple to prepare and very popular at any gathering. Experiment and discover your favorite combination!

Maki Sushi
yield: 10 rolls

* *

10 dried shiitake mushrooms, soaked
2-1/2 cups water
4 dried shrimps
1/3 cup shoyu
3 tablespoons sugar
1 package kanpyo (0.7-oz.), soaked and squeezed
10 carrot strips, 8 inches long
10 stalks watercress, 8 inches long
1 can unagi (4-oz.)
3 eggs, beaten
10 sheets sushi nori
4-1/2 cups rice, rinsed and cooked
1 teaspoon salt
1-1/4 cups "Vinegar Sauce for Sushi" (see recipe on
page 23)

Remove stems from softened mushrooms and slice caps into
1/4-inch strips. Cover and simmer mushrooms and shrimp in
water until tender, about 15 to 30 minutes. Add shoyu, sugar
and kanpyo; cook until kanpyo is tender, about 15 minutes.
Remove and drain mushrooms and kanpyo; save shoyu mixture. Cook carrots in shoyu sauce until tender, about 5 minutes; drain.

In large frying pan, spray vegetable spray and fry beaten eggs
into a thin sheet. When almost done, flip egg sheet over.
When cooked, remove and cool. Slice into long thin strips,
1/4 inch wide. Set aside. In same frying pan, add enough
water to boil watercress. Add salt to taste. When done, about
2 minutes, remove and set aside.

In small pan, cook unagi, stirring constantly and breaking
apart unagi, until heated through.

Reserve 1/4 cup sushi vinegar sauce for wetting hands while handling rice. Remove cooked rice into large container. Sprinkle 1 teaspoon salt over cooked rice before mixing in vinegar sauce. Fan and stir gently to cool. Add vinegar sauce a little at a time, turning over rice gently to mix. Adjust amount of sauce to your taste.

Arrange ingredients for sushi. Squeeze mushrooms and watercress to remove excess liquid. If kanpyo is too thin, twist 2 to 3 kanpyo strips together into 8-inch lengths.

Place a sheet of nori, shiny side down, on bamboo mat. Use the 1/4 cup vinegar sauce to wet hands while handling rice. Spread 1-1/3 cups sushi rice on nori, leaving 1-1/4 inches uncovered at farthest end. Two inches from nearest edge, arrange 1 row each of 2 teaspoons unagi, mushrooms, kanpyo, carrot, egg and watercress. Roll like a jelly roll, lifting mat when it touches rice. Continue rolling until nori completely surrounds roll. Squeeze gently and press ends within mat. Place seam side down on waxed paper. Cut into 8 slices.

Optional: Celery soaked in water and a little vinegar. If using gobo, cook first in water. When half-cooked, add mushrooms.

Ono Broiled Sushi

yield: 35 to 40 servings

* *

3 cups cooked rice
6 to 9 dried shiitake mushrooms, soaked
8-oz. imitation crab, shredded or chopped
1 container sour cream (8-oz.)
1 cup mayonnaise
1/2 cup Nori Komi Furikake, adjust to taste
4 packages Temaki Yaki Nori (0.4-oz. each, 10 sheets per
   package)

Discard mushroom stems. Squeeze out excess water; chop. In mixing bowl, mix together chopped mushrooms, crab, sour cream and mayonnaise. Place cooked rice in 9 x 13-inch pan; sprinkle furikake generously over rice. Top with crab mixture. Broil for 8 to 10 minutes, or until browned. Spoon onto nori and form into cone or roll.

Shinko Maki

yield: 32 sushi

* *

1-1/2 cups rice, rinsed and cooked
salt for sprinkling
1/2 cup "Vinegar Sauce for Sushi" (see recipe on page 23)

Remove cooked rice into container. Sprinkle a little salt to season. Fan and stir gently to cool. Add vinegar sauce, turning over rice gently to mix.

4 sheets sushi nori, 7-1/2 x 8 inches
1 whole takuwan (e.g., Hawaiian Style Honda Food Brand
(10-oz.) or Kewalo Brand Pickled Radish (10-oz.))
wasabi paste, optional
2-3 tablespoons "Vinegar Sauce for Sushi" for wetting hands

Cut sheets of nori into halves. Cut takuwan into eight 8 x 1/4 x 1/4-inch strips. Place a sheet of nori on bamboo mat; moisten fingers with vinegar sauce and spread 1/2 cup sushi rice on nori, leaving one inch uncovered at farthest end. One inch from nearest edge, smear a line of wasabi paste, if desired. Place a strip of takuwan along wasabi line. Roll like a jelly roll, lifting mat when it touches rice. Continue rolling until nori completely surrounds roll. Squeeze gently and press ends within mat. Cut each roll crosswise into halves; then cut each piece diagonally into halves.

Note: There will be leftover takuwan. Slice and serve as a side dish with your meals.

Variation: Substitute cucumber strips in place of takuwan.

Spam® Musubi

yield: 8-9 pieces

* *

1 can Spam® (12-oz.), cut into 8 to 9 slices
8-9 half sheets nori, 4 x 7 inches
2-1/2 cups rice (or 3 rice cooker measuring cups)
acrylic musubi maker mold

Rinse and cook rice. (I add 1 teaspoon salt to rice for more flavor.) Fry Spam® slices on both sides. Place mold frame on center of half sheet nori. Place cooked rice loosely halfway into mold. Place a slice of Spam® over rice and press firmly with mold press. Remove mold press and frame. (To remove musubi maker, press down center while pulling sides up.) Fold nori over rice and Spam®. Place musubi, overlapping nori side, down on plate. Wrap with waxed paper or plastic wrap.

Variation #1: Teri-Spam® Musubi

2 tablespoons sugar
2 tablespoons shoyu
1 tablespoon mirin

Heat sugar, shoyu and mirin and cook Spam® in sauce before making musubi.

Variation #2:

Sprinkle furikake over rice in mold before putting in Spam®.

Spicy Tuna

yield: 8-10 appetizer servings

* *

2 cups rice
1 pound 'ahi, chopped in small cubes
1 tablespoon tobiko (optional)
4 tablespoons mayonnaise
4 teaspoons Sriracha Hot Chili Sauce
1 teaspoon hot sesame oil
3/4 teaspoon Japanese red pepper Ichimi Togarashi
1/2 teaspoon peanut oil (or sesame oil)
3 Korean-style seasoned seaweed packets (0.23-oz. each,
   2-1/4 x 3-inch size) or use larger size Korean-style seasoned seaweed 7 x 8 inches cut in half for handroll sushi

Rinse and cook rice. While rice is cooking, combine rest of
ingredients (except Korean-style seasoned seaweed).

For handroll sushi: Spread rice on nori. Place about a teaspoonful of spicy tuna in middle and fold or roll nori. Dip in
shoyu and wasabi sauce.

For nigiri style: Refrigerate spicy tuna until ready to serve.
Cut 4 Japanese nori in half, the long way, then in thirds to
make 24 long strips. For each nigiri sushi, press about 2-1/2
tablespoons rice into a thumb shaped mound about 2 x 1 x 1
inch in size. Wrap a nori strip around rice. Place in platter
and cover with waxed paper. Just before serving, place about
a teaspoonful of spicy tuna on top.

Note: Stacee and Derek Nishibata enjoy spicy tuna sushi at
sushi bars. They developed this recipe so they could also
enjoy it at home. Thank you for sharing your recipe with us.
Don and I love it, too. It is really ono!

Note: Substitute tobiko for spicy tuna.

Temaki Roll

yield: 20-30 pieces

* *

3 packages Temaki Yaki Nori (0.4-oz. each, 10 sheets per package)
3 cups rice
1/2 cup rice vinegar
2 tablespoons sugar
1 tablespoon salt

Rinse and cook rice. Combine rice vinegar, sugar and salt. Combine cooked rice with vinegar sauce.

Sesame Sauce:

1/2 cup mayonnaise
2 teaspoons honey
2 teaspoons roasted sesame seeds
1/2 teaspoon sesame oil

Mix sesame sauce ingredients and set aside.

Filling Suggestions:

imitation crab sticks, cut lengthwise into halves or thirds
cucumber, seeded and cut into thin strips
avocado slices, sprinkled with lemon juice
radish sprouts
3 eggs, beaten and thinly fried, sliced into thin strips
shrimp, cleaned and cooked
kamaboko, slivered
'ahi poke

Select 3 or 4 fillings of your choice. On a large tray, arrange all ingredients, including rice, temaki nori and sesame sauce. For each serving, spoon a small amount of rice into the center of a piece of nori; top with one or several of the filling ingredients on the tray. Add sesame sauce, if desired. Roll into a cone or cylinder.

Somen or Soba Sushi

yield: 6 sushi rolls

* *

1 bundle somen (8-oz.), or soba noodles
6 sushi nori sheets

Cook noodles according to package directions and drain. Divide into 6 portions. Roll in sheets of nori with any of the following ingredients:

2 eggs, fried thin and thinly sliced
1 block kamaboko, sliced in thin strips
1 cucumber, sliced in thin strips
celery, sliced in thin strips
carrots, slivered
1 can tuna

Refrigerate sushi rolls at least an hour before cutting. Cut each sushi roll in 8 pieces and serve with sauce for dipping.

Dipping Sauce:

3 tablespoons brown sugar
3 tablespoons vinegar
4 tablespoons shoyu
5 tablespoons soup stock
1 teaspoon salt
1 teaspoon sesame oil

Note: Very light and refreshing! May be prepared a day before and kept in refrigerator for 2 to 3 days.

Pūpū–Meat

Barbecue Sticks

yield: about 30 sticks

* *

2 pounds boneless crossrib roast, cut into 1/4-inch slices
    (ask butcher to do this)
30 bamboo skewers (8 inches long), soaked in water

Marinade:

1 cup shoyu
3/4 cup sugar
1/8 cup water
1/2 inch fresh ginger, grated
1 clove garlic, crushed

Combine marinade ingredients. Cut meat slices into strips about 1 inch wide. Soak in marinade for about 30 minutes. String strips onto skewers in an undulating style. Grill on hibachi

Note: Remember the wonderful smell of teriyaki meat being grilled and eating barbecue sticks at school carnivals? Somehow skewering the strips of teriyaki makes it even juicier and tastier.

Easy Spareribs

yield: 2-4 appetizer servings

* *

1 pound babyback ribs
1 tablespoon white wine
2 tablespoons balsamic vinegar
3 tablespoons shoyu
4 tablespoons sugar
5 tablespoons water

Place spareribs and rest of ingredients into pan. Cover and bring to a boil. Lower heat and cook until meat is tender (about 45 minutes). Turn over and marinate ribs with sauce occasionally. When done, cut ribs apart and serve.

Note: Monitor the sauce while cooking and don't let it run dry and burn. If there is a lot of sauce at the end, you may turn the heat on high and boil up the liquid.

Fried Ginger Pork

yield: 6-8 appetizer servings

* *

2 pounds boneless pork butt, cut in bite-size pieces
   (about 1-inch cubes)
1/4 cup sesame oil
1 cup onion, finely minced
1 large clove garlic, crushed
1/2 cup shoyu
1 tablespoon fresh ginger, chopped
1 teaspoon sugar
2 tablespoons vinegar

Mix together chopped ginger and sugar; set aside. Heat sesame oil and brown pork on all sides on medium-high heat. Add onions and garlic; cook on medium heat until onions are soft. Add shoyu, ginger and sugar mixture and vinegar. Cover and simmer 10 minutes or until done. Serve pork cubes with toothpicks.

Note: This is an old ono pūpū recipe shared by Jean Yoshikane many years ago when we taught at Puohala Elementary School. She says it's also delicious when the pork is cut in thick slices, cooked and placed in Chinese buns.

Gyoza (Pot Stickers)

yield: about 48 pieces

* *

1-1/2 pounds ground pork
2 stalks green onion, chopped
1/2 cup Chinese cabbage, shredded
3 tablespoons shoyu
1 tablespoon sesame oil
2 packages mundoo wrappers (12-oz. each)
oil for frying

Mix together ground pork, green onion, Chinese cabbage, shoyu and sesame oil. Spoon about 1 tablespoon of pork mixture onto mundoo wrapper. Moisten the edges with water, then press together to seal completely. Place about 2 tablespoons of oil onto bottom of a nonstick frying pan. Fry both sides of gyoza in hot oil for about 3 minutes. Place enough water (about 1/2 cup) to cover bottom of pan. Put lid on pan and steam for a couple of minutes or until water evaporates.

Serve with sauce or with ponzu-shoyu, if desired.

Sauce:

2 tablespoons shoyu
2 tablespoons vinegar
1/2 to 1 teaspoon La Yu (hot Chinese sesame oil)

Kalbi

yield: 12-14 appetizer servings

* *

3-1/2 pounds thinly sliced beef short ribs

Marinade:

3/4 cup shoyu
1/3 cup water
3 to 4 cloves garlic, minced or grated
2 teaspoons fresh ginger, minced or grated
4 tablespoons honey or brown sugar
2 tablespoons sesame oil
1-1/2 tablespoons roasted sesame seeds
1/2 cup green onions, chopped

Combine marinade ingredients and marinate short ribs. Place short ribs in well-sealed container or plastic bag. Marinate 30 to 45 minutes in refrigerator, flipping container over occasionally to marinate all pieces. Grill on hibachi. Cut between bone sections for pūpū-size pieces.

Lumpia
yield: about 40 pieces

✳ ✳

1 pound ground pork
2 cloves garlic, minced
1/4 pound shrimp, minced
3 to 4 dried shiitake mushrooms, soaked, then minced
1 small carrot, grated
1/2 pound green beans, French cut
1 small onion, minced
1/2 can water chestnuts (half of 8-oz. can), minced
salt and pepper, to taste
1 package bean sprouts (12-oz.)
40 lumpia wrappers
oil for frying

Fry ground pork with garlic in 2 teaspoons oil. Add shrimp, shiitake, carrots, green beans, onion, water chestnuts and seasonings and fry. Add bean sprouts and toss only until sprouts are slightly wilted. Drain well; cool.

Put about 2 tablespoons of filling on lumpia wrapper. Wrap envelope style. Wet edge to seal. Fry in about 1/2 inch oil until brown. Be careful when turning not to pierce lumpia or it will splatter. Drain on paper towel. Serve with dipping Sauce.

Dipping Sauce:

1/2 tablespoon cornstarch
1/2 cup water
1/2 cup vinegar
1/2 cup sugar
1 teaspoon shoyu
1 clove garlic, minced
salt and pepper, to taste

Mini Laulau Pūpū

yield: 25-30 pieces

* *

1 pound lūʻau leaves
1/2 pound salted butterfish, cut into 1-inch-square pieces
1/2 pound boneless stew or chuck roast, cut into 1-inch
  cubes
1/2 teaspoon Hawaiian salt
6 tī leaves
25 to 30 toothpicks

Cut off stems of lūʻau leaves. Wash and cut leaves into 2-inch strips. Sprinkle salt over meat cubes and toss gently. Place a piece of meat and a piece of fish on one end of lūʻau leaf. Roll meat and fish and secure with 1 toothpick. Line steamer with tī leaves. Place mini laulau pūpū on tī leaves and cover with additional tī leaves. Steam for 2 hours. Serve hot.

Note: When rolling lūʻau leaf, adjust by adding smaller pieces of leaf to strip. Left over lūʻau leaves may be cooked with pork or meat for another meal.

Manapua

yield: 24 buns

* *

Bun Dough:

1 package dry yeast
3 tablespoons lukewarm water
2 cups warm water
1-1/2 tablespoons oil
3/4 cup sugar
3/4 teaspoon salt
6 cups flour
1/2 teaspoon oil

Dissolve yeast in 3 tablespoons water and let stand until yeast softens. Mix remaining water, oil, sugar and salt until sugar is dissolved. Add yeast mixture.

In large mixing bowl, add flour and 1/2 of liquid mixture together. Knead together until all liquid is absorbed. Add remaining liquid and knead again until ball of dough is smooth. (Dough is ready when long strands form on outside of ball.)

Coat outside of dough with remaining oil. Cover bowl with plastic wrap and let sit in warm room for 1 hour to rise double in size. Punch dough to deflate and let rise second time (1 hour). Place dough in refrigerator for 3 to 4 hours to rise further.

Filling:

1 cup water
2 tablespoons cornstarch
2 tablespoons sugar
1 tablespoon oyster sauce
1/2 teaspoon salt
1 pound char siu, diced
3 drops red food color

Mix water, cornstarch, sugar, oyster sauce and salt in pot and bring to boil for 1 minute, stirring constantly. Add char siu and food color; remove from heat and set aside to cool. Divide filling into 24 portions.

To prepare manapua:

Cut 24 2-inch-square sheets of waxed paper or pastry paper and brush one side with oil or coat with non-stick cooking spray.

Punch down dough and separate into 24 pieces. Flatten on non-stick surface (i.e., plastic cutting board) to about a 3-inch circle and place filling in center of dough. Gather up edges carefully to center of bun and pinch dough together to seal. Place pinched side down onto waxed paper.

Preheat large steamer pot. Place buns about 2 inches apart in steamer and cover. Steam for 15 to 20 minutes. Turn off heat and let stand for another 5 minutes. **(Do not open lid.)** Serve hot.

Peppered Steak

yield: 4-6 appetizer servings

* *

1-1/2 to 2 pounds flank steak

Marinade:

2 tablespoons shoyu
2 tablespoons lemon juice
1/4 cup vegetable oil
1 teaspoon pepper
1 teaspoon celery salt
2 tablespoons green onion, chopped
2 cloves garlic, finely chopped

Marinate flank steak for 2 hours or overnight in refrigerator. Broil to desired doneness. Slice into thin strips and serve.

Pipikaula
(Beef Jerky, Hawaiian-Style)
yield: 4-6 appetizer pieces

* *

2 pounds flank steak

Marinade:

1/2 cup shoyu
1/4 cup sake
1 tablespoon liquid smoke
1 tablespoon sugar
1 teaspoon salt
pepper, to taste
1 small piece fresh ginger, minced
1 clove garlic, minced
1 Hawaiian chili pepper, seeded and minced

Cut meat with the grain 2 inches wide. Combine marinade ingredients. Marinate meat overnight in refrigerator, turning several times. Drain meat and arrange on cooling racks on baking sheet. Dry meat at 200°F for 4 to 7 hours. (Longer time will result in drier pipikaula.) To serve, slice and fry in a little oil for 1 to 2 minutes. Serve hot or cold with poi.

Note: Pipikaula may be stored in refrigerator up to 5 days or in freezer for 6 to 8 months.

Pork Adobo Pūpū

yield: 6-8 appetizer servings

* *

2 pounds boneless pork butt, cut in bite-size pieces
(about 1-inch cubes)
2-1/2 teaspoons Hawaiian salt

Rub pork pieces thoroughly with salt; let stand for 2 hours.

Marinade:

1/2 cup vinegar
3 to 4 cloves garlic, minced
1/2 teaspoon freshly cracked black pepper
1/2 teaspoon crushed red pepper
1 teaspoon liquid smoke (e.g., Wright's® Natural Hickory
Seasoning Liquid Smoke)

Combine marinade ingredients and marinate pork 6 to 7
hours or overnight. Remove pork; reserve marinade. In large
skillet over medium-high heat, brown pork on all sides. Pour
reserved marinade over pork and simmer 15 to 20 minutes.

Pūpū-Style Spareribs

yield: 15-20 appetizer servings

* *

5 pounds spareribs, cut into 1-1/2-inch pieces
4 cloves garlic, crushed
1 large piece ginger root, crushed
1/2 teaspoon salt

Sauce:

1 cup sugar
1 cup shoyu
1 cup catsup
1/3 cup oyster sauce

In large pot, combine spareribs, garlic, ginger and salt. Add water to cover spareribs; bring to boil. Lower heat and simmer 1-1/2 to 2 hours or until spareribs are tender. Drain. Combine sauce ingredients and marinate spareribs in sauce overnight in the refrigerator.

Place spareribs on rack of broiler pan and broil for 7 to 10 minutes, basting with remaining sauce. Turn and broil for 5 to 7 minutes more.

Shish Kabob

yield: 36 skewers

* *

2 pounds boneless sirloin steak, cut in 1-inch cubes
2 green peppers, cut in 1-inch squares
1 large onion (Maui onion preferred), cut in 1-inch squares
1 to 2 firm tomatoes, cut in bite-size pieces (green pepper
  size)
36 bamboo skewers (8 inches long), soaked in water

Marinade:

1/2 cup shoyu
1/3 cup sugar
1 clove garlic, crushed
1 inch fresh ginger, crushed

Marinate meat about 10 to 15 minutes. Skewer in order:
green pepper, meat, onion, tomato, meat, green pepper, meat,
onion and green pepper. (Or skewer to your own preference.
However, begin and end with green peppers to hold everything together.) Grill on hibachi.

Note: This is one of our family's favorite pūpū. The vegetables grilled with the slightly marinated meat makes a very
tasty combination.

Siu Mai

yield: about 40 pieces

* *

4 dried shiitake mushrooms, soaked
1 pound ground pork
1/2 pound shrimp, cleaned and minced
1/4 cup water chestnuts, minced
1/4 cup green onion, minced
1 egg, slightly beaten
1-1/2 to 2 teaspoons salt
1 teaspoon sugar
1 teaspoon shoyu
1/4 teaspoon sesame oil
pepper, to taste
2 tablespoons cornstarch
2 packages won ton wrappers (10-oz. each)

Remove stems from mushrooms and mince caps. Combine all ingredients (except won ton wrappers). Place about 1 tablespoon pork mixture in center of each wrapper. Moisten and gather edges of wrapper around filling, leaving tops open and shaping corners to form petals. Place on greased rack and steam over boiling water for 20 minutes.

Note: For easier handling, corners can be pre-trimmed into curves for more uniform petals. For left over wrappers, cut into thin strips, deep fry in hot oil for crispy crunchies to garnish green salads.

Spam® Won Ton

yield: about 115 won ton pieces

* *

1 can Spam® (12-oz.), grated
3 blocks kamaboko (6-oz. each), grated
1-1/2 packages cream cheese (12-oz. total), softened
3 packages won ton wrappers (12-oz. each)
Oil for deep-frying

Mix together and fill won ton wrappers with about a teaspoonful of mixture. Wet fingertip and moisten inner edges with water. Fold wrapper in half and press to seal edges. Deep-fry in hot oil on medium heat until golden brown. Adjust heat as necessary. Drain on paper towels.

Note: Refrigerate left over won ton wrappers for use at a later time.

Spam® Won Ton with Green Chilies

yield: about 65-70 pieces

* *

1 can Spam® (12-oz.), grated or shredded
4 dried shiitake mushrooms, soaked and chopped
1 can chopped green chilies (4.5-oz.)
1/2 can water chestnuts (half of 8-oz. can), chopped
1/3 pound shrimp, cleaned and chopped
1 egg, slightly beaten
1 stalk green onion, chopped
2 packages won ton pi (12-oz. each)
Oil for deep-frying

Mix Spam®, mushroom, chilies, water chestnuts, shrimp, egg and green onion together. Fill each won ton skin with a teaspoon of the filling. Dip fingertip in water and moisten inner edges of wrapper. Fold in half and press to seal. Heat oil and deep-fry until golden brown. Drain on paper towels. Serve with shoyu and mustard sauce.

Note: Extra wrappers can be stored in refrigerator.

Spring Rolls

yield: 8-10 appetizer servings

* *

1 package Menlo® Lumpia Wrap (16-oz.), 30 wrappers
1 pound ground beef (pork or chicken)
2 tablespoons oil
1 package chop suey vegetables (9-oz.)
1 package long rice (2-oz.)
2 eggs, slightly beaten
1 small onion, minced
1 package imitation crab (about 1/2 pound), coarsely
    shredded
1 tablespoon oyster sauce
pepper and salt, to taste
garlic powder, to taste
oil for deep-frying

Defrost lumpia wrappers in refrigerator a day before using.

Soak long rice in water for 10 minutes. Cut in 1 inch lengths; set aside. Heat oil in frying pan; sauté onion. Add ground beef and rest of ingredients (except lumpia wrappers and oil). Cook together until bean sprouts are done but not limp.

Place one tablespoonful of mixture onto lumpia. Wrap envelope style and seal by wetting the last edge. Deep-fry in medium hot oil until lightly browned. Drain on paper towels.

Serve with Vietnamese Lumpia Sauce (see recipe on page 84).

Stuffed Fried Lotus Root

yield: 4-6 appetizer servings

* *

2 sections lotus root, peeled and cut into 1/4-inch slices
2 eggs, slightly beaten
3/4 cup flour

Stuffing:

1/2 pound ground beef
1/2 teaspoon salt
1/8 teaspoon pepper
1-1/2 tablespoons shoyu
1/8 teaspoon sesame oil
1 small clove garlic, crushed
1 tablespoon green onion, finely chopped

Combine stuffing ingredients. Place about 1 tablespoon on each slice of lotus root. Press, filling holes. Dredge stuffed lotus roots in flour; then dip in eggs. Fry in 1 inch oil until golden brown on both sides. Serve hot with Hot Dipping Sauce.

Hot Dipping Sauce:

1 tablespoon Vinegar
2 tablespoons shoyu
1 teaspoon sugar
1 teaspoon sesame oil
1 teaspoon Tabasco® sauce
1 teaspoon Ko-chu-jang sauce

Note: Depending upon the quality and size of the lotus root, you may need to make some adjustments in filling the holes of all the slices, taking from some and adding more to others.

Won Ton

yield: about 40-50 pieces

* *

1/2 pound ground pork
4 medium size shrimps, cleaned and chopped
4 water chestnuts, minced
1/2 teaspoon salt
1/4 cup green onion, finely chopped
1/4 teaspoon sugar
1 to 2 packages won ton pi (12-oz. each)
oil for deep-frying

Combine all ingredients (except won ton pi and oil). Place about 1/2 teaspoon of the mixture in each won ton wrapper. Dampen edges and fold diagonally to form triangle. Next, dampen one of the opposite corners of the triangle and fold the two narrow ends together in the center. Press tightly; then fold down halfway.

Deep-fry in hot oil until a light golden brown. Drain on paper towels. Serve with Shoyu-Mustard Sauce or with Won Ton Dipping Sauce.

Shoyu-Mustard Sauce:

1/2 tablespoon Colman's® Mustard (dry mustard)
1/2 tablespoon water
2 tablespoons shoyu

Put dry mustard in small bowl. Slowly add water, blending thoroughly until smooth. Add shoyu and mix together.

Won Ton Dipping Sauce:

1 tablespoon oil
1/2 teaspoon sesame oil

1 tablespoon oyster sauce
2 tablespoons shoyu
1 teaspoon sugar
pepper, to taste

Note: A 12-oz. package has about 39 to 40 wrappers.

Taco Won Ton
yield: about 60 pieces

* *

1 pound ground beef
1 package taco mix (1-oz.)
1/2 can refried beans (half of 16-oz.)
1/2 cup shredded Cheddar cheese
2 packages won ton pi (12-oz. each)

Brown ground beef. Drain oil. Add taco mix, beans and cheese. Mix well. Place about 1 teaspoonful of ground beef mixture onto won ton pi. Wet inside edges of won ton pi, fold in half and press edges to seal. Deep-fry. Drain on paper towel. Serve with taco sauce or salsa.

Note: Refrigerate any leftover won ton pi. Won ton pi may be cut into thin strips and deep-fried. The crisp and crunchy won ton may be used as garnish for vegetable salads.

Teriyaki Meatballs

yield: 6 dozen meatballs

* *

1-1/2 pounds ground beef or ground chicken
2 eggs, beaten
2 tablespoons flour
1 teaspoon salt
pepper, to taste

Sauce:

1/4 cup sugar
1/3 cup shoyu
2 tablespoons cornstarch
1 can beef broth (14.5-oz.)
1/4 cup sake
2 teaspoons fresh ginger, minced
2 teaspoons garlic, minced

Combine meat, eggs, flour, salt and pepper. Shape into small balls about 3/4 to 1 inch in diameter. Bake in large greased baking pan at 400°F for 14 to 17 minutes.

In a skillet, combine sugar, shoyu and cornstarch. Stir in broth, sake, ginger and garlic. Cook until mixture thickens slightly, stirring constantly. Add meatballs and serve.

Pūpū–Chicken

Buffalo Wings

yield: 12-18 pieces

* *

12 to 18 chicken wings
1/2 cup flour
1/4 teaspoon salt
1/4 teaspoon cayenne pepper
1/4 teaspoon paprika

Combine flour, salt, cayenne pepper and paprika; place in plastic bag. Add chicken wings and shake to coat evenly. Refrigerate wings for about an hour. Remove from refrigerator and let sit 30 minutes before cooking.

1/4 cup butter
1/4 cup hot sauce (e.g., Red Devil Cayenne Pepper Sauce)
1/4 teaspoon garlic, grated
oil for deep-frying

Melt butter and mix in hot sauce and garlic; set aside.

Heat oil to 350°F and fry chicken wings for about 10 minutes, or until dark brown. Remove and pour hot sauce over and stir.

Suggestion: Serve with celery sticks and Bleu Cheese Dressing or Ranch Dressing.

Note: I got this recipe from someone who got it based on a well-known restaurant's buffalo wings. Fantastic taste!

Easy Macnut Chicken Drummettes

yield: about 6-8 appetizer servings

* *

2 pounds chicken drummettes
1 egg, beaten
1/4 cup milk
1/2 cup butter (1 block), melted

Flour Mixture:

1 cup flour
2 teaspoons salt
1 teaspoon baking soda
2 teaspoons paprika
dash pepper
5 tablespoons sesame seeds
1/4 cup macadamia nuts, chopped

Mix together egg and milk. Dip chicken in milk and egg mixture and roll in flour mixture. Place chicken and butter in foil-lined 9 x 13-inch pan and bake at 400°F for 30 minutes. Turn chicken over and bake for another 30 minutes.

Fried Chicken Drummettes

yield: 8-10 appetizer servings

* *

3 pounds chicken drummettes
1 tablespoon Hawaiian salt (or less, adjust to taste)

Rub Hawaiian salt all over chicken wings and let sit for 30 minutes.

Flour Mixture:

2 cups cornstarch
1/2 cup flour
1 tablespoon garlic salt
1 teaspoon pepper

Combine flour mixture in plastic bag.

2 eggs, beaten
1/2 teaspoon salt
oil for frying, 1 inch deep

Heat oil in large, heavy skillet on medium-high heat (350°F). Mix egg and salt together. Dip chicken in egg. Place in flour mixture and shake well until coated. Fry chicken, turning chicken over when brown and cook until done. Test for doneness. Drain on paper towels.

Garlic Chicken

yield: 10-12 appetizer servings

* *

4 pounds chicken wings
1 cup flour
1 cup panko
4 tablespoons garlic salt
1/2 teaspoon pepper
oil for deep-frying

Combine flour, panko, garlic salt and pepper and mix well. Put flour mixture in gallon-size plastic bag. Pat chicken with paper towel to remove excess liquid and place about a fourth of chicken in plastic bag. Shake and coat each piece evenly with flour mixture. Deep-fry in hot oil on medium to high heat until chicken is golden brown. Drain on paper towels. Repeat until all pieces are cooked.

Dipping Sauce:

1 cup shoyu
1 cup sugar
3/4 cup water
1/2 teaspoon fresh ginger, grated
1/2 teaspoon garlic, minced
3 stalks green onion, minced

Whisk shoyu, sugar and water until sugar is dissolved. Stir in ginger, garlic and green onion. Set aside at room temperature. Serve as a dipping sauce for chicken wings.

Oven-Barbecued Chicken Wings

yield: 8-10 appetizer servings

* *

3 pounds chicken wings
1/4 teaspoon salt
1/8 teaspoon pepper
1-1/2 teaspoons paprika
1/4 cup peanut oil

Arrange chicken wings in large pan in a single layer. Season with salt, pepper and paprika. Drizzle chicken with peanut oil; mix to evenly coat. Bake at 400°F for 15 minutes, or until chicken is golden.

Sauce:

1 cup ketchup
1/4 cup peanut oil
1/4 cup honey
1/4 cup butter, melted
1 tablespoon spicy brown mustard
6 tablespoons vinegar
2 tablespoons Worcestershire sauce
1 clove garlic, crushed
1-1/2 teaspoons paprika
1 teaspoon hot pepper sauce

While chicken is baking, combine sauce ingredients in saucepan and bring to boil. Remove from heat. Brush chicken with sauce and continue cooking chicken for an additional 40 to 45 minutes, turning and basting with sauce every 10 minutes. Test for doneness. Serve warm.

Parmesan Chicken Pūpū

yield: 6-8 appetizer servings

* * * * * * * * * * * * * * * * * * * *

2 pounds chicken drummettes
3/4 cup Parmesan cheese, grated
2 tablespoons fresh parsley, chopped
1 teaspoon salt
2 teaspoons oregano
2 teaspoons paprika
1/2 teaspoon pepper
1/2 cup butter, melted

Combine Parmesan cheese, parsley, salt, oregano, paprika and pepper; place in plastic bag. Rinse and drain chicken; pat dry. Place in bowl. Pour melted butter over and mix together. Put chicken in plastic bag. Shake to coat. Place in large foil-lined pan and bake at 350°F for 1 hour.

Sesame Seed Chicken

yield: 6-8 appetizer servings

* *

2 to 3 pounds chicken drummettes
oil for deep-frying

Marinade:

4 tablespoons flour
8 tablespoons cornstarch
4 tablespoons sugar
1-1/2 teaspoons salt
5 tablespoons shoyu
2 eggs
2 cloves garlic, minced
1 stalk green onion, chopped
2 tablespoons sesame seeds

Mix marinade ingredients until well blended. Marinate chicken overnight in refrigerator, stirring occasionally. Heat oil and deep-fry chicken. Drain on paper towels.

Note: Whenever Jennifer comes back to Hawai'i, she has her favorite okazu place where she always orders sesame chicken. She asked me for a recipe like it. After testing several recipes, she finally said, "This is it!" It was Grandma Watanabe's old recipe.

Sweet-Sour Chicken Wings

yield: 6-8 appetizer servings

* *

2 pounds chicken wings
garlic salt, to taste
2 eggs, well beaten
1 cup corn starch or mochiko
oil for frying

Sauce:

1 teaspoon chicken instant bouillon dissolved in 1/2 cup
    water
3 tablespoons shoyu
3 tablespoons ketchup
1/2 cup sugar
1/2 cup vinegar
1/2 teaspoon salt

Sprinkle wings with garlic salt and let sit for 1/2 hour. Roll in beaten eggs and then in cornstarch. Fry chicken in hot oil until slightly brown. Place browned chicken wings in 9 x 13-inch pan lined with foil.

Combine sauce ingredients and heat. Pour all of the sauce over wings and bake at 350°F for 30 to 45 minutes, turning chicken after 15 minutes to brown evenly. Remove from sauce and serve.

Tasty Chicken Pūpū

yield: about 6-8 appetizer servings

* *

2-1/2 pounds chicken drummettes
1 tablespoon Hawaiian salt
3 tablespoons vinegar
1 inch piece fresh ginger, grated
2 to 3 cloves garlic, minced

Combine salt, vinegar, ginger and garlic. Soak chicken in mixture for at least 1 hour. Broil on hibachi.

Note: Very easy and simple to prepare. A great tasting pūpū!

Mochiko Chicken (p.114) and 'Ahi Limu Poke (p.2)

Hot Crab Dip (p.16)

Shish Kabob (p.50) and California Inside Out Sushi (p.24)

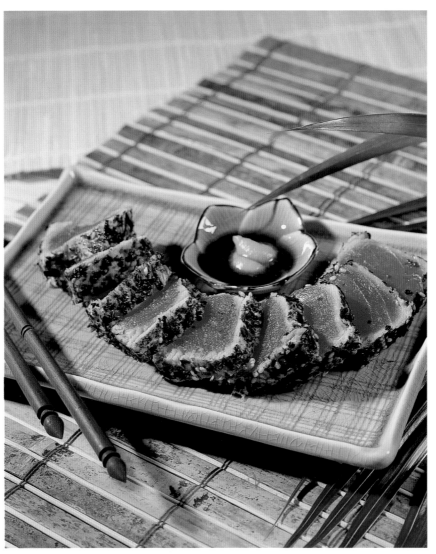

Furikake Seared 'Ahi (p.77)

Evie's Local-Style Party Mix (p.95)

Buffalo Wings (p.60)

Lomi Salmon on Skewers (p.78)

Stuffed Aburage with Somen (p.122)

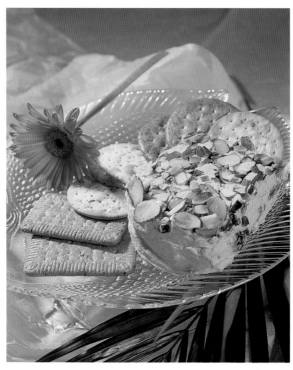

Curry Mango Cream Cheese Spread (p.14)

Clams and Ground Pork Pūpū (p.71)

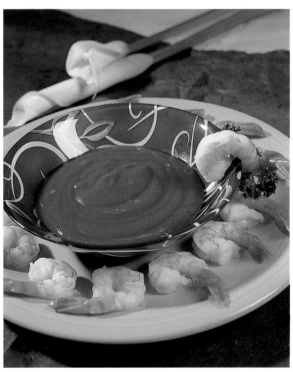

Cocktail Shrimp (p.72)

Oyster Bacon Wrap (p.81)

Yaki Tori Sticks

yield: about 20 sticks

* *

2 pounds chicken thighs, boneless and skinless, cut into
    1 to 1-1/2-inch squares
20 barbecue skewers (8 inches long), soaked in water
1 to 2 green peppers, cut into 1-inch squares
1 Maui onion, cut into 1-inch pieces or wedges

Marinade:

3 tablespoons sugar
5 tablespoons shoyu
1 tablespoon sherry or sake
1/2 teaspoon salt
1/2 teaspoon sesame oil
1 clove garlic, crushed

Mix marinade ingredients and soak chicken in sauce 5 hours
or overnight in refrigerator. To make yaki tori sticks, skewer
green pepper, chicken and onions on barbecue sticks. Begin
with green pepper and end with green pepper. Use about 3
chicken pieces with onion pieces in between. Grill on
hibachi.

Pūpū–Seafood

Clams and Ground Pork Pūpū

yield: about 8-10 appetizer servings

* *

1 tray ground pork (about 3/4 pound)
1 to 2 teaspoons garlic salt
1 inch piece fresh ginger, crushed
2 to 3 trays fresh clams (about 2 to 3 pounds)
1 egg, beaten
1/4 cup green onion, chopped
Worcestershire sauce, to taste (optional)

Place clams in container and cover with water until ready to use. Brown ground pork with garlic salt and ginger. When pork is lightly brown, drain clams and add to pork; cover and steam for about 5 minutes, or until clams open up. Mix in beaten egg and green onion. Sprinkle Worcestershire sauce, if desired.

Note: This is one of David Chun's favorite pūpū, given to him by a good friend. It's easy to prepare and the ground pork mixed in with the clams has a great taste. His wife, Marilyn, also likes it served with rice.

Cocktail Shrimp
yield: 50-60 pieces

* *

2 quarts water
1 bay leaf
juice of one lemon
rind of one lemon
1 can beer
2 pounds shrimp (31 to 40 count), peeled and deveined

Combine all ingredients (except shrimp) and bring water to aggressive boil. Add shrimp and stir, whirling through the boiling water. Cover tightly and remove from heat. Allow to stand for 5 minutes exactly. Then drain through colander. Run shrimp under cold water to cool. Chill and arrange on platter with dipping sauce.

Dipping Sauce:

1 cup catsup
2 teaspoons wasabi paste
juice of one lemon

Note: From 1 to 5 pounds of shrimp may be used with this recipe. This is definitely for shrimp lovers. It's "crunchy," cooked just right, with a light fresh taste. Our Popo just loves this shrimp! We like the 31 to 40 count best, but you can use the 26 to 30 count, if desired.

Crab Cakes
yield: 8 pieces

* *

1-1/2 pounds cooked crab (Kona or Dungeness)
1/3 cup mayonnaise
1 teaspoon Dijon mustard
1 tablespoon onion or parsely, minced (optional)
3/4 cup fine panko, divided
2 tablespoons oil

Remove crab meat from shell (about 1 cup). Shred large
pieces. Combine crab meat, mayonnaise, mustard and 1/4
cup of the panko. Mix well. Shape mixture into 8 portions,
forming round, thick discs. Coat crab cakes with the remaining 1/2-cup panko.

Heat a large non-stick skillet over medium heat and add oil.
When oil is hot, fry crab cakes until golden brown and crisp
on each side. Drain on paper towel and serve immediately.

Crab Stuffed Mushrooms

yield: 30 pieces

* *

30 medium mushrooms
1/2 pound imitation crab
1/3 cup black olives, finely chopped
1/4 cup mayonnaise
2 tablespoons parsley, chopped
2 teaspoons lemon juice
1/4 teaspoon garlic powder
1/4 teaspoon onion powder
grated Parmesan cheese for sprinkling

Remove stems from mushrooms; mince stems. Flake crab; add minced mushroom stems, olives, mayonnaise, parsley, lemon juice and garlic and onion powders. Fill mushroom caps with crab mixture. Sprinkle with cheese. Place on baking sheets. Cover with foil and bake at 400°F for 12 to 15 minutes. Uncover and continue baking about 5 more minutes or until golden brown.

Note: Stuffed mushrooms may be prepared ahead of time and kept in a covered container in refrigerator until ready to bake.

Deep-Fried Oysters
yield: about 18 oysters

* *

1 jar fresh oysters (1 quart)
salt and pepper, to taste
1/2 cup flour
2 eggs, beaten
1 cup fine panko
oil for deep-frying

Rinse and drain oysters. Salt and pepper both sides. Roll oysters in flour, dip into beaten egg and coat with panko. Cook in heated oil. Drain on paper towels to remove excess oil.

Note: If you like deep-fried oysters served at Chinese restaurants, here it is!

Easy Shrimp Skewers
yield: about 30 skewers

* *

3 pounds shrimp, 31 to 40 count
1 bottle Kraft® Zesty Italian dressing (16-oz.)
1 package barbecue skewers (8-inch skewers), soaked in
    water

Remove shells and devein shrimp. Soak shrimp in Italian dressing 5 hours or longer in refrigerator. Skewer 3 shrimps in "C" shape with tail-side down on each stick. Cook on hibachi over coals.

Fishcake and Spam® Pūpū

yield: 70-80 pieces

* *

2 pounds raw Chinese fishcake
1 can Spam® (12-oz.), minced
1 can water chestnuts (8-oz.), minced
1/2 onion, minced
3 to 4 stalks green onion, minced
3 eggs
3 to 4 tablespoons oyster sauce
pepper to taste (optional)
Chinese parsley, finely chopped (optional)
oil for frying

Mix all ingredients together. Drop by teaspoonful into 1-1/2-inches deep hot oil. Cook until brown. Serve on bed of shredded cabbage with hot mustard and shoyu dipping sauce.

Note: Use 2 teaspoons for safe handling. Use one teaspoon to scoop fishcake mixture and the other teaspoon to scrape off and drop fishcake into hot oil.

Furikake Seared 'Ahi

yield: 4-6 appetizer servings

* *

1 pound 'ahi fillet, sliced into pieces 3/4-inch thick
3 to 4 tablespoons furikake for coating
2 to 3 teaspoons oil

Dipping Sauce:

2 tablespoons shoyu
wasabi, to taste

Coat 'ahi pieces with furikake. Sear 'ahi in hot oil in non-stick skillet on medium-high heat, keeping the middle raw. Slice 'ahi, sashimi style. Mix shoyu and wasabi to desired taste and use as dipping sauce.

Namako (or Konnyaku) Pūpū

yield: 2-4 appetizer servings

* *

1 cup namako, sliced, or 2 pieces konnyaku, sliced
4 tablespoons sugar
4 tablespoons fresh lemon juice
1 teaspoon salt
1-1/2 cups daikon, grated and water squeezed out.

Combine all ingredients. Refrigerate.

Lomi Salmon on Skewers

yield: about 50 pieces

* *

1/2 pound salted salmon
1 small Maui onion, cut into 1/2-inch cubes
1 to 2 firm medium tomatoes, cut into 1/2-inch cubes
1 stalk green onion, cut into 1-inch lengths
1/2 bag poi (8-oz.)
50 large toothpicks

Rinse salmon and soak in fresh water for 1 to 2 hours. Drain and remove skin and bones; cut into 1/2-inch cubes. Skewer a piece of onion, tomato, green onion and then salmon onto a toothpick, shish kabob style. Continue until all ingredients have been used.

Mix poi with water until of dipping consistency. Place poi in a small bowl on a platter and arrange lomi salmon skewers around it.

Mimi's Shrimp

yield: about 15 appetizer servings

* *

3 pounds shrimp (21 to 25 count)

Marinade:

1 cup Canola oil
2 teaspoons shoyu
3 tablespoons honey
3 teaspoons Hawaiian salt (pulverized with mortar and
    pestle)
2 cloves garlic, grated
dash of Tabasco® sauce

Do not peel shrimp. Cut shrimp from back and remove vein. Butterfly shrimp and lay flat.

Mix together oil, shoyu, honey, pulverized Hawaiian salt and garlic. Add a few drops of Tabasco® sauce. Keep stirring mixture as you dip each shrimp in the marinade. Lay flat in a pan for 1 hour. Grill on hibachi.

Note: This is still the best tasting grilled shrimp! Everyone loves this. Thank you, Mimi.

Octopus (Tako) Pūpū with Miso Sauce

yield: 3-4 appetizer servings

* *

1 pound cooked octopus, cooled

Slice thinly and serve with miso sauce.

Miso sauce:

1 cup miso
3 tablespoons vinegar
3 tablespoons sugar
2 tablespoons sake
2 tablespoons mirin

Mix well.

Note: I love tako with miso sauce! We always had this for our New Year's get together ever since I was little. Now that supermarkets provide cooked tako, it makes it much easier to prepare this dish.

Oyster Bacon Wrap

yield: about 20-24 pieces

* *

2 jars fresh oysters (10-oz. each)
1 tablespoon olive oil
4 cloves garlic, finely chopped
1 bunch fresh spinach, cleaned (or 1 package baby spinach,
    6-oz).
1/4 cup water
1 package bacon slices (12-oz.), cut slices in half
1 tablespoon American parsley, chopped (for garnish),
    optional
20 to 24 toothpicks

Put oysters in strainer and rinse with water; drain and set
aside. Heat olive oil in pot and add garlic. When garlic is
lightly browned, add spinach. Toss lightly and add water.
Sauté until spinach is limp and turns a darker green. (Do not
boil and overcook.) Drain and set aside to cool.

Lay 1/2 bacon strip on chopping board and add oyster (if too
big, cut in half or thirds) and 1 to 2 teaspoons of spinach.
Wrap with strip of bacon and fasten with toothpick. Lay in
foil-lined baking pan with toothpick facing up.

Bake at 350°F for 30 to 45 minutes or until bacon browns.
Transfer oysters onto serving tray. Sprinkle parsley on top of
oysters to garnish, if desired, and serve warm.

Note: Fresh oysters may be found in the refrigerated section
at the grocery.

Oyster Rolls

yield: 40-50 rolls

* *

2 pounds ground pork
1 to 1-1/2 pounds raw Chinese fishcake
2 cans smoked oysters (3-oz. each), drained and chopped
1 can water chestnuts (8-oz.), drained and minced
3/4 cup green onion, chopped
3/4 cup Chinese parsley, chopped
1 teaspoon oyster sauce
1 package panko fine bread crumbs (4-oz.)
oil for frying

In non-stick skillet, fry pork, breaking into bits. Drain fat and let pork cool.

In large bowl, mix cooked pork with remaining ingredients (except for the panko and oil). Shape into rolls, using about 1 tablespoon per roll. Coat each roll with panko. Heat about 1 inch of oil in skillet over medium temperature. Fry rolls until brown. Drain on paper towels.

Note: Great hot or cold! Serve with dry mustard and shoyu mixture.

Salt and Pepper Shrimp

yield: about 26-30 pieces

* *

1 pound shrimp, medium size (26 to 30 count)
pinch salt and pepper to taste
1/2 cup cornstarch for coating
1/4 cup oil
2 to 3 cloves garlic, finely minced
1 Hawaiian chili pepper, seeded and cut into strips length-
　　wise
1/4 cup green onion, finely sliced
pinch seasoned 5 spices salt*

Devein and rinse shrimp. Leave shell on. Drain and pat dry with paper towel. Sprinkle salt and pepper on shrimp. Place cornstarch in plastic bag. Put shrimp in and toss together to coat.

Heat oil on medium-high in non-stick pan. Stir-fry shrimp; set aside. Heat pan on medium-high again. Add more oil if necessary. Stir-fry garlic first, then add chili pepper strips and green onion. Put back shrimp; sprinkle seasoned 5 spices salt. Toss together once and serve.

To prepare 5 spices salt, lightly brown 1/4 cup Hawaiian salt (or regular salt) in frying pan on low heat without oil. Add pinch 5 spices and mix together. The seasoned 5 spices salt can also be used to season chicken.

Variation: Use 1 pound Kuhuku shrimp, medium size, with head on. Prepare shrimp by trimming "hair" near head of shrimp with kitchen scissors.

Note: This is my sister-in-law, Amy Hee's, best pūpū! It is absolutely delicious! You'll be getting raves on this dish.

Shrimp Lumpia

yield: 30 pieces

* *

30 shrimp (31 to 40 count size) about 1 pound, cleaned
and cut to lay flat
1 to 2 carrots, cut into 30 carrot sticks about the length of
the shrimp
1 package string beans (8-oz.), cut to length of shrimp (30
pieces)
1 package bean sprouts (10-oz.)
30 square lumpia wrappers (frozen Menlo® Pastry Wrapper/
Balutan-NG-Lumpia), thawed
oil for deep-frying

Carefully separate lumpia wrappers. Lay one shrimp, carrot
stick, and string bean along one end of lumpia wrapper
(about 2 inches from edge closest to you). Place a very small
handful of bean sprouts over shrimp and vegetables. Fold end
over shrimp and vegetables and roll once. Fold over sides
and roll. Place end down. Repeat until all are done. Fry in
1/2 inch hot oil on medium until brown and crisp. Drain on
paper towels. Serve with Vietnamese Lumpia Sauce.

Vietnamese Lumpia Sauce:

1/2 cup fish sauce (Nguyen Chat Nuoc Mam)
1/2 cup water
1/3 cup plus 1 tablespoon sugar (adjust to taste)
5 cloves garlic, crushed with garlic press
3 tablespoons lemon juice
Hawaiian chili pepper, optional

Combine fish sauce, water, sugar, garlic and lemon juice. Cut and use 1/4 inch of pointed end of chili pepper to begin with (very hot). Remove seeds if any. Mix in chili pepper and remove. Adjust to your taste.

Note: Sayoko Watanabe created this pūpū when she was running late one day and she had promised to bring lumpia for a party. She improvised and came up with this tasty dish. It was a big hit! Her Vietnamese Lumpia Sauce is also a winner!

Bacon-Wrapped Shrimp
yield: 26-30 pieces

* *

1 pound shrimp (26 to 30 count)
1/4 cup shoyu
1 tablespoon sugar
1/4 teaspoon fresh ginger, grated
13 to 15 water chestnuts, sliced in half
13 to 15 strips bacon, cut in half
26 to 30 bamboo skewers (6 inches long), soaked in water

Clean and devein shrimp, but leave tails on. Marinate shrimp in shoyu, sugar and ginger for a few minutes. In lightly oiled non-stick pan, lightly sear shrimp on both sides until halfway cooked. Remove from heat; cool enough to handle. Press a water chestnut against shrimp and wrap with bacon. Skewer shrimp horizontally. Sear in hot pan with bacon seam side down. Cook until bacon is crispy on both sides. Drain on paper towels.

Seared 'Ahi

yield: 4-6 appetizer servings

* *

1 pound 'ahi
garlic salt to taste
pepper, to taste
1 tablespoon oil
lettuce, finely sliced

Cut 'ahi into sashimi blocks, about 1 x 1-1/2-inches. Sprinkle with garlic salt and pepper. Heat frying pan; add oil. Fry sashimi blocks, about 15 to 20 seconds on each side. (Fish should be rare inside.) Place lettuce on platter. Slice seared 'ahi as you would sashimi and arrange on bed of lettuce. Serve with dipping sauce.

Dipping Sauce:

1 tablespoon fresh ginger, finely slivered
1 teaspoon green onion, finely chopped
2 tablespoons oil
2 tablespoons shoyu

Place ginger and green onion into a small dish. Heat oil in small pot until very hot; pour over ginger and green onion. Immediately add shoyu.

Shrimp Tempura

yield: 6-8 appetizer servings

* *

1 pound shrimp (26 to 30 count)
oil for deep-frying

Batter:

1 cup flour
1 egg
1/2 teaspoon baking powder
3/4 cup chilled water

Shell and devein shrimp leaving tails on. Lightly slash underside of each shrimp diagonally to prevent curling.

Mix batter ingredients with chopsticks until slightly lumpy. (Begin with 1/2 cup chilled water and add more if necessary.) Holding tail, coat shrimp with batter. Fry in hot oil until golden color. Serve immediately with tempura sauce below or Vietnamese Lumpia Sauce, see page 84.

Tempura Sauce:

1/2 cup chicken broth
2 tablespoons shoyu
2 tablespoons mirin
grated daikon (optional)
grated fresh ginger (optional)

In a saucepan, combine chicken broth, shoyu and mirin. Heat until warm. To serve, put sauce in individual serving dishes. Put a little daikon and ginger in each dish, if desired.

Hint: Do not overbeat batter. You should be able to see some of the shrimp color after dipping in batter.

Shrimp Toast

yield: 48 pieces

* *

1 pound shrimp, cleaned and minced
1/4 cup onion, minced
1/2 cup water chestnuts, minced
1 teaspoon green onion or chives, minced
1 egg, beaten
1-1/2 teaspoons salt
1/2 teaspoon sugar
1 tablespoon cornstarch
1 teaspoon sherry
1/4 teaspoon sesame oil
12 slices sandwich-style bread
oil for deep-frying

Combine all ingredients (except bread and oil). Mix well. Cut each bread slice in fourths. Spread shrimp mixture on each piece. Fry in hot oil, shrimp side down, for only a few seconds as shrimp cooks readily. Drain on paper towels and serve hot.

Note: Not necessary to trim crusts, but you may do so if preferred.

Squid Pūpū (Fried Calamari)

yield: 8-10 servings

* *

1 box frozen squid (3 pounds), thawed
1 cup corn starch or flour
1 tablespoon garlic salt
pepper
oil for deep frying

Clean squid and cut into 1/4 to 1/2-inch slices; drain thoroughly. Combine corn starch, garlic salt and pepper. Coat squid in corn starch and drop pieces one-by-one in heated oil. Deep-fry until brown. (Be careful of splatters.) Drain on paper towels.

Note: To clean squid, pull tentacles and draw out innards. Remove cartilage and rub off skin. Rinse, flushing out insides. If desired, tentacles may also be used. Cut tentacles just below eyes and discard eyes section.

Pūpū–Variety

Aburage Pūpū

yield: 8-10 appetizer servings

* *

2 packages aburage (2-oz. each), 8 pieces total
1 package shredded cod fish (4-oz.)
1/2 cup green onion, chopped
1 to 2 medium chili peppers, seeded and chopped

Sauce:

3 tablespoons sesame oil
4 tablespoons shoyu
1 tablespoon vinegar
3 tablespoons sugar
2 cloves garlic, minced
2 tablespoons roasted sesame seeds (optional)

Mix sauce ingredients until sugar is dissolved.

Cut aburage into strips and rinse in hot water. Squeeze out excess water. Lightly rinse cod fish in warm water. Place aburage, green onion, chili pepper and cod fish in bowl and toss. Add sauce and mix well together. Chill before serving.

Boiled Peanuts, Chinese-Style

yield: 10-12 appetizer servings

* *

1 pound raw peanuts
1 to 2 tablespoons salt
2 to 3 star anise

Rinse peanuts several times, or until water is clear. Cover peanuts with water. Add salt and star anise. Bring to boil. Lower heat and simmer, covered, for 1 to 2 hours, frequently stirring peanuts. Taste peanuts for doneness desired. Do not overcook.

Note: There are many varieties of peanuts. Some are better for roasting, others for boiling. Shop around for your favorite. I prefer the raw peanuts packaged by Exotic Food Distributors sold at Longs Store for this recipe.

Chili Burrito Rolls

yield: 64 appetizer servings

* *

1 can chili (15-oz.)
1 package cream cheese (8-oz.)
1 cup onion, chopped
1 package burrito wraps (1 pound size)
sour cream (optional)
taco sauce or salsa

Melt cream cheese slowly, stirring on low heat. Add chili and onion and cook on medium heat until heated through. Set aside to cool. Spread on burrito wrap. Spread desired amount of sour cream, if desired. Roll burrito and refrigerate to chill. Cut into 8 pieces. Serve with taco sauce or salsa.

Deviled Eggs

yield: 24 pieces

* *

12 large hard-boiled eggs, cooled
mayonnaise, to moisten
curry powder, to taste
salt and pepper, to taste

Peel eggs and slice lengthwise. Pop the yolks out into food processor or bowl. (Keep the whites in a separate dish.) Add a dash of curry powder, salt and pepper to taste. Begin with less seasoning. Mash yolks. Mix in mayonnaise to make it into frosting consistency. Add more curry, salt or pepper as needed.

Fill a pastry bag fitted with a "star" tip and squeeze filling into egg whites. Or just fill egg whites with spoonfuls of the yolk mixture.

Evie's Local-Style Party Mix

yield: about 6-1/2 quarts

* *

1 box Crispix® (12-oz. each)
1/2 box Corn Chex® or Rice Chex® (half of 15.6-oz. box)
2 cups snack mix (e.g. Gardetto's® Snack Mix or Kirkland
    Crunchy Snack Mix) or thin stick pretzels
2 cups salted macadamia nuts
1 jar Nori Komi Furikake (1.9-oz. each)
2 cups arare

Sauce:

1/2 cup butter (1 block)
1/4 cup Karo® light corn syrup
1/2 teaspoon garlic salt
1/4 teaspoon onion powder
1/2 tablespoon Worcestershire sauce

Melt all sauce ingredients in saucepan, set aside.

Divide Crispix®, Corn Chex®, snack mix or pretzels and macadamia nuts evenly into 2 large roasting pans. Pour 1/2 of mixture over each pan; gently mix. Sprinkle 1/2 jar of furikake into each pan; toss. Bake 1 hour at 250°F, tossing every 15 minutes. Cool and add arare.

Note: Recipe may be doubled. This makes a great gift to share with relatives and friends for the holidays. The children especially like the furikake and arare in this party mix!

Furikake Arare Popcorn

yield: 8 cups

* *

8 cups popped corn
1/4 cup melted butter
1/2 cup Nori Komi Furikake
1 cup arare

Pour melted butter over popcorn. Sprinkle furikake. Add arare. Eat immediately.

Microwave Boiled Peanuts

yield: 10-12 appetizer servings

* *

1 pound peanuts
1/4 cup Hawaiian salt

Wash peanuts and place in bowl. Cover peanuts with hot water and 1/4 cup salt. Put weight on to hold peanuts in water. Soak overnight.

Microwave half of the peanuts. Place in container with water and cover with plastic wrap. Microwave on HIGH for 5 minutes. Stir peanuts and microwave an additional 5 minutes. Take bowl of peanuts out of microwave and allow to sit in water and cool. Repeat with the other half.

Note: For less wet peanuts, remove and drain. For weight, I use a slightly smaller bowl filled with water to press down peanuts.

Green Onion Pretzels

yield: about 90 pretzels

* *

1 bunch green onions, minced (about 1/2 cup)
1 egg, beaten
1 can evaporated milk (13-oz.)
3/4 can water (use evaporated milk can), about 1 cup
1 box cornstarch (16-oz.)
1/2 cup flour
3 teaspoons salt
1/2 teaspoon pepper
oil for deep-frying

Chop, then finely mince green onion; set aside in small bowl. Heat oil to 350°F. Place rosette iron in oil to heat up.

In large bowl, beat egg with whisk. Add evaporated milk and water; mix together. Add cornstarch, flour, salt and pepper to liquid and mix together. Run through strainer so that batter is smooth and free of lumps. Add enough batter to bowl of minced green onions so that it is "soupy."

Pour some of the batter into a small bowl about the size of a rice bowl. Add about a teaspoon of the "soupy" green onion mixture and stir together. Dip hot iron into this mixture and return to oil. Cook until pretzels are slightly browned, turning once. Drain on paper towels.

Continue adding the green onion mixture to batter in small bowl, adjusting more or less green onion according to your taste.

Note: This is time consuming and a little difficult for a beginner. But it is also a huge favorite with all the Hee family. Amy Hee, my sister-in-law, adjusted and perfected this one and only original recipe. This has been our secret family recipe that we are now sharing with you.

Lavosh

yield: 8-10 appetizer servings

* *

2-3/4 cups flour
1/4 cup sugar
1/2 teaspoon salt
1/2 teaspoon baking soda
1 tablespoon sesame seeds
1 tablespoon poppy seeds
3/4 cup butter (1-1/2 blocks)
1 cup buttermilk

Sift together dry ingredients. Add seeds. Cut butter into dry ingredients. Add buttermilk. Mix together. Sprinkle flour on cookie sheet. Get about a baseball size of dough and press down. Cover with waxed paper and roll out thinly. Remove waxed paper and bake at 325°F to 350°F for 12 to 15 minutes or until light brown.

Hint: Check sides. If brown, sides may be cracked off, while middle part is returned to oven. Lavosh may be flipped over so top and bottom are crispy.

Note: This is the best lavosh I ever tasted. Jean Tanimoto gave me this recipe over 30 years ago and it still remains my favorite!

Onion Rings

yield: 8-10 servings

* *

3 large onions, cut crosswise into 1/2-inch rounds
ice water
1 cup flour
1/2 cup cornstarch
1 teaspoon baking soda
1/2 teaspoon salt
oil for deep-frying

Separate onions into rings. Soak in bowl of ice water with ice cubes for 1 hour. Combine dry ingredients in large bowl. Add 1-1/2 cups of ice water and whisk until the batter is smooth. Refrigerate for 1 hour. Heat oil for deep frying. Coat onion rings in batter; drop the rings, one by one, into hot oil. Fry, turning once until crisp and golden brown. Drain well on paper towels. Sprinkle with salt and serve hot.

Potato Skin with
Imitation Crab Filling

yield: 12 pieces

* *

6 small potatoes
4 tablespoons butter, melted
salt and pepper, to taste

Scrub potatoes with brush. Place potatoes directly on oven rack and bake at 400°F for 45 to 60 minutes or until done.* Allow to cool 20 to 30 minutes. Cut potatoes in half lengthwise. Scoop out pulp, leaving a 1/4-inch shell. (Use pulp for mashed potatoes.) Place potato skins on cookie sheet. Brush inside and outside of shell with butter. Broil 5 to 8 minutes or until edges are brown. Sprinkle with salt and pepper. For extra crispy potato skins, fry skins in hot oil.

Filling:

1/2 small onion, chopped
2 cloves garlic, minced
1 tablespoon butter
salt and pepper, to taste
1 can mushrooms, stems and pieces (4-oz.), drained
1/3 cup white wine
1/2 pound imitation crab, shredded
mayonnaise, to moisten

Saute onion and garlic in butter. Season with salt and pepper. Add mushrooms and wine. Bring to boil and cook until liquid evaporates. Cool. Add imitation crab. Add enough mayonnaise to bind. Mix well and stuff potato skins. Broil until golden.

Test doneness by pressing potato between fingers. (Use hot pad for protection.) Potato is done if it feels soft.

Ogo Kim Chee

yield: 6-8 appetizer servings

* *

1 pound seaweed, cleaned and separated into smaller
   pieces

Place seaweed in colander and pour boiling water over;
drain. Rinse with cool water; drain. Place in bowl and set
aside.

Sauce:

1/3 cup vinegar
1/4 cup sugar
2 tablespoons shoyu
1-1/2 teaspoons roasted sesame seeds
1 stalk green onion, chopped
1 chili pepper, seeded and minced
1 clove garlic, grated
1 inch piece fresh ginger, grated

Combine sauce ingredients and pour over seaweed. Chill
before serving.

Sesame Pancake Croquettes Pimetees Snack

yield: 9 cups

* *

1 bag sesame pancake croquettes® pimetees (14-oz.)*

Sauce:

1/2 cup butter (1 block)
1/4 cup sugar
1/4 cup Karo® light corn syrup
1-1/2 tablespoons shoyu

Boil together sauce ingredients, stirring until sugar is dissolved. Pour sauce over chips and coat well. Bake at 250°F to 300°F for 1 hour, stirring every 15 minutes. Transfer chips to another pan to cool. Mix with spoon to separate.

Note: At this time I only know of one place to purchase a bag of sesame pancake croquettes pimetees—at Ranch 99. But everyone who has tasted this has requested this recipe and has made the trip there. Thanks to Roberta Tokumaru who shared this recipe with the Aikahi Elementary School teachers.

Spicy Edamame (Soybeans)

yield: about 4 appetizer servings

* *

1 pound frozen edamame
8 cups water
1 tablespoon salt
1 to 2 cloves garlic, minced
1 Hawaiian chili pepper, remove seeds and mince
1 to 2 tablespoons salt, to taste

Boil water and add 1 tablespoon salt. Place frozen edamame into salted boiling water. Bring to boil again and cook for a few minutes. Drain well and return to pot. While edamame is still hot, add rest of ingredients and toss until well-coated. Refrigerate overnight. Serve cold, or warm in microwave just before serving.

Spinach Rolls

yield: about 80 pieces

* *

2 boxes chopped spinach (10-oz. each), thaw and
   squeeze excess water
1 container sour cream (8-oz.)
1 cup mayonnaise
1/2 cup bacon bits, (Hormel® Real Bacon Bits preferred)
1 package Hidden Valley® Original Ranch® Dressing (1-oz.)
1/4 cup green onion, chopped
1/4 cup water chestnut, chopped
1 package flour tortillas (17.5-oz.), 10 soft taco size tortillas

Mix together all ingredients (except tortillas) until completely blended. Divide mixture into 10 parts (about 1/3
cup each). Spread evenly on tortillas and roll. Wrap each
roll individually in waxed paper. Refrigerate overnight in
covered container or 3 hours in freezer prior to cutting for
easier slicing. Trim ends before slicing, if desired. Slice
into 8 pieces.

Veggie Pizza

yield: 9 x 13-inch pan

* *

Crust:

1 tube Pillsbury Crescent Rolls (8-oz.)

Press unrolled dough in 9 x 13-inch pan. Bake at 375°F for 10 minutes or until golden. Cool.

Filling:

1 package cream cheese (8-oz.), softened
2/3 cup mayonnaise
1 to 2 tablespoons Ranch-style package dressing

Blend filling ingredients together until smooth. Spread over cooled crust.

Topping:

1 carrot, peeled into slivers
1 small bunch broccoli, sliced
1 small head cauliflower, sliced
1 cucumber, seeded and sliced
1 can sliced olives (2.25-oz.), drained
1 red bell pepper, sliced
1 package grated Cheddar cheese (8-oz.)

Place vegetables and olives on top of filling and sprinkle with grated Cheddar cheese. Press vegetables into filling. Refrigerate. Cut into squares and serve.

Warabi Appetizer

yield: 8-10 servings

* *

1 bunch warabi (about 30 stalks)
1 package shredded codfish (1.75-oz.)
1/2 onion, thinly sliced
2 firm tomatoes, cubed

Dressing:

1/4 cup shoyu
1/2 cup sugar
2/3 cup lemon juice (about 4 lemons)
1/4 teaspoon garlic salt

Wash warabi under running water, removing "hair" follicles. Cut into 1-inch lengths. Cook warabi in boiling water for 1 to 2 minutes. Drain and immediately place in ice cold water. Drain and set aside.

Soak codfish in water for 10 to 15 minutes; drain and shred. Combine warabi, codfish, onion and tomatoes in mixing bowl. Mix dressing ingredients together and pour over warabi mixture; toss gently. Chill before serving.

Note: One of the good things about living in Hilo on the Big Island is that you always have a supply of fresh warabi available. For the rest of us, be sure to visit the Farmer's Market in downtown Hilo and pick up a bunch or two to bring back home. Warabi can be wrapped in wet newspaper, and covered with a plastic bag keeps very well in the refrigerator for about a week.

Potluck

Crispy Gau Gee

yield: 48-60 pieces

* *

Filling:

1/2 pound ground pork
1/2 pound shrimp, deveined, coarsely chopped
1/4 cup water chestnuts, chopped
1/4 cup dry shiitake mushrooms, softened (stems removed) and chopped
1/4 cup green onions, chopped
1 egg

Seasoning:

1 tablespoon cornstarch
1 tablespoon oyster sauce
1 teaspoon sugar
1 teaspoon shoyu
1/2 teaspoon salt
1/4 teaspoon pepper

Wrapper:

2 packages won ton pi (10-oz.each)

Mix all filling ingredients. Mix in seasoning. Place 1 generous teaspoonful filling in center of wrapper. Moisten edges of wrapper and fold wrapper in half to a rectangular shape. Press edges together to seal. Deep-fry in oil until golden brown. Drain on paper towels and serve with dipping sauce.

Dipping Sauce:
Option 1: *Local Style* Mix together 3 tablespoons Colman's® Mustard with 2 teaspoons water to make a paste. Add 1/4 teaspoon sesame oil and 4 tablespoons shoyu. Mix thoroughly.

Option 2: *Sweet Sour Sauce* Mix 1/2 cup vinegar, 2 table-spoons ketchup, 6 tablespoons sugar, 1/8 cup water with 1/2 teaspoon cornstarch. Cook over medium heat until thickened. Set aside to cool.

Option 3: Kikkoman or Lee Kum Kee's Chinese Sweet Sour Sauce

Option 4: Mae Ploy's™ Thai Sweet Chili Sauce

Chili

yield: 15-20 servings

* *

1 pound ground beef
1 onion, chopped
2 Portuguese sausages (10-oz. each), sliced
1 tablespoon oil
1 teaspoon salt
1 teaspoon sugar
1 teaspoon pepper
1 tablespoon chili powder
2 cans whole tomatoes (28-oz. each), drained and coarsely
    chopped
2 cans chili beans (15-oz. each)
1 can small red beans (15-oz.), drained
1 can tomato sauce (8-oz.)

Heat oil and brown together hamburger, onion and Portuguese sausage. Add rest of ingredients and simmer mixture, uncovered, for 2 hours.

California Pan Sushi

yield: 9 x 13-inch pan

* *

3 cups rice
1 package imitation crab sticks (10-oz.), shredded
1 cup mayonnaise
1 ripe avocado
1 cucumber, cut in thin 1-inch strips
1 container radish sprouts (4-oz.), trim roots off
20 to 30 sheets of seasoned Temaki nori

Rinse and cook rice. When rice cools, lay rice in pan. (Do not press down.) Mix crab and mayonnaise. Lay over rice. Spoon avocado over crab. Top with cucumber and radish sprouts. Spoon California sushi into a sheet of seasoned nori and fold.

Gon Lo Mein

yield: 10-12 servings

* *

2 pounds fried chow mein noodles
1/4 cup oyster sauce
1/4 cup sesame oil
oil for stir-frying
Hawaiian salt, to season
1/4 pound char siu, slivered, for garnish
Chinese parsley, chopped, for garnish

Vegetables:

1 small onion, slivered
2 stalks celery, julienne cut
1 small carrot, julienne cut
1/4 pound snow peas
1 package bean sprout mixture (12-oz.)
6 dried shiitake mushrooms, softened in water, sliced

Combine chow mein noodles with oyster sauce and sesame oil and marinate for 1 hour. In heavy frying pan or wok, heat oil and stir-fry noodles. Place on platter, set aside.

Stir-fry lightly each vegetable separately in oil and Hawaiian salt (except mushrooms). Set aside. Stir-fry mushrooms without salt and add all ingredients (except char siu and Chinese parsley) into the pan and toss together. Place over noodles and garnish with char siu and Chinese parsley.

Korean Chicken Wings

yield: 12-15 appetizer servings

* *

5 pounds chicken wings
2 cups flour and cornstarch combination
2 tablespoons salt
oil for deep-frying

Sauce:

2 tablespoons sugar
1/2 cup shoyu
3 cloves garlic, finely minced
2 Hawaiian chili peppers, seeded and minced
1/2 cup green onions, thinly chopped
2 tablespoons roasted sesame seeds (optional)

Combine sauce ingredients in small bowl. Set aside.

Mix flour and salt in large plastic bag. Place a batch of chicken wings in flour; shake to coat. Deep-fry. Place on paper towels to drain. Dip wings once in sauce just to coat and place on serving platter. Repeat until all wings are cooked and dipped in sauce.

Lasagna

yield: 10 x 14-inch pan

* *

2 pounds ground beef
1 tablespoon oil
1 clove garlic, minced
1 onion, chopped
1 green pepper, chopped
1 can tomato sauce (15-oz.)
1 can tomato sauce (8-oz.)
2 teaspoons salt
2 cans basil, garlic and oregano tomato paste (6-oz. each)
3 cans water (measure with tomato paste can)
2 envelopes spaghetti sauce mix (1.37-oz. each)
1 box extra-wide lasagna noodles (16-oz.)
1 package mozzarella cheese slices (6-oz.)

Heat oil; brown garlic slightly. Add onion and green pepper and cook until tender. Add meat; do not overcook the meat. Add rest of ingredients (except noodles and mozzarella cheese slices) and simmer about 1 hour.

Cook noodles according to package directions. Rinse with cold water; drain.

Alternate layers of noodles and meat mixture in 10 x 14-inch pan, ending with meat mixture. Top with cheese slices. Bake, uncovered, at 325°F for 30 to 45 minutes or until cheese is lightly browned.

Mochiko Chicken

yield: 12-15 servings

* *

5 pounds chicken thighs, deboned, or chicken wings
4 eggs, beaten
10 tablespoons shoyu
6 tablespoons sugar
8 tablespoons mochiko
8 tablespoons cornstarch
4 cloves garlic, minced
1 teaspoon salt
1/2 cup green onion, finely chopped
1 tablespoon sesame seeds
1 teaspoon fresh ginger, grated
oil for frying

Mix everything (except chicken and oil). Marinate chicken for 5 hours or overnight in refrigerator. Fry chicken in 1-inch hot oil until golden brown on both sides. Cool and cut into slices.

Note: If desired, discard chicken skin before marinating. Tastes great with or without skin and it can be prepared a day ahead. This is one of the all time favorites with locals.

Mun Doo

yield: about 54 pieces

* *

1/2 pound ground pork
1/2 pound ground beef
1 package bean sprouts (12-oz.), blanched, minced and
    squeezed dry
2 cups kim chee, minced and squeezed dry
1 block firm tofu (20-oz.), drained and squeezed dry
1 teaspoon salt
1/8 teaspoon pepper
2 packages mun doo wrappers (12-oz. each)
oil for deep-frying

Brown pork, drain and cool. In large bowl, combine cooked pork, ground beef, bean sprouts, kim chee, tofu, salt and pepper; mix well.

To form mun doo, moisten edges of wrapper with water. Put 1 tablespoon of mixture in center of each wrapper. Fold in half; pinch edges together to seal. Heat oil to 375°F. Fry mun doo until lightly browned. Serve with Ko Choo Jung Dipping Sauce or vinegar-shoyu sauce.

Koo Choo Jung Dipping Sauce:

1/3 cup shoyu
1/3 cup vinegar
1/3 cup sugar
3 tablespoons koo choo jung
3 tablespoons green onion, chopped
1 tablespoon sesame seed (optional)

Combine all ingredients.

Potato and Macaroni Salad

yield: about 25 servings

* *

3 to 4 medium potatoes, boiled, peeled and cut into small
   cubes
1 package elbow macaroni (16-oz.)
3 to 4 eggs, hard-boiled and diced
2 tablespoons onion, finely diced
1 to 2 stalks celery, finely diced
2 tablespoons sweet pickle relish
1 package imitation crab (8-oz.), shredded
1 block kamaboko (6-oz.), shredded
1/4 carrot, grated
1 cup frozen peas, thawed
mayonnaise, to moisten
salt and pepper, to taste

Cook macaroni according to package directions. Rinse and
drain thoroughly in colander, turning over occasionally until
macaroni looks dry (about 30 minutes). In small bowl, combine onion, celery and sweet pickle relish. Set aside.

After all items are cooled, combine all ingredients in large
container (discard excess liquid from sweet pickle relish).
Mix together. Refrigerate.

Note: This is my mom's recipe and my husband Don's
favorite potato and macaroni salad which I always prepare
for special occasions.

Hint: Be sure that the macaroni is drained thoroughly and
dry before mixing.

Seafood Salad

yield: 9 x 13-inch pan

* *

1/2 pound shrimp, clean and cut into bite-size pieces
1 small tray scallops (about 0.36-pound), rinsed and cut into
    bite-size pieces
1/2 pound imitation crab, cut into bite-size pieces
1 small head broccoli, cut into bite-size pieces
1 envelope onion soup mix
1 can cream of mushroom soup, family-size (26-oz.)
2 cups mayonnaise
8 ounces Cheddar cheese, shredded
8 ounces Monterey Jack cheese, shredded
1-1/2 tubes Ritz® crackers (about 50 pieces), crushed

Combine and mix all ingredients (except cheese and crackers) in 9 x 13-inch pan. Sprinkle cheese, covering entire pan. Cover with Ritz® crackers and bake at 300°F for 30 minutes. May be served hot or cold.

Shrimp and Kamaboko Tempura

yield: about 50 pieces

* *

6 to 8 medium shrimp, cleaned and chopped
1 block kamaboko (6-oz.), chopped
1 cup water chestnuts, finely chopped
1 stalk green onion, chopped
oil for deep-frying

Batter:

3/4 cup flour
1/2 teaspoon salt
1 teaspoon sugar
1/4 cup ice water
1 egg, slightly beaten

Combine flour, salt and sugar; set aside. Combine water and egg and add to flour mixture. Stir only to moisten the dry ingredients (not runny and thin). Add kamaboko, shrimp, water chestnuts and green onion. Mix well together. Drop by teaspoonfuls into heated oil. Fry until light brown. Drain on paper towels. Serve hot.

Note: For safety, use 2 teaspoons, one to scoop mixture and the other to scrape off into the oil. This recipe tastes like the tempura at Shirokiya, really great. Try the batter with vegetables such as string beans and gobo.

Somen Salad

yield: 9 x 13-inch pan

* *

1 package somen (8-oz.)
1 small head iceberg lettuce, shredded
3 green onions, finely chopped
Chinese parsley, chopped (optional)
1 Japanese cucumber, slivered
1 kamaboko (6-oz.), slivered
3 eggs, beaten and fried, thinly sliced into 2-inch strips
1/4 pound char siu or ham, slivered

Dressing:

1 to 2 tablespoons roasted sesame seeds
4 tablespoons sugar
6 tablespoons vinegar
4 tablespoons shoyu
1-1/2 teaspoons salt
1/2 cup oil

Break somen noodles in half and cook according to package directions. Rinse with cold water and drain; cool. Place somen noodles on bottom of pan. Layer in order the rest of the ingredients. Refrigerate.

Note: When ready to serve, place dressing on the side. Each person can then use the desired amount of dressing to his taste. This also prevents the salad from getting soggy.

Warabi Sushi Rice

yield: 12-15 servings

* *

Vinegar Sauce:

1/2 cup sugar
5/8 cup rice vinegar
2 teaspoons salt

Combine sauce ingredients and cook on medium heat until boiling. Cool and set aside.

1 bunch warabi (about 25 to 30 stalks), parboiled and cut
    into 1/3-inch slices
3 tablespoons oil
1 tablespoon dried shrimp, finely diced
2 pieces aburage (half of 2-oz. package), finely chopped
1 carrot, finely diced
4 dry shiitake mushrooms, soaked and finely diced
1/4 cup kurome, soaked and coarsely chopped
1/2 block kamaboko (half of 6.5-oz. block), finely diced
1 can ajitsuke seasoned baby clams (6-oz.)
1/2 cup shoyu
1/3 cup sugar
4-1/2 cups rice

Prepare all ingredients before cooking rice so that when rice is cooking, you can time the cooking of the vegetables so that they will be ready to toss together with hot rice.

Rinse rice and cook. While rice is cooking heat oil in large frying pan, add shrimp; stir-fry. Add aburage and stir-fry 3 to 5 minutes or until aburage gets crispy and not limp. Add carrots, shiitake and kurome and stir-fry on medium-high heat for 3 minutes. Lower heat and cook longer as needed to soften carrots. Add clams (including juice), shoyu and sugar; mix everything together. Add warabi and stir over medium-high heat for 2 to 3 minutes. Mix in kamaboko and turn off heat. Drain vegetable mixture in colander.

While rice is still hot, mix with vinegar sauce. Add vegetable mixture and toss well so that mixture is evenly distributed throughout rice. Cool before covering.

Note: See page 106, "Warabi Appetizer" for information on warabi.

Taegu Ocean Salad Linguine
yield: about 8-10 servings

✳ ✳

1 package linguine (8-oz.)
3 ounces taegu
2 Japanese cucumbers, seeded and sliced in 1-inch strips
8 ounces imitation crab, shredded
8 ounces fresh green ocean salad
1/2 bottle furikake (half of 1.9-oz.)
Tropics® Oriental Dressing (12-oz.), adjust to taste
Chinese parsley, to garnish (optional)

Break linguine into thirds and cook according to package directions; drain and cool. Mix linguine with taegu, cucumbers, imitation crab and ocean salad. Just before serving, mix in desired amount of furikake and Tropics® Oriental Dressing. Garnish with Chinese parsley, if desired.

Stuffed Aburage with Somen

yield: 48 pieces

* *

6 packages fully cooked and seasoned fried bean curd
   (3.88-oz. each), 8 pieces per package, rectangle type
   (e.g., Inari Sushi-No-Moto)
1 package somen (8-oz.)
2 blocks kamaboko (6-oz. each), sliced into thin strips
8 ounces green ocean salad
6 ounces Tropics® Oriental Dressing (half of 12-oz. bottle),
   adjust to taste

Prepare seasoned fried bean curd (aburage) according to package directions and set aside. Reserve juices.

Break somen noodles in half before cooking. Cook somen according to directions on package. Drain thoroughly; cool.

Mix together somen, kamaboko, green ocean salad, oriental dressing and juice from aburage. Squeeze aburage gently to remove excess liquid and stuff mixture into aburage. Refrigerate.

Note: Very light and refreshing. Very easy to prepare and very popular at potlucks. Also tasty without the aburage and eaten as a salad.

Glossary

* *

aburage	deep-fried tofu, fried bean curd
'ahi	yellowfin tuna, shibi (Japanese)
aku	skipjack tuna, bonito or katsuo
arare	Japanese rice crackers
char siu	roasted sweet red pork
Chinese parsley	cilantro
daikon	white radish or turnip
edamame	soybeans
fishcake	angelfish mashed with water and salt
five spices powder	blend of Chinese star anise, cloves, fennel, peppercorns and cinnamon
furikake	rice condiment
gau gee	Chinese dumpling, usually deep-fried
gon lo mein	noodles with meat and vegetables
green ocean salad	deep sea seasoned seaweed
guacamole	avocado dip
gyoza	Japanese meat and vegetable dumpling
hana ebi	colored shrimp powder
Hawaiian salt	coarse sea salt
hibachi	outdoor cooking grill
'inamona	roasted, pounded and salted kukui nut
kalbi	Korean barbecued short ribs, kalbi
kamaboko	steamed fish cake
kanpyo	dried strips of gourd
kim chee	Korean spicy pickled vegetables
ko choo jung	Korean sauce made from mochi rice and chili peppers
konnyaku	tuber root flour cake
kurome	dried black seaweed
laulau	steamed bundle of meat in tī leaves
lavosh	Armenian flat bread
limu	seaweed
limu kohu	type of seaweed
lomi	massage, rub or crush ingredients with fingers
lomi salmon	salted salmon and tomatoes
long rice	translucent mung bean noodles
lū'au leaves	taro leaves
lumpia	Filipino spring roll filled with meat, vegetables or fruit
maki	to roll

mirin	sweet rice wine
miso	fermented soybean paste
mochiko	glutinous rice flour
mun doo	Korean meat and vegetable dumpling
musubi	rice ball
namako	sea cucumber
namasu	vinegar-flavored food
nori	dried seaweed sheets
norimaki	sushi rolled in nori
ogo	Japanese term for seaweed, red stringy seaweed found in Hawaiʻi
oyster sauce	oyster-flavored sauce
panko	flour meal for breading
pipikaula	dried beef, jerky
poi	steamed and mashed taro
poke	cut-up pieces of raw fish with seasonings
ponzu	citrus-seasoned shoyu
pūpū	appetizer or hors d'oeuvre
sake	Japanese rice wine
shiitake	dried mushrooms
shinko maki	takuwan-filled sushi
shiofuke konbu	chopped salted sea kelp
shish kabob	meat, chicken, shrimp, etc. on skewers
shoyu	soy sauce
siu mai	Chinese meat and vegetable dumpling
somen	fine wheat-flour noodles
sushi	vinegar-flavored rice
taegu	spiced-flavored codfish
tako	octopus
takuwan	pickled turnip
temaki	hand-rolled sushi
tempura	fritters
teriyaki	soy-flavored sauce
tī leaf	broad leaf of tī plant
tofu	fresh soybean curd
tortilla	Mexican flat bread made of cornmeal or wheat flour
unagi	eel
wakame	long, curling strands of seaweed
warabi	fern shoot
wasabi	Japanese horseradish, sold in paste and powdered form
won ton	wun tun, Chinese meat dumpling
won ton pi	won ton wrappers
yakitori	Japanese-style grilled chicken

Index

A

Aburage
  Aburage Pupu, 91
  Easy Cone (Inari) Sushi, 25
'Ahi
  'Ahi Limu Poke, 2
  Furikake Seared 'Ahi, 77
  Hawaiian-Style California Rolls, 26
  Seared 'Ahi, 86
  Seared 'Ahi Poke, 7
  Spicy Tuna, 33
Aku
  Aku Poke, 3
  Poke, 6
  Shoyu Poke, 8
Artichoke
  Artichoke and Crab Dip, 11
Avocado
  7-Layer Dip, 17
  California Inside Out Sushi, 24
  California Pan Sushi, 110
  Hawaiian-Style California Rolls, 26
  Temaki Roll, 34

B

Bacon-Wrapped Shrimp, 85
Barbecue Sticks, 37
Black Olives
  7-Layer Dip, 17
  Crab-Stuffed Mushrooms,74
Boiled Peanuts, Chinese Style, 92
Buffalo Wings, 60
Bean Sprouts
  Gon Lo Mein, 111
  Lumpia, 42
  Mun Doo, 115
  Shrimp Lumpia, 84
Broccoli
  Seafood Salad, 117
  Veggie Pizza, 105

C

California Inside Out Sushi, 24
California Pan Sushi, 110
Carrot
  Easy Cone (Inari) Sushi, 25
  Gon Lo Mein, 111
  Lumpia, 42
  Maki Sushi, 28
  Shrimp Lumpia, 84
Caviar Spread, 12
Cheddar Cheese
  7-Layer Dip, 17
  Hot Crab Dip, 16
  Spicy Hot Bean Dip, 18
  Taco Won Ton, 57
Chicken
  Buffalo Wings, 60
  Easy Macnut Chicken Drummettes, 61
  Fried Chicken Drummettes, 62
  Garlic Chicken, 63
  Parmesan Chicken Pupu, 65
  Sesame Seed Chicken, 66
  Sweet-Sour Chicken Wings, 67
  Tasty Chicken Pupu, 68
  Yaki Tori Sticks, 69
Chili, 109
Chili Burrito Rolls, 93
Chili Pepper Water, 2
Chili Salsa
  7-Layer Dip, 17
Chinese Parsley
  Vela-Bailey Almost Homemade Salsa, 20
Clams
  Clams and Ground Pork Pupu, 71
  Clam Dip, 13
  Spinach Dip, 19
Cocktail Shrimp, 72
Crab Cakes, 72

Cream Cheese
  Chili Burrito Rolls, 93
  Spam Won Ton, 52
  Spicy Hot Bean Dip, 18
Cucumber
  California Inside Out Sushi, 24
  California Pan Sushi, 110
  Hawaiian-Style California Rolls, 26
  Imitation Crab Poke, 3
  Taegu Ocean Salad Linguine, 121
  Temaki Roll, 34
  Veggie Pizza, 105
Curry Mango Cream Cheese Spread,
  14
Crab
  Artichoke and Crab Dip, 11
  Crab Cakes, 73
  Crab-Stuffed Mushrooms, 74
  Crispy Gau Gee, 108
  Hot Crab Dip, 16
  Kamaboko-Crab Dip, 16
Crispy Gau Gee, 108

D
Deviled Eggs, 94
Deep-Fried Oysters, 75
Dips and Spreads
  7-Layer Dip, 17
  Artichoke and Crab Dip, 11
  Caviar Spread, 12
  Clam Dip, 13
  Curry Mango Cream Cheese
    Spead, 14
  Guacamole, 15
  Hot Crab Dip, 16
  Kamaboko-Crab Dip, 16
  Spicy Hot Bean Dip, 18
  Spinach Dip, 19
  Vela-Bailey Almost Homemade
    Salsa, 20
  Vienna Sausage Spread, 21
Dried Shrimp
  Maki Sushi, 28
  Vinegar Sauce for Sushi, 23

E
Easy Cone (Inari) Sushi, 25

Easy Macnut Chicken Drummettes, 61
Easy Shrimp Skewers, 75
Easy Spareribs, 38
Eggs
  Deviled Eggs, 94
  Maki Sushi, 28
  Temaki Roll, 34
Evie's Local-Style Party Mix, 95

F
Fish
  'Ahi Limu Poke, 2
  Aku Poke, 3
  Hawaiian-Style California Rolls, 26
  Poke, 6
  Seared 'Ahi Poke, 7
  Shoyu Poke, 8
Fishcake and Spam® Pupu, 76
Fried Chicken Drummettes, 62
Fried Ginger Pork, 39
Furikake Nori
  Furikake Arare Popcorn, 96
  Furikake Seared 'Ahi, 77
  Layered Sushi, 27
  Ono Broiled Sushi, 30

G
Garlic Chicken, 63
Gon Lo Mein, 111
Green Beans
  Lumpia, 42
  Shrimp Lumpia, 84
Green Onion Pretzels, 97
Green Pepper
  Shish Kabob, 50
Ground Beef
  Chili, 109
  Lasagna, 113
  Mun Doo, 115
  Spring Rolls, 54
  Taco Won Ton, 57
Ground Pork
  Clams and Ground Pork Pupu, 71
  Gyoza (Pot Stickers), 40
  Lumpia, 42
  Mun Doo, 115
  Oyster Rolls, 82

Siu Mai, 51
Spring Rolls, 54
Won Ton, 56
Guacamole, 15
Gyoza, 40

H
Hawaiian-Style California Rolls, 26
Hot Crab Dip, 16

I
Imitation Crab
  Artichoke and Crab Dip, 11
  California Inside Out Sushi, 24
  California Pan Sushi, 110
  Crab-Stuffed Mushrooms, 74
  Hawaiian-Style California Rolls, 26
  Hot Crab Dip, 16
  Imitation Crab Poke, 3
  Kamaboko-Crab Dip, 16
  Ono Broiled Sushi, 30
  Potato and Macaroni Salad, 116
  Spring Rolls, 54

K
Kalbi, 41
Kamaboko
  Kamaboko-Crab Dip, 16
  Potato and Macaroni Salad, 116
  Spam Won Ton, 52
  Temaki Roll, 34
Korean Chicken Wings, 112

L
Lasagna, 113
Lavosh, 98
Layered Sushi, 27
Lomi Salmon on Skewers, 78
Lumpia, 42

M
Maki Sushi, 28
Manapua, 44
Artichoke and Crab Dip, 11
Meat
  Barbecue Sticks, 37
  Easy Spareribs, 38

Fried Ginger Pork, 39
Gyoza (Pot Stickers), 40
Kalbi, 41
Lumpia, 42
Manapua, 44
Mini Laulau Pupu, 43
Peppered Steak, 46
Pipikaula (Beef Jerky, Hawaiian
  Style), 47
Pork Adobo Pupu, 48
Pupu-Style Spareribs, 49
Shish Kabob, 50
Siu Mai, 51
Spam® Won Ton, 52
Spam® Won Ton with Green
  Chilies, 53
Spring Rolls, 54
Stuffed Fried Lotus Root, 55
Taco Won Ton, 57
Teriyaki Meatballs, 58
Won Ton, 56
Microwave Boiled Peanuts, 96
Mimi's Shrimp, 79
Mini Laulau Pupu, 43
Mochiko Chicken, 114
Mun Doo, 115

N
Namako (or Konnyaku) Pupu, 77
O
Octopus (Tako) Pupu with Miso
  Sauce, 80
Ogo (Limu)
  'Ahi Limu Poke, 2
  Aku Poke, 3
  Ogo Kim Chee, 101
  Poke, 6
  Seared 'Ahi Poke, 7
  Tofu Poke, 8
Onion Rings, 99
Ono Broiled Sushi, 30
Ono Poke, 4
Ono Shrimp Poke, 5
Oven-Barbecued Chicken Wings, 64
Oysters
  Deep-Fried Oysters, 75
  Oyster Bacon Wrap, 81

Oyster Rolls, 82

P

Parmesan Cheese
  Artichoke and Crab Dip, 11
  Parmesan Chicken Pupu, 65
Peanuts
  Boiled Peanuts, Chinese Style, 92
  Microwave Boiled Peanuts, 96
Peppered Steak, 46
Pipikaula (Beef Jerky, Hawaiian Style),
  47
Poke
  'Ahi Limu Poke, 2
  Aku Poke, 3
  Imitation Crab Poke, 3
  Ono Poke, 4
  Ono Shrimp Poke, 5
  Poke, 6
  Seared 'Ahi Poke, 7
  Shoyu Poke, 8
  Tako Poke, 9
  Tofu Poke, 8
Pork Adobo Pupu, 48
Potluck
  California Pan Sushi, 110
  Chili, 109
  Crispy Gau Gee, 108
  Gon Lo Mein, 111
  Korean Chicken Wings, 112
  Lasagna, 113
  Mochiko Chicken, 114
  Mun Doo, 115
  Potato and Macaroni Salad, 116
  Seafood Salad, 117
  Shrimp and Kamaboko Tempura, 118
  Somen Salad, 119
  Stuffed Aburage with Somen, 122
  Taegu Ocean Salad Linguine, 121
  Warabi Sushi Rice, 120
Pupu-Style Spareribs, 49
Potato and Macaroni Salad, 116
Potato Skin With Imitation Crab
  Filling, 100

R

Refried Beans

7-Layer Dip, 17
Spicy Hot Bean Dip, 18
Taco Won Ton, 57

S

Salt and Pepper Shrimp, 83
Seafood
  Bacon-Wrapped Shrimp, 85
  Clams and Ground Pork Pupu, 71
  Cocktail Shrimp, 72
  Crab Cakes, 73
  Crab-Stuffed Mushrooms, 74
  Deep-Fried Oysters, 75
  Easy Shrimp Skewers, 75
  Fishcake and Spam® Pupu, 76
  Furikake Seared 'Ahi, 77
  Lomi Salmon on Skewers, 78
  Mimi's Shrimp, 79
  Namako (or Konnyaku) Pupu, 77
  Octopus (Tako) Pupu with Miso
    Sauce, 80
  Oyster Bacon Wrap, 81
  Oyster Rolls, 82
  Salt and Pepper Shrimp, 83
  Seared 'Ahi, 86
  Shrimp Lumpia, 84
  Shrimp Tempura, 87
  Shrimp Toast, 88
  Squid Pupu (Fried Calamari), 89
Seafood Salad, 117
Seared 'Ahi, 86
Seared 'Ahi Poke, 7
Sesame Pancake Croquettes,
  Pimetees Snack, 102
7-Layer Dip, 17
Sesame Seed Chicken, 66
Shiitake Mushrooms
  Crispy Gau Gee, 108
  Easy Cone (Inari) Sushi, 25
  Gon Lo Mein, 111
  Maki Sushi, 28
  Lumpia, 42
Shinko Maki, 31
Shish Kabob, 50
Siu Mai, 51
Shoyu Poke, 8

Shrimp
  Bacon-Wrapped Shrimp, 85
  Easy Shrimp Skewers, 75
  Lumpia, 42
  Mimi's Shrimp, 79
  Salt and Pepper Shrimp, 83
  Shrimp and Kamaboko Tempura,
    118
  Shrimp Lumpia, 84
  Shrimp Tempura, 87
  Shrimp Toast, 88
  Spam® Won Ton, 52
  Won Ton, 56
Siu Mai, 51
Somen or Soba Sushi, 35
Somen Salad, 119
Sour Cream
  7-Layer Dip, 17
  Ono Broiled Sushi, 30
  Spicy Hot Bean Dip, 18
  Spinach Dip, 19
Spam®
  Fishcake and Spam® Pupu, 76
  Spam® Musubi, 32
  Spam® Won Ton, 52
  Spam® Won Ton with Green
    Chilies, 53
Spicy Edamame (Soybeans), 103
Spicy Hot Bean Dip, 18
Spicy Tuna, 33
Spinach Dip, 19
Spinach Roll, 104
Spring Rolls, 54
Squid Pupu (Fried Calamari), 89
Stuffed Aburage with Somen, 122
Stuffed Fried Lotus Root, 55
Sushi
  California Inside Out Sushi, 24
  Easy Cone (Inari) Sushi, 25
  Hawaiian-Style California Rolls, 26
  Layered Sushi, 27
  Maki Sushi, 28
  Ono Broiled Sushi, 30
  Shinko Maki, 31
  Somen or Soba Sushi, 35
  Spam® Musubi, 32
  Spicy Tuna, 33

  Temaki Roll (California Roll), 34
  Vinegar Sauce for Sushi, 23
Sweet-Sour Chicken Wings, 67

T
Taco Won Ton, 57
Taegu Ocean Salad Linguine, 121
Tasty Chicken Pupu, 68
Temaki Roll, 34
Teriyaki Meatballs, 58
Tofu Poke, 8
Tomatoes
  7-Layer Dip, 17
  Lomi Salmon on Skewers, 78
  Shish Kabob, 50
  Vela-Bailey Almost Homemade
    Salsa, 20

U
Unagi
  Maki Sushi, 28

V
Variety
  Aburage Pupu, 91
  Boiled Peanuts, Chinese Style, 92
  Chili Burrito Rolls, 93
  Deviled Eggs, 94
  Evie's Local-Style Party Mix, 95
  Furikake Arare Popcorn, 96
  Green Onion Pretzels, 97
  Lavosh, 98
  Microwave Boiled Peanuts, 96
  Ogo Kim Chee, 101
  Onion Rings, 99
  Potato Skin with Imitation Crab
    Filling, 100
  Sesame Pancake Croquettes
    Pimetees Snack, 102
  Spicy Edamame (Soybeans), 103
  Spinach Rolls, 104
  Veggie Pizza, 105
  Warabi Appetizer, 106
Veggie Pizza, 105
Vela-Bailey Almost Homemade Salsa,
  20

Vienna Sausage Spread, 21
Vinegar Sauce for Sushi, 23

W
Warabi Appetizer, 106
Warabi Sushi Rice, 120
Watercress
  Maki Sushi, 28
Water Chestnut
  Bacon-Wrapped Shrimp, 85
  Crispy Gau Gee, 108

Fishcake and Spam® Pupu, 76
Lumpia, 42
Oyster Rolls, 82
Shrimp Toast, 88
Siu Mai, 51
Spinach Dip, 19
Won Ton, 56
Won Ton, 56

Y
Yaki Tori Sticks, 69

The Working Woman's Quick Cookbook

*Healthy recipes in 30 minutes or less —
plus businesswomen's success secrets*

AMERICAN BUSINESS WOMEN'S ASSOCIATION

Published by the American Business Women's Association

Copyright© American Business Women's Association
National Headquarters
9100 Ward Parkway
P.O. Box 8728
Kansas City, Missouri 64114-0728
816-361-6621
816-361-4991 fax

Library of Congress Catalog Number: 96-85127
ISBN: 0-9652588-0-7

Edited, Designed and Manufactured by:
Favorite Recipes® Press
P.O. Box 305142
Nashville, Tennessee 37230
1-800-358-0560

Manufactured in the United States of America
First Printing: 1996   20,000 copies

Contents

A Seat at the Table 4

Come Join Our Circle 6

Nutritional Profile Guidelines 8

Appetizers & Beverages 9
    Appetizers 10
    Beverages 29

Soups & Salads 35
    Soups 36
    Salads 43

Main Dishes 65
    Meats 66
    Poultry 103
    Seafood 133
    Egg & Pasta Dishes 147

Vegetables & Side Dishes 161
    Vegetables 162
    Side Dishes & Breads 179

Desserts & Cookies 191
    Desserts 192
    Cookies 201

Cakes & Pies 211
    Cakes 212
    Pies 223

Contributors 230

Saving Fat and Calories 233

Index 235

Order Information 239

A Seat at the Table

I learned life's lessons in the kitchen. As I stepped off the school bus and climbed the tall hill called Poplar Street, Mom was waiting for me in the kitchen. As she started dinner, I'd pull up a chair next to her at the countertop. I'd stir while she talked about work and I about school. My sister Brenda and I took turns setting the table. When Dad arrived home from work, he'd join our kitchen conversations. The kitchen was the heart of our home.

In a home where both parents work, everyone helps out in the kitchen. After dinner, Dad cleared the table, Mom washed dishes and Brenda and I dried them. Then it was homework time. I'd spread my algebra across the kitchen table as Dad coached me through story problems. "What do you know?" he'd ask, waiting as I studied the problem. "Now, what do you need to know?" he'd nudge until I found the solution.

While Dad became my teacher, Mom became my mentor. Our kitchen conversations were a mix of cooking and career lessons. When we made gingerbread houses for the holidays, Mom taught me lessons in teamwork, creativity and patience. As I entered high school, Mom gave me my first office job. I spent summers answering phones, filing and writing business letters. As I moved on to college, she helped me craft my first résumé at the kitchen table. Each experience we shared shaped my work ethic and lifelong learning attitude. Today I use those career lessons in my job as editor in chief of *Women in Business*®, the national magazine of the American Business Women's Association.

That's what makes *The Working Woman's Quick Cookbook* special. Besides discovering simple, healthy recipes, you'll meet working women who have command of their careers as well as their kitchens. The cookbook's contributors aren't professional chefs. They're working moms, retired businesswomen and business owners. Most of the meals can be ready to serve in 30 minutes or less. As you preheat the oven or punch the microwave buttons, pause and read their inspirational stories and business success tips.

By purchasing this book, you join working women, corporations, foundations and other individuals in funding the 50th anniversary celebration of the American Business Women's Association. Our mission is to bring together businesswomen of diverse occupations and to provide opportunities for them to help themselves and others grow personally and professionally through leadership, education, networking support and national recognition.

Just as I learned valuable lessons at my family's kitchen table, ABWA is a place where working women gain the skills and confidence to pursue their dreams and find success on their own terms. Each month, 90,000 women gather in one of ABWA's 1,600 local chapters to network, share career lessons and learn new business skills. Together, we're helping working women get a seat at the corporate table.

Wendy S. Myers

Wendy S. Myers
Editor in Chief, *Women in Business*®

Come Join Our Circle

Throughout the nation, the American Business Women's Association has touched the lives of women like Diane Walters. A savvy health-care executive, Diane had no idea she was management's next prey when her hospital reorganized its staff. After feeling stripped of her professional identity, she turned to her career support network—the American Business Women's Association. Friends hand-carried her résumé to prospective employers, boosted her confidence and shared job-hunting advice.

Now wiser about her career, Diane understands the value of business leagues like ABWA. "No one is responsible for your career but you," says Diane, who now works as a nurse manager at University Medical Center in Tucson, Arizona.

That's why lifelong learning and support networks like the American Business Women's Association are survival tools for today's working women. Lifetime employability means you seek growth, make an ongoing effort to improve your skills and can adapt and synthesize your skills into other positions and industries. ABWA's network includes more than 90,000 members and 1,600 local chapters in the United States and Puerto Rico. Through business-skills training, ABWA helps working women get the skills that pay the bills. The association offers continuing education credit programs, leadership-development training, local chapters, regional and national conventions, scholarship programs and *Women in Business*®, ABWA's national bimonthly magazine.

The American Business Women's Association is the pathway to business and personal success for working women like Vickey Smith. Her supervisor introduced Vickey to ABWA and helped shape her attitude about lifelong learning. "Even though GTE has provided training during my career, I became serious about developing my educational path and pursing my degree," says Vickey, a staff administrator at the GTE regional office in Marion, Ohio. "ABWA seminars, programs and monthly chapter meetings have been instrumental in three promotions to upper-management positions."

Since women in all occupations—from *Fortune 500* managers to business owners—belong to ABWA, you can tap a powerful career network.

Beverly Jo Couch, a material management supervisor for AT&T in Oklahoma City, relies on her ABWA support network to keep her career grounded. "By understanding what different women face in their jobs, I find out that I'm not alone," she says. "Something may be stressing me out and I find out that it's bothering someone else. If I want to vent job frustrations, I have several members I can call. They're a great support group."

That support is a valuable resource for ABWA's 11,000-plus business owners who range from the president of a North Carolina corporation with 17,000 employees to a self-employed hula instructor in Honolulu. In local chapters, entrepreneurs can share their expertise, find new customers and have a circle of friends who cheer them on. "My circle of ABWA friends and business advisers helps me solve problems and share entrepreneurial ideas," says Becky Early, who owns Arrow Supply Co. in Charlotte, North Carolina, and served as ABWA's 1994 national president.

ABWA also follows women through their career life span. The association's PrimeTime Connection program helps businesswomen make the transition from work to retirement. Designed for retired businesswomen, the program offers local chapters with flexible meeting times, travel discounts, a newsletter, seminars and other benefits.

Surrounded by a circle of friends in an ABWA chapter, you can develop leadership and business skills that ensure lifetime employability. Local chapters provide a "learning laboratory" for women to explore and test their abilities in a supportive and inspirational environment. For membership information or a list of chapters near you, write the American Business Women's Association, 9100 Ward Parkway, P.O. Box 8728, Kansas City, Missouri 64114-0728; call (816) 361-6621 or fax (816) 361-4991.

Come join our circle.

Nutritional Profile Guidelines

The editors have attempted to present recipes in a form that allows approximate nutritional values to be computed. Persons with dietary or health problems or whose diets require close monitoring should not rely solely on the nutritional information provided. They should consult their physicians or a registered dietitian for specific information.

Abbreviations for Nutritional Profile

Cal — Calories	T Fat — Total Fat	Sod — Sodium
Prot — Protein	Chol — Cholesterol	g — grams
Carbo — Carbohydrates	Fiber — Dietary Fiber	mg — milligrams

Nutritional information for these recipes is computed from information derived from many sources, including materials supplied by the United States Department of Agriculture, computer databanks and journals in which the information is assumed to be in the public domain. However, many specialty items, new products and processed foods may not be available from these sources or may vary from the average values used in these profiles. More information on new and/or specific products may be obtained by reading the nutrient labels. Unless otherwise specified, the nutritional profile of these recipes is based on all measurements being level.

▲ Artificial sweeteners vary in use and strength so should be used "to taste," using the recipe ingredients as a guideline. Sweeteners using aspartame (NutraSweet® and Equal®) should not be used as a sweetener in recipes involving prolonged heating which reduces the sweet taste. For further information on the use of these sweeteners, refer to package information.

▲ Alcoholic ingredients have been analyzed for basic ingredients, although cooking causes the evaporation of alcohol, thus decreasing caloric content.

▲ Buttermilk, sour cream and yogurt are the types available commercially.

▲ Cake mixes, which are prepared using package directions, include 3 eggs and 1/2 cup oil.

▲ Chicken, cooked for boning and chopping, has been roasted; this method yields the lowest caloric values.

▲ Cottage cheese is cream-style with 4.2% creaming mixture. Dry curd cottage cheese has no creaming mixture.

▲ Eggs are all large. To avoid raw eggs that may carry salmonella as in eggnog or 6-week muffin batter, use an equivalent amount of commercial egg substitute.

▲ Flour is unsifted all-purpose flour.

▲ Garnishes, serving suggestions and other optional additions and variations are not included in the profile.

▲ Margarine and butter are regular, not whipped or presoftened.

▲ Milk is whole milk, 3.5% butterfat. Lowfat milk is 1% butterfat. Evaporated milk is whole milk with 60% of the water removed.

▲ Oil is any type of vegetable cooking oil. Shortening is hydrogenated vegetable shortening.

▲ Salt and other ingredients to taste as noted in the ingredients have not been included in the nutritional profile.

▲ If a choice of ingredients has been given, the nutritional profile information reflects the first option. If a choice of amounts has been given, the nutritional profile reflects the greater amount.

The Working Woman's Quick Cookbook

Appetizers & Beverages

Cooking Up Knowledge

While Judy Gatewood works in the kitchen, she listens to educational or self-improvement cassettes. As co-owner and corporate secretary-treasurer of Gatewood Roofing Inc. in Topeka, Kansas, Judy looks for simple ways to get more business-skills training—and squeeze it into her busy schedule.

While cooking her family's favorite recipes, she prepares herself for success. Judy's favorite audiotapes include "Strategies for Career Success" (Nightengale Conant) by Sharon Crain and "The Psychology of Winning" (Simon & Schuster Audio) by Denis E. Waitley.

Appetizers

Establish a Career You'll Enjoy

At 70, Pat Malone still accepts challenges and seizes opportunities. After 40 years in the "corporate cocoon," she is turning a new page in her life as an independent consultant in aviation, law and motivation. "When a reporter asked if he could use my age in an article, I said, 'My Lord, yes! That's the whole point—that at 70, there's someone who's just finishing up one career and starting another,' " says the former manager for Delta Air Lines in Atlanta.

As a businesswoman who's been down the road and back—a couple of times—Pat feels some women seek a job simply to make big bucks rather than establish a career they'll enjoy. The most important thing, she says, is to do what you want to do and be happy. "My philosophy is that every woman has got to look at her options. Once you decide what you want to do, set your goals and do it with grace and a sense of humor," says the 1995 Top Ten Business Woman of ABWA and 1986 national president. "I found out a long time ago I couldn't be Superwoman. I kept getting my cape caught in the door."

Artichoke Dip

2   *(9-ounce) cans artichoke hearts, drained, chopped*
1¹/₂   *cups freshly grated Parmesan cheese*
2   *cups mayonnaise*
    Minced garlic to taste
    Salt and pepper to taste

▲ Preheat the oven to 350 degrees.

▲ Combine the artichoke hearts, cheese and mayonnaise in a bowl and mix well. Season with the garlic, salt and pepper. Spoon into a 1¹/₂-quart casserole.

▲ Bake for 30 minutes.

▲ Yield: 18 servings.

Approx Per Serving: Cal 221; Prot 4 g; Carbo 2 g; T Fat 22 g; 88% Calories from Fat; Chol 21 mg; Fiber 0 g; Sod 387 mg

Maureen Welling, Owner, Flying Bridge II Restaurant
Englewood, Florida

Spring Garden Dip

1   *cup sour cream*
¹/₄   *cup mayonnaise*
2   *teaspoons sugar*
¹/₂   *teaspoon salt*
¹/₄   *teaspoon white pepper*
1   *clove of garlic, minced*
¹/₄   *cup minced green bell pepper, drained*
¹/₄   *cup minced green onions, drained*
¹/₄   *cup minced cucumber, drained*
¹/₄   *cup minced radishes, drained*
¹/₄   *cup minced celery, drained*

▲ Blend the sour cream, mayonnaise, sugar, salt, white pepper and garlic in a bowl. Stir in the green pepper, green onions, cucumber, radishes and celery.

▲ Serve with crudités or crackers.

▲ Yield: 20 servings.

Approx Per Serving: Cal 48; Prot <1 g; Carbo 1 g; T Fat 5 g; 85% Calories from Fat; Chol 7 mg; Fiber <1 g; Sod 77 mg

Hot Chipped Beef Dip

16   *ounces cream cheese, softened*

2   *cups sour cream*

2   *tablespoons dried onion flakes*

1/2   *teaspoon garlic powder*

2   *(2-ounce) packages chipped beef, chopped*

1/2   *cup chopped pecans*

▲ Preheat the oven to 350 degrees.

▲ Blend the cream cheese and sour cream in a bowl. Add the onion flakes and garlic powder. Stir in the chipped beef.

▲ Spoon into a 1-quart baking dish sprayed with nonstick cooking spray. Top with the pecans.

▲ Bake for 20 minutes or until the edges are bubbly.

▲ Serve hot with crackers or fresh vegetables.

▲ May be prepared ahead and stored in the refrigerator or freezer. May be prepared in 2 smaller baking dishes; bake one now and freeze the other for later use.

▲ Yield: 30 servings.

Approx Per Serving: Cal 105; Prot 3 g; Carbo 2 g; T Fat 10 g; 84% Calories from Fat; Chol 25 mg; Fiber <1 g; Sod 184 mg

Marie Fretz, Graphic Arts Coordinator, Honeywell, Inc.
Perkasie, Pennsylvania

Clam Dip in Bread

1	(16-ounce) round loaf sourdough bread
16	ounces cream cheese, softened
16	drops of Tabasco sauce
1¹/₂	teaspoons seasoned salt
1	tablespoon chopped parsley
2	(6-ounce) cans minced clams
2¹/₂	teaspoons garlic powder
1¹/₂	teaspoons Beau Monde seasoning
¹/₂	cup clam juice
1	(16-ounce) loaf French bread, cut into pieces

▲ Preheat the oven to 300 degrees.

▲ Cut the top from the sourdough bread. Remove and reserve the inside of the loaf.

▲ Mix the cream cheese, Tabasco sauce, seasoned salt, parsley, clams, garlic powder, seasoning and clam juice in a bowl. Spoon into the bread bowl. Replace the top.

▲ Wrap the bread bowl twice with foil. Place on a baking sheet.

▲ Bake for 2 hours.

▲ Use the French bread pieces and reserved sourdough bread for dipping.

▲ Yield: 30 servings.

Approx Per Serving: Cal 145; Prot 5 g; Carbo 17 g; T Fat 6 g; 39% Calories
  from Fat; Chol 21 mg; Fiber 1 g; Sod 350 mg

Susie Dreiling, Marketing Coordinator/Consultant, Visible Changes
St. Louis, Missouri

Appetizers

Sherried Hot Crab Meat

8 ounces cream cheese, softened
1 tablespoon mayonnaise
2 tablespoons dry sherry
1 teaspoon lemon juice
1/8 teaspoon Tabasco sauce, or to taste
1 (7-ounce) can crab meat, drained
1/3 cup sliced almonds

▲ Preheat the oven to 350 degrees.

▲ Mix the cream cheese, mayonnaise, sherry, lemon juice and Tabasco sauce in a bowl. Stir in the crab meat. Spoon into a shallow baking dish. Top with the almonds.

▲ Bake for 15 to 20 minutes or until heated through and bubbly.

▲ Serve with crackers.

▲ Yield: 8 servings.

Approx Per Serving: Cal 162; Prot 8 g; Carbo 2 g; T Fat 14 g; 75% Calories from Fat; Chol 54 mg; Fiber <1 g; Sod 177 mg

Marianne Cobarrubias, Corporate Communications Assistant
The Timberland Company
West Newbury, Massachusetts

Shrimp Dip

1/2 cup light mayonnaise
1/4 cup lemon yogurt
1 (4-ounce) can tiny shrimp, drained
2 tablespoons prepared horseradish
2 tablespoons finely chopped green onions
1 tablespoon catsup

▲ Combine the mayonnaise, yogurt, shrimp, horseradish, green onions and catsup in a bowl; mix well. Chill until serving time.

▲ Serve with chips, crackers or vegetables.

▲ Yield: 20 servings.

Approx Per Serving: Cal 26; Prot 2 g; Carbo 2 g; T Fat 1 g; 48% Calories from Fat; Chol 12 mg; Fiber <1 g; Sod 53 mg

Donna Gustafson, Information System Coordinator, City of Lincoln
Lincoln, Nebraska

Taco Dip

1	*pound ground beef*
1	*(16-ounce) can refried beans*
2	*(4-ounce) cans diced green chiles*
1	*(12-ounce) jar hot or mild salsa*
1	*cup shredded Monterey Jack cheese*
1	*cup shredded Cheddar cheese*
1	*cup guacamole*
1	*cup sour cream*
1/4	*cup chopped green onions or sliced black olives*

▲ Brown the ground beef in a skillet, stirring until crumbly; drain.

▲ Layer the beans, green chiles, ground beef, salsa, Monterey Jack cheese and Cheddar cheese in a microwave-safe dish.

▲ Microwave on High for 10 minutes or until the cheeses melt.

▲ Spread with the guacamole and sour cream. Top with the green onions.

▲ Serve with tortilla chips as a dip.

▲ May roll up leftovers in soft tortillas burrito-style and reheat in microwave.

▲ Yield: 20 servings.

Approx Per Serving: Cal 165; Prot 10 g; Carbo 7 g; T Fat 10 g; 54% Calories from Fat; Chol 33 mg; Fiber 2 g; Sod 44 mg

Marianne Cobarrubias, Corporate Communications Assistant
The Timberland Company
West Newbury, Massachusetts

Crab Meat Mousse

1	envelope unflavored gelatin
8	ounces cream cheese
1	small onion, grated
1	(10-ounce) can cream of mushroom soup
1	cup mayonnaise
12	ounces fresh or canned crab meat
1	tablespoon each Worcestershire sauce and warm water
1	cup finely chopped celery

▲ Soften the gelatin in a small amount of cold water.

▲ Combine the cream cheese, onion and soup in a saucepan. Cook until heated through, stirring until smooth.

▲ Stir in the mayonnaise, crab meat, Worcestershire sauce, gelatin, water and celery. Spoon into a 4-cup mold. Chill for 8 to 10 hours or until firm.

▲ Yield: 20 servings.

Approx Per Serving: Cal 156; Prot 5 g; Carbo 2 g; T Fat 14 g; 81% Calories from Fat; Chol 36 mg; Fiber <1 g; Sod 281 mg

Linda Gibson, Sales, Gerrard Packaging Systems
Vancouver, Washington

Salmon Spread

2	(6-ounce) packages smoked salmon
9	ounces whipped cream cheese, softened
3	green onions, finely chopped
	Lemon juice to taste
	Garlic to taste

▲ Combine the salmon, cream cheese, green onions, lemon juice and garlic in a bowl; mix well.

▲ Chill for 3 hours or longer. Spread on French bread or rye rounds.

▲ May substitute 1 cup crab meat for the salmon.

▲ Yield: 6 servings.

Approx Per Serving: Cal 220; Prot 12 g; Carbo 3 g; T Fat 18 g; 72% Calories from Fat; Chol 59 mg; Fiber <1 g; Sod 597 mg

Marianne Cobarrubias, Corporate Communications Assistant
The Timberland Company
West Newbury, Massachusetts

Betty's Oven Seafood Spread

12	ounces cream cheese, softened
1/3	cup minced green bell pepper
1/3	cup chopped green onions
2	tablespoons lemon juice
1/2	teaspoon Worcestershire sauce
1/2	teaspoon salt
1/8	teaspoon garlic powder, or to taste
1	(6-ounce) can crab meat
1	(4-ounce) can shrimp, drained
1	(6-ounce) can clams
2	tablespoons slivered almonds

▲ Preheat the oven to 350 degrees.

▲ Combine the cream cheese, green pepper, green onions, lemon juice, Worcestershire sauce, salt and garlic powder in a bowl; mix well. Stir in the crab meat, shrimp and clams.

▲ Spoon into a 1-quart casserole. Sprinkle with the almonds.

▲ Bake until bubbly and heated through.

▲ Yield: 40 servings.

Approx Per Serving: Cal 44; Prot 3 g; Carbo 1 g; T Fat 3 g; 68% Calories
from Fat; Chol 20 mg; Fiber <1 g; Sod 78 mg

Debbie Harvil, Office Manager, Brentwood Chiropractic Clinic
Brentwood, Tennessee

Roasted Garlic

1 *whole head of garlic*
1 *teaspoon olive oil*

▲ Preheat the oven to 350 degrees.

▲ Peel the garlic, leaving the head intact. Drizzle with the olive oil. Wrap tightly in foil. Place on a baking sheet.

▲ Bake for 1 hour or until cooked through.

▲ Squeeze individual cloves onto fresh French bread or a baked potato.

▲ Garlic roasted in the skin without exposure to the air has a mellower flavor than raw garlic.

▲ May be cooked on a grill for 35 minutes while barbecuing other foods.

▲ Yield: 6 servings.

Approx Per Serving: Cal 13; Prot <1 g; Carbo 1 g; T Fat 1 g; 52% Calories from Fat; Chol 0 mg; Fiber <1 g; Sod 1 mg

Marianne Cobarrubias, Corporate Communications Assistant
The Timberland Company
West Newbury, Massachusetts

Jezebel

1 *(8-ounce) jar apple jelly*
1 *(12-ounce) jar pineapple preserves*
1/2 *cup prepared horseradish*
1/4 *cup prepared mustard*
Pepper to taste
8 *ounces cream cheese*

▲ Combine the jelly, preserves, horseradish, mustard and pepper in a bowl. Chill for 8 to 10 hours.

▲ Pour over the cream cheese.

▲ Serve with butter crackers.

▲ Yield: 20 servings.

Approx Per Serving: Cal 116; Prot 1 g; Carbo 20 g; T Fat 4 g; 31% Calories from Fat; Chol 13 mg; Fiber <1 g; Sod 89 mg

Louise P. Ce Balt, Owner and President, Wimpy's Bar & Grille
Roseville, Michigan

Almond-Ham Roll-Ups

8	ounces cream cheese, softened
2	tablespoons light mayonnaise
1	teaspoon instant minced onion
1	teaspoon Worcestershire sauce
1/4	teaspoon dry mustard
1/4	teaspoon paprika
1/8	teaspoon pepper
1/8	teaspoon hot sauce
1	tablespoon finely chopped toasted almonds
1	(12-ounce) package thinly sliced boiled ham

▲ Combine the cream cheese, mayonnaise, onion, Worcestershire sauce, mustard, paprika, pepper, hot sauce and almonds in a bowl; mix well.

▲ Spread 1 tablespoon of the mixture on each ham slice. Roll up as for a jelly roll, starting at the short end. Wrap in plastic wrap. Let stand for several hours.

▲ Cut each roll into 3/4-inch slices.

▲ May be prepared ahead and stored in the refrigerator or placed in the freezer for up to 1 month. Thaw at room temperature for 1 hour before serving.

▲ Yield: 60 servings.

Approx Per Serving: Cal 26; Prot 2 g; Carbo <1 g; T Fat 2 g; 71% Calories from Fat; Chol 8 mg; Fiber <1 g; Sod 90 mg

Marvis M. Bedford, Office Manager, Environmental Protection Agency
Atlanta, Georgia

Cheese and Bacon Rolls

12   slices American cheese
12   slices whole wheat or white bread, crusts trimmed
12   slices bacon

▲ Preheat the oven to 350 degrees.

▲ Place 1 slice of cheese on each piece of bread. Roll up and wrap each with a bacon slice, securing with a wooden pick.

▲ Place on a baking sheet.

▲ Bake for 5 minutes or until the cheese melts and the bacon is cooked through.

▲ May partially cook bacon before assembling.

▲ Yield: 12 servings.

Approx Per Serving: Cal 157; Prot 8 g; Carbo 11 g; T Fat 9 g; 52% Calories from Fat; Chol 19 mg; Fiber 1 g; Sod 456 mg

Donna Rita Weeks, Secretary, Chattanooga Human Rights
Chattanooga, Tennessee

Garden Greek Appetizer

8   ounces cream cheese, softened
8   ounces feta cheese, crumbled
1/4 cup plain yogurt
1   clove of garlic, minced
1/4 teaspoon pepper
2   tomatoes, chopped
1   medium seedless cucumber, chopped
3   green onions, finely chopped
3   black olives, finely chopped

▲ Process the cream cheese, feta cheese, yogurt, garlic and pepper in a food processor until smooth.

▲ Spread the mixture in a 10-inch pie plate. Chill until firm.

▲ Top with the tomatoes, cucumber, green onions and black olives. Serve with miniature pitas or assorted breads and crackers.

▲ Yield: 12 servings.

Approx Per Serving: Cal 129; Prot 5 g; Carbo 4 g; T Fat 11 g; 75% Calories from Fat; Chol 38 mg; Fiber 1 g; Sod 278 mg

Hot Curried Cheese Appetizers

  6 English muffins, split into halves
  8 ounces sharp Cheddar cheese, shredded
 $1/2$ cup mayonnaise
 $1/4$ teaspoon curry powder
 $1/4$ cup chopped green onions or scallions
 $1/4$ teaspoon salt
  1 (2-ounce) can pitted black olives, sliced

▲ Preheat the broiler.

▲ Cut each muffin half into 4 wedges.

▲ Combine the cheese, mayonnaise, curry powder, green onions and salt
  in a medium bowl, stirring gently until evenly mixed. Add the olives,
  stirring gently until the olives are evenly distributed.

▲ Spread the cream cheese mixture on each muffin wedge. Place on an
  11x15-inch baking sheet.

▲ Broil 3 inches from broiler for 2 minutes or until bubbly.

▲ Serve hot.

▲ Yield: 48 servings.

Approx Per Serving: Cal 54; Prot 2 g; Carbo 4 g; T Fat 4 g; 61% Calories
   from Fat; Chol 6 mg; Fiber <1 g; Sod 94 mg

Janis C. Peterson, Sales Assistant, Paine Webber
Palm Beach Gardens, Florida

Appetizers

Crabbettes

4   ounces sharp Cheddar cheese, shredded
1/2 cup butter, shredded
6   ounces fresh or frozen white crab meat, drained
6   English muffins, split into halves

▲ Preheat the broiler.

▲ Mix the cheese and butter in a bowl. Stir in the crab meat.

▲ Spread the mixture on each muffin half. Cut each piece into quarters. Place on a baking sheet or broiler pan.

▲ Broil for 5 minutes.

▲ Serve hot.

▲ May be prepared ahead and frozen on a baking sheet covered tightly with freezer-strength foil. Will keep in freezer for up to 1 month.

▲ Yield: 48 servings.

Approx Per Serving: Cal 32; Prot 2 g; Carbo 4 g; T Fat 1 g; 28% Calories from Fat; Chol 6 mg; Fiber <1 g; Sod 59 mg

Jane W. Deibler, 1980 ABWA District Vice President, Mary Kay Consultant
Lancaster, Pennsylvania

Crab-Mushroom Canapés

3	slices bacon, cut into pieces
4	ounces mushrooms, sliced
1/4	cup chopped onion
1	cup crab meat
1	cup shredded Swiss cheese
1/3	cup grated Parmesan cheese
1/2	cup mayonnaise
6	English muffins, cut into halves
2	tablespoons butter, softened
	Cayenne and paprika to taste

▲ Preheat the oven to 400 degrees.

▲ Cook the bacon in a skillet over medium heat until crisp; remove the bacon and drain on paper towels.

▲ Sauté the mushrooms and onion in the bacon drippings in the skillet until the mushrooms begin to brown; drain. Let cool.

▲ Mix the crab meat, Swiss cheese, Parmesan cheese and mayonnaise in a bowl. Stir in the mushroom mixture.

▲ Spread the muffin halves with butter. Top with the crab meat mixture. Place on a baking sheet.

▲ Bake for 15 minutes. Cut each muffin piece into halves. Sprinkle with the cayenne and paprika.

▲ Yield: 24 servings.

Approx Per Serving: Cal 109; Prot 4 g; Carbo 7 g; T Fat 7 g; 58% Calories from Fat; Chol 16 mg; Fiber <1 g; Sod 166 mg

Diane Cullen, Community Volunteer, Retired
Beaverton, Oregon

Green Chile Cocktail Fingers

1   *(4-ounce) can chopped green chiles*
1   *(3-ounce) jar bacon bits*
1   *pound sharp Cheddar cheese, shredded*
6   *eggs*
1/8 *teaspoon Tabasco sauce, or to taste*
    Salt and pepper to taste

▲ Preheat the oven to 350 degrees.

▲ Layer the green chiles, bacon bits and cheese in a greased 6x9-inch glass baking dish.

▲ Beat the eggs in a bowl. Season with the Tabasco sauce, salt and pepper. Pour over the cheese.

▲ Bake for 30 minutes. Cut into finger-sized pieces. Serve warm.

▲ Yield: 16 servings.

Approx Per Serving: Cal 170; Prot 12 g; Carbo 3 g; T Fat 12 g; 65% Calories
   from Fat; Chol 109 mg; Fiber <1 g; Sod 398 mg

Pam Powers, Broker/Owner, Preferred Real Estate Center
Hendersonville, North Carolina

Quick Nachos

1/3 *(7-ounce) package tortilla chips*
8   *ounces ground beef, browned, drained*
1   *small onion, chopped*
1   *large tomato, chopped*
4   *ounces mozzarella cheese, shredded*
4   *ounces Cheddar cheese, shredded*

▲ Line a microwave-safe plate with the tortilla chips. Top with layers of ground beef, onion and tomato. Sprinkle with the mozzarella cheese and Cheddar cheese.

▲ Microwave for 3 minutes or until the cheeses melt.

▲ May top with salsa, jalapeño peppers, sour cream and/or guacamole.

▲ Yield: 6 servings.

Approx Per Serving: Cal 278; Prot 18 g; Carbo 10 g; T Fat 19 g; 60% Calories
   from Fat; Chol 63 mg; Fiber 1 g; Sod 269 mg

Rita Mary Weir, Assistant Manager, Wal-Mart
Exeter, New Hampshire

Pita Wedges

6   pita pockets
2   tablespoons olive oil
1   cup each shredded mozzarella cheese and grated Parmesan cheese
    Garlic powder and oregano to taste

▲ Preheat the oven to 350 degrees.

▲ Place the pita pockets on a baking sheet. Brush each piece with olive oil. Sprinkle with the mozzarella cheese and Parmesan cheese. Season with the garlic powder and oregano.

▲ Bake for 10 to 15 minutes or until heated through and cheese is melted. Cut each pita into quarters.

▲ May use cooked broccoli, asparagus and/or pepperoni as toppings. May be prepared ahead and reheated in a toaster oven.

▲ Yield: 24 servings.

Approx Per Serving: Cal 84; Prot 4 g; Carbo 9 g; T Fat 4 g; 43% Calories from Fat; Chol 7 mg; Fiber <1 g; Sod 176 mg

Nancy O. Lundy, Administrative/Personnel Assistant, Fred F. Groff, Inc.
Lancaster, Pennsylvania

Oyster Cracker Snacks

1   (1-pound) package oyster crackers
1   envelope ranch salad dressing mix
1¹/₂   tablespoons dillweed
¹/₂   tablespoon lemon pepper
³/₄   cup vegetable oil

▲ Combine the crackers, salad dressing mix, dillweed and lemon pepper in a large jar or covered plastic bowl; shake well.

▲ Pour the vegetable oil over the mixture and mix well. Let stand for 24 hours, shaking occasionally.

▲ May add 1 tablespoon garlic salt to the mixture.

▲ Yield: 30 servings.

Approx Per Serving: Cal 117; Prot 1 g; Carbo 12 g; T Fat 7 g; 56% Calories from Fat; Chol 0 mg; Fiber <1 g; Sod 302 mg

Lois Francis, 1990 ABWA District Vice President, Sales Support Manager
Great American Opportunities
Nashville, Tennessee

Pizza Burgers

1   pound ground beef, browned, drained
1   teaspoon oregano
1/4   cup chopped onion
2   teaspoons Tabasco sauce
1   clove of garlic, minced
1   (10-ounce) can cream of mushroom soup
1   (6-ounce) can tomato paste
1   (16-ounce) loaf party rye bread, cut into slices
1   cup shredded mozzarella cheese

▲ Preheat the oven to 350 degrees.

▲ Combine the ground beef, oregano, onion, Tabasco sauce, garlic, mushroom soup and tomato paste in a bowl; mix well.

▲ Spread on the bread slices. Top with the cheese.

▲ Bake for 15 minutes.

▲ Yield: 36 servings.

Approx Per Serving: Cal 79; Prot 5 g; Carbo 8 g; T Fat 3 g; 35% Calories from Fat; Chol 12 mg; Fiber 1 g; Sod 206 mg

Marianne Cobarrubias, Corporate Communications Assistant
The Timberland Company
West Newbury, Massachusetts

Stuffed Mushrooms

16   medium or large fresh mushrooms
1   to 2 tablespoons lemon juice or lime juice
4   ounces cream cheese, softened
1/4   teaspoon garlic powder
1   teaspoon chopped parsley, chives or green onions

▲ Remove the stems from the mushrooms; mince the stems. Sprinkle the caps with lemon juice and toss lightly to prevent discoloring.

▲ Beat the cream cheese in a mixer bowl until light and fluffy. Add the garlic powder, parsley and minced stems.

▲ Fill the mushroom caps with the mixture, using a pastry bag or spoon. Garnish with additional parsley. Serve cold.

▲ May be prepared 1 to 2 days ahead and stored in the refrigerator. Recipe may be doubled.

▲ Yield: 16 servings.

Approx Per Serving: Cal 30; Prot 1 g; Carbo 1 g; T Fat 3 g; 73% Calories from Fat; Chol 8 mg; Fiber <1 g; Sod 22 mg

Margaret-Haley S. Moya, National Airspace Systems Operations Manager
Federal Aviation Administration
Longmont, Colorado

Zucchini Balls

2   zucchini, grated
6   eggs
1   sleeve crackers, crushed
1/2   cup grated Parmesan cheese
1   tablespoon each salt (or to taste) and pepper

▲ Mix the squash with the eggs in a bowl. Stir in the cracker crumbs. Add the cheese, salt and pepper.

▲ Drop by desired size spoonfuls into a nonstick skillet. Fry for 15 to 20 minutes or until browned.

▲ Yield: 6 servings.

Approx Per Serving: Cal 219; Prot 13 g; Carbo 20 g; T Fat 10 g; 41% Calories from Fat; Chol 219 mg; Fiber 2 g; Sod 1546 mg

Marianne Cobarrubias, Corporate Communications Assistant
The Timberland Company
West Newbury, Massachusetts

Appetizers

Aunt Sherry's Hot Dogs

1   (10-count) package hot dogs
1   cup packed brown sugar
1   cup catsup
1   cup bourbon

▲ Cut each hot dog diagonally into 8 pieces.

▲ Combine the hot dogs, brown sugar, catsup and bourbon in a saucepan. Cook over medium heat until the brown sugar dissolves and the mixture is bubbly, stirring constantly. Reduce the heat to low. Simmer, covered, for 1 hour or until the sauce is syrupy, stirring occasionally.

▲ Serve in a small fondue pot or other warmer. Spear each hot dog piece with a wooden pick.

▲ Best if refrigerated for 24 hours before reheating and serving. May be frozen. Sauce will stain plastic dishes or utensils.

▲ Yield: 80 servings.

Approx Per Serving: Cal 41; Prot 1 g; Carbo 3 g; T Fat 2 g; 45% Calories
   from Fat; Chol 4 mg; Fiber <1 g; Sod 117 mg

Janet Reinhart, Executive Secretary, NationsBank
Houston, Texas

Stuffed Hot Dogs

8   hot dogs
3   cups mashed potatoes
1   cup shredded Monterey Jack cheese

▲ Preheat the oven to 350 degrees.

▲ Slice the hot dogs lengthwise without cutting all the way through. Spread apart and stuff with the mashed potatoes. Top with the cheese.

▲ Place on a baking sheet or in a baking pan.

▲ Bake for 6 to 8 minutes or just until heated through. Cut into bite-size pieces. Spear with wooden picks.

▲ Yield: 8 servings.

Approx Per Serving: Cal 296; Prot 11 g; Carbo 16 g; T Fat 22 g; 64% Calories
   from Fat; Chol 43 mg; Fiber 2 g; Sod 953 mg

Marianne Cobarrubias, Corporate Communications Assistant
The Timberland Company
West Newbury, Massachusetts

Beverages

Breaking Through Barriers

Jo Ann Salazar learned at an early age that life wasn't going to be easy being a woman—especially a Mexican-American woman. When she took her college admission test, she was called into the office because a mistake had been made. She was told that no girl—particularly no Mexican girl—had ever scored that high. She would have to retake the test—right then, with a proctor in the room.

Jo Ann agreed, and scored even higher. "I've spent a lot of time fighting prejudices and preconceived notions about who I am," says Jo Ann, director of public and legal services for the Colorado Bar Association in Denver and a 1995 Top Ten Business Woman of ABWA. "If you know who you are and what you can do, no one can take that away. I knew I had to get into college, so I stood my ground and said, 'You can't budge me, you can't do this because I'm a girl or because I'm Mexican!' Since then, whenever people told me I couldn't do something because I was a girl, I'd say, 'Oh, I can't? Watch me!'"

Beverages

Fireside Coffee

2	cups nonfat dairy creamer
1¹/₂	cups hot chocolate mix
1¹/₂	cups instant coffee granules
1¹/₂	cups sugar
1	teaspoon ground cinnamon
¹/₂	teaspoon ground nutmeg

▲ Combine the creamer, hot chocolate mix, coffee, sugar, cinnamon and nutmeg in a large airtight container; mix well.

▲ Combine 1 to 2 teaspoons of the mixture with 1 cup hot water in a cup for each serving.

▲ Yield: 40 servings.

Approx Per Serving: Cal 90; Prot 1 g; Carbo 17 g; T Fat 2 g; 19% Calories from Fat; Chol <1 mg; Fiber <1 g; Sod 47 mg

Spiced Tea

³/₄	cup instant tea
2	cups orange instant breakfast drink mix
1	(3-ounce) package mixed fruit gelatin
1	package instant lemonade mix
1	to 1¹/₂ cups sugar
2	teaspoons ground cinnamon

▲ Mix the tea, breakfast drink mix, gelatin, lemonade mix, sugar and cinnamon together in a large airtight container.

▲ Mix 2 tablespoons of the tea mixture or to taste with 1 cup boiling water for each serving.

▲ Yield: 40 servings.

Approx Per Serving: Cal 101; Prot <1 g; Carbo 26 g; T Fat <1 g; <1% Calories from Fat; Chol 0 mg; Fiber 0 g; Sod 8 mg

Champagne Sparkler

Juice of ¹/₂ lime
1 *ounce gin*
1 *ounce Triple Sec*
5 *ounces (about) cold Champagne*

▲ Combine the lime juice, gin, Triple Sec and some cracked ice in a cocktail shaker or heavy-duty blender container; mix well.

▲ Pour into a tall clear 8-ounce glass. Fill with the Champagne.

▲ Yield: 1 serving.

Approx Per Serving: Cal 278; Prot <1 g; Carbo 17 g; T Fat <1 g; <1% Calories from Fat; Chol 0 mg; Fiber <1 g; Sod 11 mg

Marianne Cobarrubias, Corporate Communications Assistant
The Timberland Company
West Newbury, Massachusetts

Yummy Irish Cream

2 *eggs*
1 *(14-ounce) can sweetened condensed milk*
1¹/₂ *teaspoons coconut extract*
1 *cup half-and-half*
¹/₄ *cup pineapple juice*
¹/₄ *cup chocolate syrup*
11 *to 15 ounces Scotch whisky*

▲ Beat the eggs in a bowl with a wire whisk. Add the condensed milk, flavoring, half-and-half, pineapple juice, chocolate syrup and whisky in the order listed, whisking well after each addition.

▲ May store in refrigerator for up to 2 weeks. May use egg substitute instead of eggs to reduce the danger of salmonella.

▲ Yield: 20 servings.

Approx Per Serving: Cal 146; Prot 3 g; Carbo 14 g; T Fat 4 g; 22% Calories from Fat; Chol 32 mg; Fiber <1 g; Sod 40 mg

Marianne Cobarrubias, Corporate Communications Assistant
The Timberland Company
West Newbury, Massachusetts

Cranberry Cordial

1¹/₂   *cups cranberries*
1¹/₂   *cups sugar*
    1   *(750-milliliter) bottle sauvignon blanc*

▲ Combine the cranberries and sugar in a saucepan. Cook until the sugar dissolves, stirring constantly. Add the wine and mix well.

▲ Pour into bottles and seal. Let stand in a cool place for 22 days or longer. Strain into glasses.

▲ Yield: 8 servings.

Approx Per Serving: Cal 216; Prot <1 g; Carbo 40 g; T Fat <1 g; <1% Calories from Fat; Chol 0 mg; Fiber 1 g; Sod 5 mg

Fresh Peach Daiquiri

    2   *medium fresh peaches, cut into chunks*
1¹/₂   *ounces light rum*
    1   *tablespoon lime juice*
    2   *teaspoons sugar*
¹/₂   *to 1 cup crushed ice*

▲ Combine the peaches, rum, lime juice, sugar and ice in a blender container. Process at high speed for 10 seconds.

▲ Pour into glasses. Garnish each glass with a thick peach slice.

▲ Yield: 2 servings.

Approx Per Serving: Cal 105; Prot 1 g; Carbo 15 g; T Fat <1 g; 1% Calories from Fat; Chol 0 mg; Fiber 1 g; Sod <1 mg

Edith L. Kralik, Retired
Grand Junction, Colorado

Racy Red Punch

  1   *(46-ounce) can pineapple-grapefruit juice*
  ¹/₃ *cup sugar*
  ¹/₄ *cup cinnamon candies*
  4   *cups ginger ale*

▲ Combine the pineapple-grapefruit juice, sugar and candies in a large container; mix well.

▲ Chill in the refrigerator for 30 minutes or until serving time, stirring occasionally to dissolve the candies.

▲ Add the ginger ale just before serving.

▲ Yield: 20 servings.

Approx Per Serving: Cal 72; Prot <1 g; Carbo 18 g; T Fat <1 g; 1% Calories from Fat; Chol 0 mg; Fiber <1 g; Sod 13 mg

White Wine Sangria

  3¹/₄ *cups dry white wine*
  ¹/₂ *cup orange juice*
  ¹/₃ *cup sugar*
  ¹/₄ *cup lime juice*
  ¹/₄ *cup brandy*
  ¹/₂ *pint strawberries, cut into halves*
  1   *small lime, thinly sliced*
  1   *small red Delicious apple, thinly sliced*
  1   *small orange, thinly sliced*
  1   *(7-ounce) bottle club soda*

▲ Combine the wine, orange juice, sugar, lime juice and brandy in a large pitcher, stirring until the sugar is dissolved. Stir in the fruit.

▲ Chill until serving time.

▲ Add the club soda just before serving.

▲ Yield: 9 servings.

Approx Per Serving: Cal 126; Prot <1 g; Carbo 15 g; T Fat <1 g; 1% Calories from Fat; Chol 0 mg; Fiber 1 g; Sod 9 mg

Beverages

Wine Sherbet

  1   *quart lemon sherbet*
  1   *(750-milliliter) bottle chablis*
  1   *(12-ounce) can diet lemon-lime soda*

▲ Combine the sherbet, chablis and soda in a blender container. Process until smooth.

▲ Pour into glasses.

▲ Recipe may be doubled for punch.

▲ Yield: 20 servings.

Approx Per Serving: Cal 78; Prot <1 g; Carbo 12 g; T Fat 1 g; 9% Calories
    from Fat; Chol 2 mg; Fiber 0 g; Sod 23 mg

Opal Lucas-Williams, 1968 ABWA National President
1967 ABWA National Vice President
1966 ABWA District Vice President
Executive Secretary and Editor, Retired
Little Rock, Arkansas

Guilt-Free Holiday Eggnog

  2   *egg yolks, beaten*
  4   *cups skim milk*
  2   *egg whites*
  1   *teaspoon vanilla extract*
  3   *envelopes artificial sweetener*
1/2 *teaspoon brandy extract*
    Nutmeg to taste

▲ Mix the egg yolks with the milk in a saucepan. Cook over medium heat until thickened, stirring constantly; cool.

▲ Beat the egg whites in a bowl until soft peaks form. Fold into the egg yolks gently. Add vanilla, sweetener and brandy extract. Stir gently.

▲ Chill, covered, until serving time.

▲ Pour into individual cups; sprinkle with nutmeg.

▲ Yield: 8 servings.

Approx Per Serving: Cal 65; Prot 6 g; Carbo 6 g; T Fat 2 g; 27% Calories
    from Fat; Chol 55 mg; Fiber 0 g; Sod 78 mg

The Working Woman's Quick Cookbook

Soups & Salads

Moving to the Front of the Line

Having discrimination thrown in her face helped ignite Wanda Everist Howell's passion. When she was 18, Wanda went to the local Coca-Cola plant in search of a job. She stood in line behind two young men who were given applications to fill out. When she reached the counter, she was told there were no job openings. But two men had just completed applications, so she pressed the issue. She was told that the company hired only men—except for one woman in the plant's office.

But Wanda's family taught her to always be at the front of the line, paving the way for others. "I would try something just because I was told I couldn't do it. This made me a stronger person, one who would fight to get what she wanted and not give up when things got tough," says Wanda. "When I was young, I was considered headstrong. Now that's called having a winning attitude."

Wanda has depended on her winning attitude to build a successful career as a gunnery sergeant in the U.S. Marine Corps in Havelock, North Carolina, where she recruits and counsels people entering and leaving the military. A 1995 Top Ten Business Woman of ABWA, Wanda believes employers look for self-starters with a desire to succeed.

Soups

Know Where You're Going

After years of working as both a retail buyer and sales-person, Clare Spiegel now does a little bit of everything in the fashion industry. She has a weekly radio program, models for print and television, organizes fashion shows and does consulting work. To top it off, she recently authored *Your New Fashion Image*.

Clare's advice for success is simple: Know where you're going. Make a plan. Write it down. Know what action is needed to implement the plan. And do the action with focus. "Look at what you're trying to achieve and explore all avenues to accomplish it," says the 1995 Top Ten Business Woman of ABWA who resides in Coral Springs, Florida. "Most importantly, erase all boundaries in your mind. If you can dream it, you can achieve it."

Quick Chili

  2   *pounds ground beef*
  2   *(10-ounce) cans tomato soup*
  2   *(15-ounce) cans chili beans*
 ²/₃   *cup hot salsa*
  2   *tablespoons chili powder*
  1   *cup water*

▲ Brown the ground beef in a large saucepan, stirring until crumbly;
drain. Add the tomato soup, chili beans, salsa, chili powder and water;
mix well.

▲ Bring to a boil and reduce heat. Simmer for 15 minutes to 1 hour, stirring occasionally.

▲ Yield: 10 servings.

Approx Per Serving: Cal 328; Prot 23 g; Carbo 20 g; T Fat 19 g; 50% Calories
from Fat; Chol 74 mg; Fiber 3 g; Sod 963 mg

Hodgepodge

 1¹/₂   *pounds ground turkey*
  ³/₄   *cup chopped onion*
   1   *cup chopped celery*
   1   *clove of garlic, minced*
   3   *(10-ounce) cans minestrone*
   3   *cups water*
   1   *(31-ounce) can pork and beans*
   1   *tablespoon Worcestershire sauce*
   1   *teaspoon oregano*
        Salt and pepper to taste

▲ Brown the ground turkey with the onion, celery and garlic in a stock-
pot, stirring until crumbly; drain.

▲ Stir in soup, water, pork and beans, Worcestershire sauce, oregano, salt
and pepper.

▲ Simmer for 20 minutes or until of desired consistency, stirring
occasionally. Ladle into soup bowls.

▲ Yield: 12 servings.

Approx Per Serving: Cal 263; Prot 19 g; Carbo 24 g; T Fat 11 g; 35% Calories
from Fat; Chol 48 mg; Fiber 5 g; Sod 853 mg

Soups

Paradise Soup

1   *(64-ounce) can reduced-sodium chicken broth*
6   *eggs*
6   *tablespoons (heaping) grated Parmesan cheese*
1   *teaspoon nutmeg*
¹/₂   *teaspoon grated lemon rind or lemon juice concentrate*

▲ Bring the chicken broth to a boil in a saucepan.

▲ Beat the eggs with the cheese and nutmeg in a bowl. Stir gradually into the boiling broth and reduce the heat. Add the lemon rind.

▲ Simmer for 5 minutes. Serve hot with additional Parmesan cheese.

▲ Yield: 4 servings.

Approx Per Serving: Cal 229; Prot 23 g; Carbo 3 g; T Fat 13 g; 53% Calories from Fat; Chol 325 mg; Fiber <1 g; Sod 1498 mg

Adriana Cantelli, Secretary, Cantelli Block & Brick
Sandusky, Ohio

Cheesy Potato Soup

8   *cups water*
5   *potatoes, chopped*
5   *potatoes, shredded*
1   *bunch celery*
1   *pound carrots, shredded*
1   *large onion, shredded*
4   *(10-ounce) cans cream of celery soup*
1   *pound Velveeta cheese, cubed*
2   *cups chopped ham*

▲ Place the water, potatoes, celery, carrots and onion in a large saucepan. Cook until the vegetables are tender.

▲ Add the soup, cheese and ham. Cook over low heat until the cheese melts.

▲ May reduce the fat content by using the new reduced-fat Velveeta cheese and turkey ham. Sodium content may be reduced by using one of the reduced-sodium canned soups.

▲ Yield: 24 servings.

Approx Per Serving: Cal 185; Prot 9 g; Carbo 18 g; T Fat 9 g; 43% Calories from Fat; Chol 30 mg; Fiber 2 g; Sod 830 mg

Tortilla Soup

    2   whole chicken breasts, skinned, boned
    2   cups water
    1   (14-ounce) can beef broth
    1   (14-ounce) can chicken broth
    1   (14-ounce) can tomatoes, chopped
  1/2   onion, chopped
  1/4   cup chopped green bell pepper
    1   (8-ounce) can whole kernel corn, drained
    1   teaspoon chili powder
  1/2   teaspoon ground cumin
  1/8   teaspoon pepper
    3   cups crushed tortilla chips
    4   ounces Monterey Jack cheese, shredded
    1   avocado, cubed
    2   to 3 teaspoons chopped cilantro

▲ Rinse the chicken breasts and pat dry. Cut into 1-inch cubes; set aside.

▲ Combine the water, beef broth, chicken broth, tomatoes, onion and green pepper in a saucepan. Bring to a boil. Add the cubed chicken and reduce heat.

▲ Simmer, covered, for 10 minutes. Add the corn, chili powder, cumin and pepper. Simmer, covered, for 10 minutes longer.

▲ Place crushed tortilla chips in each bowl. Ladle soup over chips; top with cheese, avocado and cilantro.

▲ Yield: 6 servings.

Approx Per Serving: Cal 369; Prot 28 g; Carbo 24 g; T Fat 19 g; 44% Calories from Fat; Chol 66 mg; Fiber 5 g; Sod 856 mg

Soups

Cucumber Soup

1   cucumber, peeled, chopped
1   cucumber, chopped
2   cups sour cream
¹/₂ medium onion, chopped
1   (10-ounce) can chicken broth
2   tablespoons chopped parsley
    Salt, pepper and nutmeg to taste

▲ Combine the cucumbers, sour cream, onion, broth, parsley, salt, pepper and nutmeg in a blender container. Process until blended. Chill, covered, in refrigerator. Pour into soup bowls.

▲ May reduce the fat content by substituting nonfat sour cream or plain yogurt for the sour cream.

▲ Garnish with a dollop of sour cream or yogurt and a bit of parsley.

▲ Yield: 6 servings.

Approx Per Serving: Cal 196; Prot 5 g; Carbo 7 g; T Fat 17 g; 75% Calories from Fat; Chol 35 mg; Fiber 1 g; Sod 339 mg

Gazpacho

1   cucumber
2   ripe tomatoes
1   green bell pepper
1   clove of garlic
³/₄ cup finely chopped mixed Italian parsley, basil, thyme and chives
1   tablespoon olive oil
3   tablespoons lemon juice
2   cups chilled vegetable stock or water
1   onion, thinly sliced

▲ Peel the cucumber. Chop the cucumber, tomatoes, green pepper and garlic very fine and combine in a bowl. Stir in the herbs.

▲ Add the olive oil, lemon juice and vegetable stock gradually. Add the onion slices. Chill for 4 hours. Garnish servings with dry bread crumbs or yogurt.

▲ Yield: 4 servings.

Approx Per Serving: Cal 86; Prot 2 g; Carbo 12 g; T Fat 4 g; 42% Calories from Fat; Chol 0 mg; Fiber 3 g; Sod 518 mg

Betty Cole, Realtor, Edina Realty
Minneapolis, Minnesota

Chilled Sweet Pepper Soup

     2   medium carrots, chopped
     1   large onion, chopped
     1   tablespoon margarine
  1¹/4   cups chicken broth
     1   yellow bell pepper, chopped
   ¹/2   teaspoon salt
     3   ounces cream cheese, softened
          Red pepper and nutmeg to taste
   ¹/2   cup milk
   ¹/2   cup sour cream
     1   to 2 tablespoons milk

▲ Sauté the carrots and onion in the margarine in a saucepan for 10 minutes or until tender. Stir in the chicken broth. Bring to a boil over medium-high heat.

▲ Stir in the bell pepper and reduce heat. Simmer, covered, for 15 minutes or until the pepper is tender. Cool slightly.

▲ Add the salt, cream cheese, red pepper and nutmeg, stirring constantly. Cook until the cheese melts.

▲ Process in a blender until smooth. Chill, covered, for 4 hours to 4 days. Blend ¹/2 cup milk into soup. Ladle into soup bowls.

▲ Blend the sour cream with enough remaining milk to thin to desired consistency. Drizzle in a circle over surface of soup; cut with knife to make a spoke pattern. Serve immediately.

▲ May reduce the fat content by using fat-free cream cheese and skim milk.

▲ Yield: 4 servings.

Approx Per Serving: Cal 355; Prot 9 g; Carbo 13 g; T Fat 31 g; 78% Calories from Fat; Chol 80 mg; Fiber 2 g; Sod 756 mg

Soups

Sweet Strawberry Soup

   2   *(10-ounce) packages frozen strawberries*
   8   *ounces plain nonfat yogurt*
   1   *cup peach nectar*
   1   *tablespoon lime juice*
   ¹/₂   *teaspoon grated lime rind*
   ¹/₂   *teaspoon vanilla extract*

▲ Process the strawberries in a food processor or blender until smooth. Add the yogurt, peach nectar, lime juice, lime rind and vanilla; process until smooth.

▲ Chill until serving time. Spoon into serving dishes; garnish with additional lime rind.

▲ Yield: 6 servings.

Approx Per Serving: Cal 77; Prot 3 g; Carbo 18 g; T Fat <1 g; 2% Calories from Fat; Chol 1 mg; Fiber 2 g; Sod 34 mg

Slang Jang

   1   *(8-ounce) can cove oysters, coarsely chopped*
   4   *(16-ounce) cans stewed tomatoes, chopped*
   ¹/₂   *cup chopped celery*
   1   *tablespoon minced onion*
   ¹/₂   *to ³/₄ cup finely shredded cabbage*
   1   *teaspoon Worcestershire sauce*
   6   *drops of Tabasco sauce*
   1   *tablespoon vinegar*
   1   *tablespoon (or more) pepper sauce*
       Salt and pepper to taste

▲ Combine the oysters, tomatoes, celery, onion, cabbage, Worcestershire sauce, Tabasco sauce, vinegar, pepper sauce, salt and pepper in a 2-quart bowl; mix well.

▲ Chill until serving time.

▲ Oysters may be drained or undrained, depending on taste.

▲ This soup is delicious as an appetizer course or a light supper on hot summer nights.

▲ Yield: 8 servings.

Approx Per Serving: Cal 83; Prot 4 g; Carbo 17 g; T Fat 1 g; 10% Calories from Fat; Chol 16 mg; Fiber 4 g; Sod 624 mg

Salads

Stretching Outside Your Comfort Zone

Networking and support from other women is essential for success, says Connie Aden. But her mentors haven't been just women. Her male supervisor at Mountain Bell/US West took her under his wing and taught her how to succeed.

She was in middle management when five upper-management positions opened. She knew she could do three of the jobs with no problems, but didn't have the skill or experience for the other two. Sure enough, her supervisor moved her into one of those positions. Even though it was a momentous accomplishment for her—she was the first woman to move into upper management at the company—Connie wasn't exactly jumping for joy. "I went into his office and told him that he was setting me up to fail," says the 1995 Top Ten Business Woman of ABWA and 1982 national president. "He told me, 'Connie, I'm setting you up to succeed because you need experience in this area in order to go further in the company. I'm not putting you in a position I don't think you can handle. I'll be right here for anything you need. I know you can do this job.' "

As it turned out, it was one of the toughest positions Connie ever had. But it was also the job that helped her pinpoint, and eventually achieve, her dream of owning her own business. "Women should welcome opportunities that are scary because you learn by experiencing," says Connie, who took an early retirement offer to start her new career as a training and management consultant in human resources. "And normally those experiences are the ones that are the most beneficial."

Salads

Cranberry Salad

1 pound fresh cranberries
8 to 10 unpeeled apples
1 orange
2 cups sugar

▲ Grind the cranberries, apples and orange with rind in a food chopper.

▲ Combine the ground fruit with the sugar in a 1¹/₂-quart bowl and mix well.

▲ Store in a covered container in the refrigerator.

▲ Yield: 6 servings.

Approx Per Serving: Cal 441; Prot 1 g; Carbo 113 g; T Fat 1 g; 2% Calories from Fat; Chol 0 mg; Fiber 9 g; Sod 1 mg

Marilyn Pedersen, 1994 ABWA District Vice President
Senior Online Documentation Consultant
Principal Mutual Life Insurance Company
Des Moines, Iowa

Finger Gelatin

4 envelopes unflavored gelatin
1 cup cold water
3 (3-ounce) packages strawberry gelatin
3 cups boiling water
¹/₄ cup sugar
2 cups bourbon

▲ Soften the unflavored gelatin in the cold water in a bowl.

▲ Dissolve the strawberry gelatin in the boiling water in a bowl. Stir in the softened gelatin until dissolved. Stir in the sugar and bourbon. Spoon into a shallow dish. Chill until firm.

▲ May also make with lime gelatin and brandy, orange gelatin and vodka or apricot gelatin and brandy.

▲ Yield: 8 servings.

Approx Per Serving: Cal 286; Prot 5 g; Carbo 35 g; T Fat <1 g; <1% Calories from Fat; Chol 0 mg; Fiber 0 g; Sod 89 mg

Marianne Cobarrubias, Corporate Communications Assistant
The Timberland Company
West Newbury, Massachusetts

Easy Fruit Salad

1   (12-ounce) can pineapple chunks
1   (16-ounce) can chunky fruit salad, drained
1   (11-ounce) can mandarin oranges, drained
3   or 4 bananas, sliced
1   small package sugar-free vanilla instant pudding mix
3   tablespoons orange breakfast drink mix

▲ Drain the pineapple, reserving the juice. Combine the pineapple with
   the fruit salad, oranges, bananas and pudding mix in a bowl.

▲ Combine the reserved pineapple juice and orange drink mix in a
   medium bowl and mix well. Add to the fruit and mix gently. Chill
   until serving time.

▲ Yield: 6 servings.

Approx Per Serving: Cal 220; Prot 1 g; Carbo 57 g; T Fat 1 g; 2% Calories
   from Fat; Chol 0 mg; Fiber 3 g; Sod 99 mg

Dr. Nancy Hughston, 1992 Top Ten Business Woman of ABWA
Veterinarian, Companion Animal Clinic
Spartanburg, South Carolina

Salads

Festive Fruit Salad

1   (20-ounce) can pineapple chunks, drained
1   (11-ounce) can mandarin oranges, drained
1   cup seedless red grapes
1/2   cup chopped pecans or walnuts
1   tablespoon sugar
1   cup sour cream
1   cup shredded coconut
1 1/2   cups miniature marshmallows

▲ Combine the pineapple, oranges, grapes and pecans in a 3-quart bowl.

▲ Add the sugar, sour cream and coconut and mix gently. Store, covered,
   in the refrigerator until chilled. Add the marshmallows at serving time
   and mix gently.

▲ Yield: 8 servings.

Approx Per Serving: Cal 277; Prot 3 g; Carbo 36 g; T Fat 15 g; 47% Calories
   from Fat; Chol 13 mg; Fiber 3 g; Sod 53 mg

Bobbi Economy, 1995 ABWA District Vice President, Executive Secretary
Florida Power & Light Company
Jupiter, Florida

Salads

Frozen Fruit Salad

³/₄   cup sugar
¹/₂   cup water
2   cups apricot nectar
1   (10-ounce) package frozen strawberries in syrup, thawed
1   (8-ounce) can crushed pineapple
4   medium bananas, sliced
2   kiwifruit, peeled, chopped

▲ Mix the sugar and water in a saucepan. Bring to a boil and reduce the heat. Simmer for 8 minutes. Cool to room temperature.

▲ Add the apricot nectar, undrained strawberries, pineapple, bananas and kiwifruit and mix gently.

▲ Spoon into foil-lined muffin cups. Freeze until firm.

▲ Remove the frozen cups to sealable plastic bags and store in the freezer.

▲ Yield: 18 servings.

Approx Per Serving: Cal 101; Prot 1 g; Carbo 26 g; T Fat <1 g; 2% Calories from Fat; Chol 0 mg; Fiber 1 g; Sod 2 mg

Vicki S. Berry, 1980 ABWA National Secretary-Treasurer
Secretary/Legal Cashier, U.S. Steel Group
Kansas City, Missouri

Low-Fat Frozen Fruit Salad

Salads

16   *ounces nonfat cream cheese, softened*
1/2   *cup whipped topping*
1/2   *cup nonfat sour cream*
1   *tablespoon mayonnaise-type salad dressing*
1/2   *cup sugar*
1   *(30-ounce) can fruit cocktail, drained*
4   *medium bananas, sliced 1/4 to 1/2 inch thick*
1   *(3-ounce) package lime gelatin*

▲ Beat the cream cheese in a mixer bowl until smooth. Add the whipped topping, sour cream, salad dressing and sugar and mix well.

▲ Fold in the fruit cocktail, bananas and dry gelatin mix.

▲ Spoon into a 9x9-inch dish and cover with plastic wrap. Freeze for 24 hours or store in freezer for up to 3 weeks.

▲ Let stand at room temperature for 15 minutes before cutting into servings.

▲ Yield: 9 servings.

Approx Per Serving: Cal 251; Prot 10 g; Carbo 50 g; T Fat 2 g; 7% Calories from Fat; Chol 9 mg; Fiber 2 g; Sod 354 mg

Kathleen D. Sanford, 1995 ABWA District Vice President
1994 American Business Woman of ABWA
Vice President of Nursing, Harrison Memorial Hospital
Bremerton, Washington

Salads

Orange Light Delight

24   *ounces low-fat cottage cheese*
4   *ounces light whipped topping*
1   *(11-ounce) can mandarin oranges, drained*
1   *(15-ounce) can juice-pack pineapple tidbits, drained*
1   *small package sugar-free orange gelatin*

▲ Combine the cottage cheese, whipped topping, oranges and pineapple in a bowl. Sprinkle the gelatin over the fruit and mix well.

▲ Chill, covered, in the refrigerator.

▲ Serve as a salad on lettuce leaves or as a dessert in compotes. Garnish with fresh orange slices.

▲ Yield: 8 servings.

Approx Per Serving: Cal 163; Prot 13 g; Carbo 22 g; T Fat 3 g; 17% Calories from Fat; Chol 7 mg; Fiber <1 g; Sod 376 mg

Joan Warlick, retired Engineering Technician
North Carolina Department of Transportation
Raleigh, North Carolina

Easy Fruity Salad

16   *ounces whipped topping*
16   *ounces cottage cheese*
1   *(16-ounce) can crushed pineapple, drained*
1   *(6-ounce) package gelatin*

▲ Combine the whipped topping and cottage cheese in a bowl. Add the pineapple and mix well.

▲ Sprinkle with the gelatin and mix well. Serve immediately or store in the refrigerator.

▲ Yield: 10 servings.

Approx Per Serving: Cal 279; Prot 8 g; Carbo 33 g; T Fat 14 g; 43% Calories from Fat; Chol 7 mg; Fiber <1 g; Sod 239 mg

Marianne Cobarrubias, Corporate Communications Assistant
The Timberland Company
West Newbury, Massachusetts

Pretzel Salad

  2   *cups crushed pretzels*
  ³/₄ *cup melted margarine*
  8   *ounces cream cheese, softened*
  1   *cup sugar*
  1   *envelope whipped topping mix, prepared*
  1   *(6-ounce) package strawberry gelatin*
  2   *cups boiling water*
  1   *cup drained crushed pineapple*
  1   *(16-ounce) package frozen strawberries in syrup, thawed*

▲ Preheat the oven to 350 degrees.

▲ Mix the crushed pretzels and margarine in a bowl. Press into a 9x13-inch baking dish. Bake for 10 minutes. Let stand until cool.

▲ Beat the cream cheese and sugar in a mixer bowl until smooth. Fold in the whipped topping. Spoon over the pretzel layer. Chill until firm.

▲ Dissolve the gelatin in the boiling water in a bowl. Stir in the pineapple and undrained strawberries. Spread over the cream cheese layer.

▲ Chill until set. Cut into squares to serve.

▲ Yield: 15 servings.

Approx Per Serving: Cal 330; Prot 4 g; Carbo 45 g; T Fat 16 g; 43% Calories
    from Fat; Chol 18 mg; Fiber 1 g; Sod 383 mg

Lois Revenaugh, 1995 ABWA District Vice President
Sales Development Manager, Flint Journal
Flint, Michigan

Apple Snicker Salad

  6   *large apples, chopped*
  6   *(2-ounce) Snickers candy bars, chopped*
 12 *ounces whipped topping*

▲ Combine the apples and candy bars in a large bowl and mix gently.

▲ Fold in the whipped topping. Chill until serving time.

▲ Yield: 12 servings.

Approx Per Serving: Cal 281; Prot 3 g; Carbo 40 g; T Fat 14 g; 42% Calories
    from Fat; Chol 3 mg; Fiber 3 g; Sod 83 mg

Gina L. Plummer, Director/Teacher, Wee Shipmates Preschool
Sidney, Iowa

Salads

Frozen Strawberry Salad

8   ounces cream cheese, softened
1   cup sugar
1   (10-ounce) package frozen strawberries, thawed
2   or 3 bananas, sliced
8   ounces whipped topping

▲ Beat the cream cheese and sugar in a mixer bowl until smooth.

▲ Add the undrained strawberries, bananas and whipped topping and mix gently.

▲ Spoon into a 9x13-inch dish. Freeze until firm. Cut into squares to serve.

▲ Yield: 15 servings.

Approx Per Serving: Cal 180; Prot 2 g; Carbo 24 g; T Fat 9 g; 45% Calories from Fat; Chol 17 mg; Fiber 1 g; Sod 49 mg

Janae Herman, Radiologic Technologist/Office Manager
Ahrlin Orthopedic, LTD
Rapid City, South Dakota

Bean and Tuna Salad

1   tablespoon fresh lemon juice
3   tablespoons olive oil
1¹/₂ tablespoons minced garlic
2   tablespoons chopped parsley
¹/₂   medium red onion, chopped
2   (15-ounce) cans navy beans, drained
2   (6-ounce) cans water-pack tuna, drained

▲ Mix the lemon juice, olive oil, garlic and parsley in a bowl.

▲ Add the onion and beans and mix well. Stir in the tuna gently.

▲ Chill, covered, until serving time.

▲ Yield: 6 servings.

Approx Per Serving: Cal 298; Prot 25 g; Carbo 33 g; T Fat 8 g; 23% Calories from Fat; Chol 17 mg; Fiber 8 g; Sod 200 mg

Judith Bliss, Fixed Assets Supervisor
University of North Carolina at Greensboro
Greensboro, North Carolina

Thai Chicken Salad

1	quart take-out chicken-fried rice
2	ribs celery, chopped
1	large carrot, chopped
2	green onions, chopped
1	(6-ounce) can water chestnuts, drained, chopped
3	to 4 tablespoons hot peanut sauce

▲ Combine the fried rice with the celery, carrot, green onions and water chestnuts in a large bowl and mix well.

▲ Add peanut sauce to taste. Chill until serving time.

▲ Yield: 10 servings.

Nutritional information for this recipe is not available.

Gail Marsh, Business Partner, B&G Associates
Lansing, Michigan

Salads

Taco Salad

1	head lettuce, torn
2	tomatoes, chopped
1	each avocado and onion, chopped
1	(16-ounce) can kidney beans or pinto beans, drained
1	cup shredded Cheddar cheese
1	pound ground beef
1/2	cup Thousand Island salad dressing
3	cups crushed tortilla chips
	Tabasco sauce to taste

▲ Combine the lettuce, tomatoes, avocado, onion, beans and cheese in a large salad bowl and mix well.

▲ Brown the ground beef in a skillet, stirring until crumbly; drain. Spread over the salad. Top with the salad dressing and crushed tortilla chips. Add Tabasco sauce if desired.

▲ Yield: 4 servings.

Approx Per Serving: Cal 998; Prot 46 g; Carbo 72 g; T Fat 61 g; 54% Calories from Fat; Chol 122 mg; Fiber 14 g; Sod 1181 mg

Marianne Cobarrubias, Corporate Communications Assistant
The Timberland Company
West Newbury, Massachusetts

Easy Linguini Salad

1   *(16-ounce) package linguini*
1   *cup chopped tomatoes*
1   *cup chopped green bell pepper*
1   *cup chopped cucumber*
1   *cup chopped pepperoni*
1   *(8-ounce) bottle fat-free Italian salad dressing*
¹/₂   *cup grated Parmesan cheese*

▲ Break the pasta into thirds. Cook using the package directions; drain.

▲ Combine with the tomatoes, green pepper, cucumber and pepperoni in a large bowl and mix well.

▲ Add the salad dressing and cheese and toss to mix.

▲ Chill until serving time.

▲ Yield: 8 servings.

Approx Per Serving: Cal 503; Prot 21 g; Carbo 49 g; T Fat 25 g; 44% Calories from Fat; Chol 44 mg; Fiber 2 g; Sod 1415 mg

Ellen M. Moore, Squadron Operations Officer, 89th Aerial Port Squadron
U.S. Air Force
Fairfax Station, Virginia

Yum-Yum Macaroni Salad

Salads

1³/4   cups uncooked elbow macaroni
 1   small onion, chopped
¹/4   green bell pepper, chopped
¹/2   cup Marzetti's salad dressing
¹/2   cup mayonnaise
       Salt and pepper to taste
¹/4   teaspoon celery seeds
 1   medium tomato, cut into wedges

▲ Cook the macaroni using the package directions for 8 to 10 minutes or until tender; drain.

▲ Combine with the onion and green pepper in a bowl. Add the salad dressing, mayonnaise, salt and pepper and mix well. Sprinkle with the celery seeds.

▲ Chill in the refrigerator for 8 hours or longer. Top with the tomato at serving time.

▲ Yield: 10 servings.

Approx Per Serving: Cal 208; Prot 3 g; Carbo 17 g; T Fat 15 g; 63% Calories
from Fat; Chol 7 mg; Fiber 1 g; Sod 158 mg

Barbara H. Rowe, Paralegal, Hardt & Vance
Richmond, Virginia

Pasta Salad

1   *(16-ounce) package fusilli or corkscrew pasta*
1   *(16-ounce) package frozen mixed vegetables*
1   *cup shredded nonfat Cheddar cheese*
1   *cup nonfat Catalina salad dressing*

▲ Cook the pasta using the package directions; drain.

▲ Place the mixed vegetables in a microwave-safe bowl. Microwave on High for 8 minutes.

▲ Combine the pasta and vegetables in a colander. Rinse with cool water and drain well.

▲ Add the cheese and salad dressing and mix well. Chill until serving time.

▲ Yield: 8 servings.

Approx Per Serving: Cal 310; Prot 14 g; Carbo 61 g; T Fat 1 g; 3% Calories from Fat; Chol 2 mg; Fiber 4 g; Sod 491 mg

Tracey Bright, 1993 Top Ten Business Woman of ABWA
County Attorney, Ector County
Odessa, Texas

Zesty Pasta Salad

2   envelopes Italian salad dressing mix
1   (16-ounce) package shell pasta
4   ounces salami, thinly sliced
4   ounces pepperoni, thinly sliced
4   ounces provolone cheese, chopped
1   (4-ounce) jar green olives, chopped
1   (4-ounce) jar black olives, chopped
3   tomatoes, chopped
2   green bell peppers, chopped
1   onion, chopped
$^1/_2$ cup chopped celery
8   ounces mushrooms, chopped

▲ Prepare the salad dressing mix using the package directions. Chill in the refrigerator.

▲ Cook the pasta using the package directions; drain and cool.

▲ Combine the salami, pepperoni, cheese, olives, tomatoes, green bell peppers, onion and celery in a large bowl and mix well.

▲ Add the salad dressing and pasta and mix gently.

▲ Chill for several hours. Stir in the mushrooms just before serving.

▲ Yield: 10 servings.

Approx Per Serving: Cal 579; Prot 14 g; Carbo 42 g; T Fat 40 g; 62% Calories from Fat; Chol 24 mg; Fiber 3 g; Sod 1330 mg

Anna Chidester, retired Administrative Technician, Department of Agriculture
Nashville, Tennessee

Salads

Marinated Bean Salad

1   cup sugar
1   cup vegetable oil
½   cup cider vinegar
1   (16-ounce) can green beans, drained
1   (16-ounce) can wax beans
1   (16-ounce) can green peas
1   (16-ounce) can whole kernel corn
1   (16-ounce) can Shoe Peg corn
1   (2-ounce) jar chopped pimento
1   bunch green onions, sliced
4   ribs celery, sliced

▲ Bring the sugar, oil and vinegar to a boil in a saucepan. Let stand until cool.

▲ Combine the beans, peas, corn, pimento, green onions and celery in a large bowl. Add the oil mixture and mix well.

▲ Chill in the refrigerator for 8 hours or longer.

▲ Yield: 15 servings.

Approx Per Serving: Cal 250; Prot 3 g; Carbo 29 g; T Fat 15 g; 51% Calories from Fat; Chol 0 mg; Fiber 3 g; Sod 398 mg

Becky Epley, 1993 Top Ten Business Woman of ABWA, Owner/Manager
Buchanan Management Company
Dallas, Texas

Broccoli Salad

1	pound fresh broccoli florets
1	cup shredded Cheddar cheese
1	cup crumbled crisp-fried bacon
$1/4$	cup chopped dill
$1/4$	cup chopped onion
$1/2$	to 1 cup mayonnaise
1	tablespoon sugar
$1/4$	cup white wine vinegar

▲ Combine the broccoli, cheese, bacon, dill and onion in a large bowl and toss gently.

▲ Combine the mayonnaise, sugar and vinegar in a small bowl and mix well.

▲ Add the dressing to the broccoli mixture and mix well. Chill until serving time.

▲ Yield: 8 servings.

Approx Per Serving: Cal 291; Prot 7 g; Carbo 7 g; T Fat 27 g; 82% Calories from Fat; Chol 34 mg; Fiber 2 g; Sod 352 mg

Betty Cole, Realtor, Edina Realty
Minneapolis, Minnesota

Salads

Napa Salad

    2   (3-ounce) packages ramen noodles
   1/4   cup butter
    1   head napa cabbage, shredded
    5   green onions, chopped
    1   cup salad oil
   2/3   cup sugar
    2   tablespoons soy sauce
   1/4   cup vinegar

▲ Break the noodles into pieces, reserving the seasoning packets for another use. Sauté in the butter in a skillet until light brown; drain.

▲ Combine the cabbage and green onions in a medium bowl.

▲ Combine the oil, sugar, soy sauce and vinegar in a covered jar and shake until well mixed.

▲ Add the dressing and noodles to the cabbage mixture just before serving and toss to mix well.

▲ Yield: 12 servings.

Approx Per Serving: Cal 304; Prot 3 g; Carbo 21 g; T Fat 24 g; 69% Calories from Fat; Chol 10 mg; Fiber 1 g; Sod 470 mg

Betty Cole, Realtor, Edina Realty
Minneapolis, Minnesota

Cauliflower Salad

1	*large head cauliflower*
2	*tomatoes, chopped*
1/2	*cup chopped green olives*
1/2	*cup chopped radishes*
1/2	*cup chopped celery*
1	*cup chopped Cheddar cheese*
1	*cup light mayonnaise*
1/3	*cup horseradish*
1/2	*cup sugar*
1	*teaspoon salt*
1/2	*teaspoon white pepper*

▲ Cut the cauliflower into bite-size pieces. Combine with the tomatoes, olives, radishes, celery and cheese in a large bowl.

▲ Combine the mayonnaise, horseradish, sugar, salt and white pepper in a small bowl and mix well.

▲ Add the dressing to the salad and mix gently. Chill until serving time.

▲ Yield: 8 servings.

Approx Per Serving: Cal 260; Prot 6 g; Carbo 26 g; T Fat 16 g; 53% Calories
   from Fat; Chol 23 mg; Fiber 2 g; Sod 857 mg

Ruth Granley Locke, Manager, Budget Bargain Center
Longview, Texas

Green and White Salad

3	*cups frozen green peas*
1/4	*cup finely chopped onion*
1	*head cauliflower, chopped*
3/4	*cup sour cream with chives*
1	*envelope buttermilk salad dressing mix*

▲ Cook the peas in boiling water to cover in a saucepan for 2 minutes; drain. Combine the peas with the onion, cauliflower, sour cream and salad dressing mix in a bowl and mix well. Chill until serving time.

▲ Yield: 10 servings.

Approx Per Serving: Cal 88; Prot 4 g; Carbo 11 g; T Fat 4 g; 38% Calories
   from Fat; Chol 8 mg; Fiber 3 g; Sod 264 mg

Melanie Mayberry, Brokerage Services Coordinator, Commodity Services, Inc.
West Des Moines, Iowa

Salads

Easy Caesar Salad

1	head Romaine lettuce, torn
1/4	cup grated Parmesan cheese
1/4	cup vegetable oil or olive oil
3	tablespoons vinegar
2	tablespoons lemon juice
1	egg
1/2	teaspoon garlic powder
1/4	teaspoon salt
1/4	teaspoon pepper
1	cup croutons

▲ Toss the lettuce and cheese in a large bowl. Chill in the refrigerator.

▲ Combine the oil, vinegar, lemon juice, egg, garlic powder, salt and pepper in a covered jar and shake to mix well.

▲ Add the dressing to the salad and toss gently. Top with the croutons.

▲ May use egg substitute instead of egg to reduce the danger of salmonella. May add anchovy paste to taste if desired.

▲ Yield: 6 servings.

Approx Per Serving: Cal 140; Prot 4 g; Carbo 6 g; T Fat 12 g; 73% Calories from Fat; Chol 39 mg; Fiber 1 g; Sod 215 mg

Kathryn A. Van Such, 1994 Top Ten Business Woman of ABWA
1990 ABWA National Secretary-Treasurer
1989 ABWA District Vice President, Optometrist
Phoenix, Arizona

Greek Salad

1   *large head Romaine lettuce, torn*
2   *medium tomatoes, cut into 1/2-inch wedges*
1   *large cucumber, sliced 1/8 inch thick*
6   *to 8 radishes, sliced*
4   *green onions, thinly sliced*
6   *ounces feta cheese, crumbled*
4   *ounces black olives*
1   *teaspoon finely chopped mint*
1/2   *cup olive oil*
3   *tablespoons fresh lemon juice*
2   *tablespoons red wine vinegar*
1/2   *teaspoon finely chopped oregano*
1   *clove of garlic, crushed*

▲ Combine the lettuce, tomatoes, cucumber, radishes, green onions, cheese and olives in a salad bowl and toss gently. Sprinkle with the mint.

▲ Whisk the olive oil, lemon juice, vinegar, oregano and garlic in a small bowl until well mixed.

▲ Add the dressing to the salad and toss lightly. Serve as a salad or with bread as a main dish.

▲ Yield: 4 servings.

Approx Per Serving: Cal 430; Prot 9 g; Carbo 14 g; T Fat 40 g; 80% Calories from Fat; Chol 38 mg; Fiber 4 g; Sod 674 mg

Dr. Barbara Pevoto, 1996 Top Ten Business Woman of ABWA
Dean of Instruction/Director of Area School, Arapohoe Community College
Littleton, Colorado

Salads

Tropical Salad with Papaya Seed Dressing

$^1/_2$	cup sugar
$^1/_2$	cup white vinegar
$^1/_4$	cup chopped onion
$^1/_2$	teaspoon dry mustard
$1^1/_2$	teaspoons salt
$^1/_2$	cup vegetable oil
2	tablespoons fresh papaya seeds
1	head Romaine lettuce
1	head leaf lettuce
1	pint strawberries, cut into halves
1	large papaya, peeled, seeded, chopped
2	avocados, peeled, sliced

▲ Combine the sugar, vinegar, onion, dry mustard and salt in a blender container and process until smooth. Add the oil gradually, processing constantly until smooth. Add the papaya seeds and process until the seeds resemble coarsely ground pepper. Store in an airtight container in the refrigerator for up to 2 days.

▲ Wash and tear the lettuce and store in a plastic bag in the refrigerator.

▲ Arrange the lettuce on a serving platter. Mound the strawberries and papaya in the center. Arrange the avocado spoke-fashion around the fruit. Drizzle with the salad dressing.

▲ Yield: 8 servings.

Approx Per Serving: Cal 294; Prot 2 g; Carbo 26 g; T Fat 22 g; 63% Calories from Fat; Chol 0 mg; Fiber 4 g; Sod 412 mg
Nutritional profile does not include papaya seeds.

Karen Maihofer, Owner, Creative Cuisine Cooking School
Estero, Florida

Radicchio and Onion Salad

Salads

 2   *heads radicchio, torn, drained*
 1   *small onion, finely chopped*
 2   *tablespoons olive oil*
 1   *tablespoon wine vinegar*
     Salt and pepper to taste

▲ Toss the radicchio and onion in a salad bowl.

▲ Add the olive oil, vinegar, salt and pepper and toss to mix well.

▲ Yield: 4 servings.

Approx Per Serving: Cal 85; Prot 1 g; Carbo 5 g; T Fat 7 g; 70% Calories
    from Fat; Chol 0 mg; Fiber <1 g; Sod 18 mg

Adriana Cantelli, Secretary, Cantelli Block and Brick
Sandusky, Ohio

Potato Salad

 6   *baking potatoes*
 1   *clove of garlic, minced*
 2   *tablespoons finely chopped parsley*
 6   *tablespoons olive oil*
 1/4   *cup wine vinegar*
     Salt and freshly ground pepper to taste

▲ Cut the potatoes into $1/2$-inch pieces. Cook in water to cover in a
saucepan just until tender; drain.

▲ Combine the garlic, parsley, olive oil, vinegar, salt and pepper in a
bowl and mix well. Add to the warm potatoes and mix gently. Spoon
into a serving bowl.

▲ Let stand to absorb flavors before serving. Serve warm or chilled.

▲ Yield: 6 servings.

Approx Per Serving: Cal 235; Prot 2 g; Carbo 27 g; T Fat 14 g; 51% Calories
    from Fat; Chol 0 mg; Fiber 2 g; Sod 7 mg

Adriana Cantelli, Secretary, Cantelli Block and Brick
Sandusky, Ohio

Salads

Sweet Sauerkraut Salad

1   quart sauerkraut
2   cups sugar
1   cup cider vinegar
1   cup chopped celery with leaves
1   cup chopped Vidalia onion
1   cup chopped carrots
1   teaspoon celery seeds

▲ Rinse the sauerkraut in a colander and drain well.

▲ Bring the sugar and vinegar to a boil in a medium saucepan over medium-high heat. Boil until the sugar dissolves. Cool to room temperature.

▲ Combine with the sauerkraut, celery, onion, carrots and celery seeds in a covered 2-quart glass container. Store in the refrigerator.

▲ Yield: 12 servings.

Approx Per Serving: Cal 156; Prot 1 g; Carbo 40 g; T Fat <1 g; 1% Calories from Fat; Chol 0 mg; Fiber 3 g; Sod 531 mg

Janet M. Priewe, Legal Secretary, Curran Law Office
Mauston, Wisconsin

Main Dishes

Tapping Into Networks

Ever hear the saying, "All the help you'll ever need is right at the end of your arm?" Professional organizations like the American Business Women's Association are the perfect place to reach out and shake hands on new business deals, says Leslie Renquist-Hughes.

A massage therapist and owner of Grand Valley Muscular Therapy in Grand Junction, Colorado, Leslie is a master of self-promotion. She markets her business by offering discounts, trading services for other members' products, donating door prizes and advertising in the group's newsletter. She also helped start a networking group for business owners, where each entrepreneur discusses a business problem and the group brainstorms solutions. "The experience has led to business referrals not only between ourselves, but with each of our extended networks of family, friends and business leads," Leslie says.

Meats

The Champion of Change

Back in her "severely domestic" days, Bonnie Coffey cross-stitched a wall hanging that still hangs in her office, inspiring her with just one word—"YAGOTTAWANNA." "If you want to make it in this world, you have to be able and willing to adapt to change," says Bonnie. "Change scares a lot of people. But remember, you always have a choice—that's what gives you control."

Bonnie's never ducked when life's thrown a curve ball her way. As the former wife of a military man, Bonnie got used to pulling up tent and heading to new territory. She's lived in 35 homes in the United States, Belgium and Japan. With the moves came new jobs and experiences. In 25 years, she's had 21 jobs, including processing loans, marketing medical services and managing a temporary agency. "When I first started moving from place to place, it was tough—people wanted stability," says Bonnie. "Now, employers are starting to look at a wide range of skills as a plus instead of a minus. That's important in these days of downsizing."

Her range of skills and interests landed her smack in the world of talk radio at KLIN-AM in Lincoln, Nebraska. Besides being co-host of the morning drive program and a call-in show with physicians, Bonnie hosts and produces her own show, "The Coffey Talk of Lincoln," a daily live call-in show. "This crazy lifestyle's taught me to back up and look at things differently," she says. "I'm like Scarlett O'Hara—tomorrow is another day. There are more opportunities waiting for me around the corner. To me, there's never a closed door—YAGOTTAWANNA."

Chuck Roast and Potatoes

   1   *(3-pound) boneless chuck roast*
1¹/₂   *pounds potatoes, peeled, cut into pieces*
   1   *(10-ounce) can golden mushroom soup*

▲ Preheat the oven to 350 degrees.

▲ Place the roast in a 10-inch baking pan. Arrange the potatoes around the roast. Spoon the soup over the roast and potatoes.

▲ Roast for 45 minutes or to desired doneness.

▲ Yield: 4 servings.

Approx Per Serving: Cal 710; Prot 67 g; Carbo 43 g; T Fat 28 g; 37% Calories from Fat; Chol 213 mg; Fiber 3 g; Sod 721 mg

Jacqueline A. Roddy, Assistant Vice President, Auditor
Brannen Banks of Florida, Inc.
Inverness, Florida

Holiday Roast

³/₄   *cup catsup*
³/₄   *cup amaretto*
¹/₃   *cup currant jelly*
  4   *to 6 dashes of Tabasco sauce*
  1   *(3-pound) sirloin roast*
1¹/₂ *teaspoons garlic pepper*

▲ Preheat the oven to 350 degrees.

▲ Combine the catsup, amaretto, jelly and Tabasco sauce in a saucepan; mix well. Bring just to the boiling point, stirring to dissolve the jelly.

▲ Rub the roast with the garlic pepper.

▲ Spray a roasting pan with nonstick cooking spray. Sear the roast in the roasting pan. Bake for 1 hour or until internal temperature reaches 150 degrees for medium-rare.

▲ Turn off the oven. Remove the roast from the oven. Pour the desired amount of sauce over the roast. Return the roast to the oven.

▲ Let stand for 10 minutes. Remove the roast to a serving platter. Serve with the remaining sauce.

▲ Yield: 12 servings.

Approx Per Serving: Cal 211; Prot 20 g; Carbo 16 g; T Fat 5 g; 20% Calories from Fat; Chol 54 mg; Fiber <1 g; Sod 229 mg

Savory Pepper Steak

1¹/₂	to 2 pounds round steak
¹/₄	cup flour
	Salt and pepper to taste
3	to 4 tablespoons vegetable oil
1	(14-ounce) can stewed tomatoes
1	cup water
³/₄	cup chopped white onion
1¹/₂	to 2 tablespoons beef gravy base
1¹/₂	to 2 tablespoons Worcestershire sauce
2	large green bell peppers, cut into strips

▲ Cut the steak into strips. Combine the flour, salt and pepper in a bowl and mix well. Coat the steak with the flour mixture.

▲ Brown the steak in hot oil in a skillet and drain.

▲ Add the tomato liquid to the steak in the skillet, reserving the tomatoes in the refrigerator.

▲ Add the water, onion and gravy base to the skillet.

▲ Simmer over low heat for 1¹/₂ to 2 hours or until the steak is tender.

▲ Stir in the Worcestershire sauce, green peppers and stewed tomatoes.

▲ Simmer for 1 hour or until the green peppers are tender. Serve over rice.

▲ Yield: 6 servings.

Approx Per Serving: Cal 297; Prot 30 g; Carbo 13 g; T Fat 14 g; 42% Calories from Fat; Chol 75 mg; Fiber 2 g; Sod 279 mg

Lori Gatewood-Murphy, Office Manager, Housemasters Home Improvement
Topeka, Kansas

Beef Stew

    3   pounds cubed round or sirloin beef
    3   large carrots, chopped
 1¹/₂   pounds small whole onions
    1   (20-ounce) can tiny green peas
    1   (20-ounce) can green beans
    1   (20-ounce) can tomatoes
    1   (10-ounce) can beef consommé
  ¹/₂   cup sauterne
  ¹/₄   cup quick-cooking tapioca
    1   tablespoon brown sugar
  ¹/₂   cup dry bread crumbs
    1   bay leaf
    1   tablespoon salt

▲ Preheat the oven to 250 degrees.

▲ Combine the beef, carrots, onions, green peas, beans, tomatoes, beef consommé, wine, tapioca, brown sugar, bread crumbs, bay leaf and salt in a large roasting pan.

▲ Bake, covered, for 6 to 7 hours or until the beef is tender. Remove the bay leaf before serving.

▲ Yield: 8 servings.

Approx Per Serving: Cal 340; Prot 38 g; Carbo 31 g; T Fat 6 g; 16% Calories from Fat; Chol 84 mg; Fiber 5 g; Sod 1423 mg

Carolyn B. Elman, Executive Director, American Business Women's Association
Kansas City, Missouri

Meats

Cheesy Beef Sandwiches

4   ounces cooked chopped beef
2   teaspoons dried minced onion
4   tablespoons butter
2   tablespoons quick-mixing flour
     White pepper to taste
1/4 teaspoon dry mustard
1   cup skim milk
4   slices bread, toasted
1   cup shredded Cheddar cheese

▲ Preheat the oven to 375 degrees.

▲ Sauté the beef with the onion in 1 tablespoon of the butter in a skillet
  for 5 minutes.

▲ Melt the remaining 3 tablespoons butter in a skillet. Stir in the flour,
  pepper and dry mustard. Cook for several minutes, stirring constantly.

▲ Add the milk gradually. Cook over medium heat until the sauce is
  thickened, stirring constantly.

▲ Layer the bread, beef, cheese and sauce in a 7x9-inch baking dish.

▲ Bake for 10 to 15 minutes or until heated through.

▲ Yield: 2 servings.

Approx Per Serving: Cal 784; Prot 42 g; Carbo 42 g; T Fat 49 g; 57% Calories
    from Fat; Chol 180 mg; Fiber 1 g; Sod 963 mg

Dianna Emerson, Independent Representative
Excel Telecommunication
Lisa Emerson, Cashier, Target
Lansing, Michigan

Quick Chimichangas

2¹/₂ *cups shredded lean roast beef*
²/₃ *cup picante sauce*
¹/₂ *onion, thinly sliced*
³/₄ *to 1 teaspoon cumin*
¹/₂ *teaspoon oregano*
  8 *large flour tortillas*
  2 *tablespoons melted margarine*
  1 *cup shredded Monterey Jack cheese*

▲ Preheat the oven to 475 degrees.

▲ Combine the beef with the picante sauce, onion, cumin and oregano in a saucepan. Simmer for 5 minutes or until most of the liquid is absorbed. Brush 1 side of each tortilla with the melted margarine.

▲ Spoon the beef mixture onto the center of the unbuttered sides of each tortilla; top with cheese. Fold 2 sides over filling; fold ends down. Place seam side down in a 9x13-inch baking dish.

▲ Bake for 13 to 15 minutes or until crisp and brown.

▲ Yield: 8 servings.

Approx Per Serving: Cal 278; Prot 17 g; Carbo 18 g; T Fat 10 g; 32% Calories from Fat; Chol 47 mg; Fiber 1 g; Sod 374 mg

Grilled Beef Bundles

  2 *pounds lean beef chuck, cubed*
  6 *medium potatoes, chopped*
  6 *tablespoons chopped onion*
¹/₂ *cup chopped parsley*
  6 *carrots, sliced ¹/₄ inch thick*
  2 *(10-ounce) cans golden mushroom soup*
     Tabasco sauce, salt and pepper to taste

▲ Cut eight 18x18-inch pieces of heavy-duty foil. Portion the beef, potatoes, onion, parsley and carrots evenly onto the foil pieces. Spread with the soup. Add Tabasco sauce, salt and pepper. Sprinkle 2 tablespoons of water over each serving. Seal packets tightly.

▲ Place in cooler or refrigerator until time to cook. Grill 2 inches from coals for 1 hour. Serve from foil packets.

▲ Yield: 8 servings.

Approx Per Serving: Cal 310; Prot 25 g; Carbo 32 g; T Fat 8 g; 25% Calories from Fat; Chol 64 mg; Fiber 3 g; Sod 630 mg

Meats

All-Purpose Coney Island Sauce

2   *pounds ground beef*
32 *ounces catsup*
2¹/₂ *teaspoons cumin*
2   *teaspoons chili powder*
2   *teaspoons salt*
1   *teaspoon pepper*
1   *teaspoon sugar*

▲ Cook the ground beef in a skillet until brown and crumbly; drain.

▲ Add the remaining ingredients; mix well. Simmer for 30 to 45 minutes or to the desired consistency.

▲ May serve over hot dogs on buns for Coney Islands. May add mushrooms, green bell peppers or other favorite ingredients and serve over a favorite pasta as spaghetti sauce. May add canned kidney beans and top with chopped onions and shredded cheese for a rich chili.

▲ Yield: 16 (¹/₂-cup) servings.

Approx Per Serving: Cal 184; Prot 13 g; Carbo 16 g; T Fat 8 g; 38% Calories from Fat; Chol 42 mg; Fiber 1 g; Sod 969 mg

Hamburgers on the Grill

2   *pounds ground beef*
1   *egg, beaten*
¹/₄ *teaspoon oregano*
1   *teaspoon salt*
1   *teaspoon pepper*
¹/₂ *cup catsup*
1   *tablespoon Worcestershire sauce*
1   *cup shredded Cheddar cheese*
1   *cup chopped onion*
12 *hamburger buns*

▲ Combine the ground beef, egg, seasonings, catsup, Worcestershire sauce, cheese and onion in a bowl; mix well.

▲ Shape into patties.

▲ Grill over hot coals until done to taste. Serve on buns.

▲ Yield: 12 servings.

Approx Per Serving: Cal 371; Prot 20 g; Carbo 27 g; T Fat 17 g; 41% Calories from Fat; Chol 77 mg; Fiber 1 g; Sod 676 mg

ABWA's Famous Beefburgers

- 25   *pounds ground beef*
- 3   *(10-ounce) cans chicken gumbo soup*
- 2   *(10-ounce) cans cream of chicken soup*
- 3/4 *cup mustard*
- 2   *envelopes instant onion soup mix*
- 3   *(10-ounce) cans cream of mushroom soup*
- 1¹/₂ *cups catsup*

▲ Brown the ground beef in a skillet, stirring until crumbly; drain.

▲ Combine the ground beef and remaining ingredients in a large roasting pan; mix well.

▲ Simmer for 30 minutes, stirring frequently.

▲ Serve on hamburger buns.

▲ Yield: 100 servings.

Approx Per Serving: Cal 273; Prot 26 g; Carbo 3 g; T Fat 17 g; 57% Calories from Fat; Chol 85 mg; Fiber <1 g; Sod 327 mg

Wilma Hyland and Karen Bappe, Registered Nurse
Nevada, Iowa

Mock Filet Mignon

- 2¹/₂ *pounds ground beef*
- 1   *cup grated carrots*
- 1   *onion, shredded*
- 1   *cup shredded Cheddar cheese*
- ¹/₂ *cup chopped green bell pepper*
- ¹/₂ *teaspoon salt*
- ¹/₂ *teaspoon pepper*
- ¹/₂ *teaspoon garlic powder*
- ¹/₄ *cup Worcestershire sauce*
- 6   *to 8 slices bacon*

▲ Combine the ground beef with the remaining ingredients except bacon in a large bowl; mix well.

▲ Shape into 10 thick patties. Wrap a bacon slice around each patty; secure with a wooden pick. Grill to the desired degree of doneness.

▲ Yield: 10 servings.

Approx Per Serving: Cal 338; Prot 30 g; Carbo 4 g; T Fat 22 g; 60% Calories from Fat; Chol 100 mg; Fiber 1 g; Sod 389 mg

Meats

Quick Salisbury Steak

1   *pound ground beef*
1   *cup flour*
1   *egg*
    Salt and pepper to taste
1   *(10-ounce) can beef gravy*

▲ Preheat the oven to 350 degrees.

▲ Combine the ground beef and flour in a bowl and mix well. Add the egg, salt and pepper; mix well.

▲ Shape into patties and arrange in a 9x9-inch baking pan.

▲ Bake, uncovered, for 20 minutes and drain. Pour the beef gravy over the patties.

▲ Bake for 15 to 20 minutes longer or until done to taste. Serve with rice or potatoes.

▲ May add onion to the patty mix. May substitute one 10-ounce can cream of mushroom soup for the beef gravy.

▲ Yield: 6 servings.

Approx Per Serving: Cal 279; Prot 22 g; Carbo 18 g; T Fat 13 g; 41% Calories from Fat; Chol 93 mg; Fiber 1 g; Sod 316 mg

Sandy Reed, Payroll Supervisor, Inland Container
Martinsville, Indiana

Sweet-and-Sour Ground Beef

Meats

1/2   cup milk
8   ounces ground beef
1/2   cup soft bread crumbs
1/4   teaspoon salt
1/4   cup chopped onion
1   tablespoon vegetable oil
1   tablespoon vinegar
2   tablespoons sugar
1   tablespoon Worcestershire sauce
1/2   cup catsup

▲ Combine the milk, ground beef, bread crumbs, salt and onion in a bowl and mix well. Shape into balls.

▲ Brown the meatballs in the oil in a skillet and drain.

▲ Combine the vinegar, sugar, Worcestershire sauce and catsup in a small bowl. Pour over the meatballs.

▲ Simmer over low heat for 30 minutes.

▲ Yield: 4 servings.

Approx Per Serving: Cal 251; Prot 15 g; Carbo 21 g; T Fat 13 g; 44% Calories from Fat; Chol 47 mg; Fiber 1 g; Sod 612 mg

Evalyn K. S. Inn, 1976 Top Ten Business Woman of ABWA
Audiologist, Self-Employed
Honolulu, Hawaii

Meats

Beef and Rice Skillet Dinner

1	*pound ground beef*
1	*large onion, chopped*
2¹/₂	*cups water*
1	*cup uncooked rice*
3	*beef bouillon cubes, crushed*
¹/₂	*teaspoon dry mustard*
1	*medium green bell pepper, chopped*
1	*medium tomato, chopped*
1	*cup shredded Monterey Jack cheese*

▲ Brown the ground beef with the onion in a skillet, stirring until the ground beef is crumbly; drain.

▲ Add the water, rice, bouillon cubes and dry mustard. Bring to a boil over medium heat. Reduce the heat.

▲ Simmer, covered, for 25 minutes or until the liquid is absorbed.

▲ Stir in the green pepper and tomato. Sprinkle the cheese over the top. Remove from the heat.

▲ Let stand, covered, for 2 to 3 minutes or until the cheese is melted.

▲ Yield: 8 servings.

Approx Per Serving: Cal 277; Prot 18 g; Carbo 22 g; T Fat 13 g; 41% Calories from Fat; Chol 55 mg; Fiber 1 g; Sod 433 mg

Hallie M. Head, Secretary, Indiana University Medical Center
Indianapolis, Indiana

Chow Mein Casserole

1¹/₂   pounds ground beef
   2   small onions, chopped
   1   cup chopped celery
   1   (10-ounce) can cream of mushroom soup
   1   (10-ounce) can cream of chicken soup
 ¹/₂   cup uncooked rice
   1   (3-ounce) can chow mein noodles
   1   to 2 tablespoons soy sauce
 ¹/₄   teaspoon pepper
   1   cup water

▲ Preheat the oven to 350 degrees.

▲ Brown the ground beef in a skillet, stirring until crumbly; drain.

▲ Add the onions, celery, soups and rice.

▲ Reserve ¹/₂ cup of the chow mein noodles. Add the remaining noodles, soy sauce, pepper and water to the ground beef mixture and mix well.

▲ Spoon into a large baking dish. Sprinkle reserved noodles over the top.

▲ Bake, covered, for 30 minutes. Remove the cover. Bake for 5 minutes longer.

▲ Yield: 6 servings.

Approx Per Serving: Cal 494; Prot 30 g; Carbo 31 g; T Fat 27 g; 50% Calories from Fat; Chol 89 mg; Fiber 2 g; Sod 1295 mg

*Gina L. Plummer, Teacher-Director, Wee Shipmates Preschool
Sidney, Iowa*

Wednesday-Night Special

4	ounces ground beef
	Salt and pepper to taste
2	(10-ounce) cans old-fashioned vegetable soup
1¹/₂	cups uncooked instant rice
¹/₂	cup frozen corn
1	cup water
1	cup shredded Cheddar cheese

▲ Preheat the oven to 350 degrees.

▲ Brown the ground beef with salt and pepper in a skillet, stirring until crumbly; drain. Add the soup, rice, corn and water; mix well. Spoon into a 9x9-inch baking dish.

▲ Bake for 25 minutes. Sprinkle the cheese over the top. Bake for several minutes longer or until the cheese is melted.

▲ Yield: 4 servings.

Approx Per Serving: Cal 423; Prot 24 g; Carbo 47 g; T Fat 16 g; 33% Calories from Fat; Chol 57 mg; Fiber 2 g; Sod 1357 mg

Judith M. Bastian, Teller Specialist, First Union
Matthews, North Carolina

Mom's Goulash

1	pound ground beef
1	small onion, chopped
	Salt, pepper and garlic salt to taste
1	(10-ounce) can cream of mushroom soup
1	package Velveeta shells and cheese

▲ Brown the ground beef with the onion, salt, pepper and garlic salt in a skillet, stirring until the ground beef crumbly; drain. Add the soup; mix well.

▲ Prepare the shells and cheese using the package directions. Stir into the ground beef mixture. Heat to serving temperature.

▲ Serve with crackers or rolls.

▲ Yield: 4 servings.

Approx Per Serving: Cal 604; Prot 39 g; Carbo 40 g; T Fat 31 g; 47% Calories from Fat; Chol 115 mg; Fiber 1 g; Sod 1451 mg

Kathy Wells, Accounting Coordinator, Baylor University
Waco, Texas

Spaghetti Lasagna

1	cup finely chopped onions
2	tablespoons butter or margarine
1¹/₂	pounds ground beef
1	(16-ounce) can tomatoes
1	(6-ounce) can tomato paste
1	(4-ounce) can mushrooms
1	teaspoon garlic salt
2	teaspoons oregano
¹/₂	teaspoon rosemary
¹/₄	teaspoon pepper
1	(8-ounce) package spaghetti noodles
16	ounces cottage cheese
³/₄	cup grated Parmesan cheese
8	ounces sliced mozzarella cheese

▲ Preheat the oven to 350 degrees.

▲ Sauté the onions in the butter in a skillet. Add the ground beef. Cook until the beef is brown, stirring until crumbly; drain.

▲ Add the tomatoes, tomato paste, undrained mushrooms, garlic salt, oregano, rosemary and pepper. Simmer, uncovered, for 30 minutes, stirring occasionally.

▲ Cook the spaghetti noodles using package directions. Drain the noodles and rinse.

▲ Place ¹/₃ of the ground beef sauce in a 9x13-inch baking dish. Layer the noodles, cottage cheese, remaining ground beef sauce, Parmesan cheese and mozzarella cheese ¹/₂ at a time over the top.

▲ Bake for 25 to 35 minutes or until brown and bubbly.

▲ Yield: 8 servings.

Approx Per Serving: Cal 538; Prot 41 g; Carbo 33 g; T Fat 27 g; 45% Calories from Fat; Chol 109 mg; Fiber 3 g; Sod 1163 mg

Maxine Budde Ross, Executive Director, C. A. Perkins Co., Inc.
Vancouver, Washington

Meats

Microwave Lasagna

1¹/₂   *pounds ground beef*
1   *(28-ounce) can spaghetti sauce*
¹/₂   *cup water*
6   *to 8 uncooked lasagna noodles*
16   *ounces cottage cheese*
3   *cups shredded mozzarella cheese*
¹/₂   *cup grated Parmesan cheese*

▲ Crumble the ground beef into a microwave-safe colander; place the colander in a 9-inch pie plate.

▲ Microwave, covered with waxed paper, on High for 5 to 6 minutes or until the beef is no longer pink, stirring after 3 minutes.

▲ Combine the beef, spaghetti sauce and water in a bowl; mix well.

▲ Place ¹/₃ of the ground beef sauce in a lightly greased baking dish. Layer the noodles, cottage cheese, mozzarella cheese and remaining ground beef sauce ¹/₂ at a time over the top. Sprinkle with half the Parmesan cheese. Cover tightly with heavy-duty plastic wrap, folding back a corner to allow steam to escape.

▲ Microwave on Medium for 32 to 35 minutes, giving the dish a half turn after 15 minutes.

▲ Remove the cover. Sprinkle with the remaining Parmesan cheese.

▲ Microwave on Medium for 2 minutes longer. Garnish with green bell pepper rings.

▲ May substitute dry red wine for the water and sliced cheese for shredded mozzarella cheese.

▲ Yield: 6 servings.

Approx Per Serving: Cal 771; Prot 55 g; Carbo 45 g; T Fat 41 g; 48% Calories from Fat; Chol 146 mg; Fiber 3 g; Sod 1388 mg

Sandra Stanfield, Revenue Officer, IRS
Lakeland, Florida

Microwave Mexican Manicotti

Meats

8	ounces ground beef
1	cup refried beans
1	teaspoon oregano
1/2	teaspoon cumin
8	uncooked manicotti shells
1 1/4	cups water
1	cup picante sauce
1	cup nonfat sour cream
1/4	cup chopped green onions
1/4	cup sliced olives
1/2	cup shredded Monterey Jack cheese

▲ Combine the ground beef, refried beans, oregano and cumin in a bowl; mix well.

▲ Pack into the manicotti shells. Arrange the shells in a 9x13-inch glass baking dish.

▲ Pour a mixture of the water and picante sauce over the shells.

▲ Microwave on High for 10 minutes. Turn the shells over.

▲ Microwave on Medium for 17 to 19 minutes or until the shells are tender.

▲ Mix the sour cream with the green onions and olives. Spoon over the shells. Sprinkle with the cheese.

▲ Microwave until the cheese melts.

▲ Yield: 8 servings.

Approx Per Serving: Cal 310; Prot 14 g; Carbo 32 g; T Fat 10 g; 29% Calories from Fat; Chol 38 mg; Fiber 5 g; Sod 418 mg

Enchilada Casserole

2	*pounds ground beef*
1	*onion, chopped*
2	*(10-ounce) cans cream of chicken soup*
1	*(12-ounce) can evaporated milk*
1	*pound Velveeta cheese, grated*
1	*(4-ounce) can green chiles, drained*
1	*(10-ounce) can mild enchilada sauce*
12	*flour tortillas*

▲ Preheat the oven to 350 degrees.

▲ Brown the ground beef with the onion in a skillet, stirring until the ground beef is crumbly; drain.

▲ Add the soup, evaporated milk, cheese, green chiles and enchilada sauce; mix well.

▲ Layer the tortillas and ground beef mixture ¹/₂ at a time in a 3-quart baking dish.

▲ Bake, covered with foil, for 30 to 40 minutes or until brown and bubbly.

▲ May substitute one 10-ounce can cream of mushroom soup for 1 can of the chicken soup.

▲ Yield: 12 servings.

Approx Per Serving: Cal 542; Prot 32 g; Carbo 30 g; T Fat 33 g; 54% Calories from Fat; Chol 112 mg; Fiber 2 g; Sod 1317 mg

Judy Gatewood, 1994 ABWA District Vice President
Co-Owner, Corporate Secretary-Treasurer, Gatewood Roofing, Inc.
Topeka, Kansas

Meats

Berry's Mexican Delight

1¹/₂   *pounds lean ground beef*

  1   *(16-ounce) can refried beans*

  1   *onion, chopped*

  2   *(10-ounce) cans enchilada sauce*

  1   *package taco seasoning mix*

  1   *(10-count) package large flour tortillas*

12   *ounces mozzarella cheese, shredded*

▲ Preheat the oven to 350 degrees.

▲ Cook the ground beef in boiling water to cover in a large saucepan until no longer pink; drain.

▲ Add the refried beans, onion, 1 can of the enchilada sauce and taco seasoning mix; mix well.

▲ Layer half the tortillas over the bottom and up the sides of a 9x13-inch baking dish. Layer all the ground beef sauce, remaining tortillas and remaining 1 can enchilada sauce over the top. Sprinkle with the mozzarella cheese.

▲ Bake for 40 minutes or until brown and the cheese is melted.

▲ Yield: 15 servings.

Approx Per Serving: Cal 379; Prot 21 g; Carbo 32 g; T Fat 19 g; 44% Calories
    from Fat; Chol 64 mg; Fiber 4 g; Sod 693 mg

Cydney Berry, 1993 ABWA National Vice President
1992 ABWA District Vice President
Executive Assistant, Demoss Tool and Die, Inc.
Lawrence, Indiana

Olé Casserole

2¹/₂ pounds extra lean ground beef
  1 medium onion, chopped
  1 (10-ounce) package corn tortillas, cut into quarters
³/₄ pound Cheddar cheese, shredded
  1 (10-ounce) can cream of mushroom soup
  1 (10-ounce) can cream of chicken soup
  1 (8-ounce) can evaporated milk
  1 (8-ounce) bottle taco sauce
  1 (4-ounce) can green chiles

▲ Preheat the oven to 350 degrees.

▲ Brown the ground beef with the onion in a skillet, stirring until the ground beef is crumbly.

▲ Line a greased shallow 2-quart baking dish with about 12 of the tortilla quarters. Alternate layers of the ground beef mixture, cheese and remaining tortillas in the prepared dish, ending with the tortillas.

▲ Combine the soups, evaporated milk, taco sauce and green chiles in a bowl and mix well. Pour over the layers.

▲ Bake for 45 minutes.

▲ Yield: 8 servings.

Approx Per Serving: Cal 676; Prot 48 g; Carbo 33 g; T Fat 40 g; 53% Calories from Fat; Chol 162 mg; Fiber 3 g; Sod 1443 mg

Wanda M. Rutherford, retired Realtor/Property Manager
Olympia, Washington

Tex-Mex Bake

1	*pound ground beef*
1	*(10-ounce) package frozen corn, thawed, drained*
1	*cup chopped onion*
1	*cup chopped green bell pepper*
1	*cup mild salsa*
1	*teaspoon ground cumin*
1/2	*teaspoon salt*
1	*(8-ounce) package corn muffin mix*

▲ Preheat the oven to 400 degrees.

▲ Brown the ground beef in a skillet, stirring until crumbly; drain.

▲ Combine the ground beef, corn, onion, green pepper, salsa, cumin and salt in a bowl and mix well.

▲ Spoon into a 9-inch square baking dish. Cover with foil.

▲ Bake for 30 minutes.

▲ Prepare the muffin mix using the package directions. Spoon the mixture over the ground beef, spreading to seal edges.

▲ Bake for 20 to 25 minutes longer or until golden brown.

▲ Yield: 6 servings.

Approx Per Serving: Cal 424; Prot 23 g; Carbo 45 g; T Fat 17 g; 35% Calories from Fat; Chol 93 mg; Fiber 4 g; Sod 885 mg

Joleen Mitchell, Computer Programmer/Analyst
American Mutual Life Insurance
West Des Moines, Iowa

Mexican Jumbo

1	*pound ground beef*
1	*onion, chopped*
1	*(16-ounce) can kidney beans*
1	*(4-ounce) can chopped black olives*
8	*ounces Cheddar cheese, shredded*
2	*teaspoons chili powder*
1¹/₂	*cups water*
¹/₂	*teaspoon salt*
1	*(12-ounce) package corn chips*

▲ Brown the ground beef in a skillet, stirring until crumbly and drain.

▲ Add the onion, beans, olives, cheese, chili powder, water and salt. Bring to a boil, stirring frequently. Reduce the heat.

▲ Simmer for 5 minutes, stirring occasionally.

▲ Layer the corn chips in a serving bowl. Spoon the ground beef mixture over the chips.

▲ May substitute pinto beans for kidney beans.

▲ Yield: 6 servings.

Approx Per Serving: Cal 715; Prot 34 g; Carbo 47 g; T Fat 44 g; 55% Calories from Fat; Chol 96 mg; Fiber 8 g; Sod 1191 mg

Marianne Cobarrubias, Corporate Communications Assistant
The Timberland Company
West Newbury, Maine

Mexican-Style Spaghetti

3	*pounds ground round*
1	*teaspoon seasoned salt*
1	*teaspoon seasoned pepper*
1/4	*teaspoon garlic powder*
1	*medium onion, chopped*
1	*tablespoon (heaping) chili powder*
1	*(15-ounce) can tomato sauce*
6	*ounces water*
1	*(16-ounce) package thin spaghetti*
2	*cups 1-inch cubes Velveeta cheese*
1/2	*cup grated Parmesan cheese*

▲ Brown the ground round in a skillet, stirring until crumbly and drain.

▲ Add the seasoned salt, seasoned pepper and garlic powder; mix
well. Add the onion.

▲ Simmer over medium heat for 2 minutes, stirring occasionally.

▲ Stir in the chili powder, tomato sauce and water. Simmer over low heat
for 15 minutes, stirring occasionally.

▲ Cook the spaghetti using the package directions and drain well.

▲ Add cheese to the sauce. Cook over very low heat for 5 minutes.
Spoon the spaghetti into a serving bowl. Add the sauce and sprinkle
with Parmesan cheese.

▲ Yield: 6 servings.

Approx Per Serving: Cal 1021; Prot 75 g; Carbo 65 g; T Fat 50 g; 45% Calories
from Fat; Chol 219 mg; Fiber 4 g; Sod 1607 mg

Janis C. Peterson, Sales Assistant, Paine Webber
Palm Beach Gardens, Florida

Texas Corn Chip Pie

2 *(22-ounce) cans chili*
1 *(16-ounce) package small corn chips*
1 *large onion, chopped*
16 *ounces Cheddar cheese, shredded*

▲ Preheat the oven to 325 degrees.

▲ Heat the chili in a saucepan over medium heat, stirring frequently.

▲ Layer the corn chips, chili, onion and cheese ¹/₃ at a time in a 9x13-inch baking dish.

▲ Bake for 20 minutes or until the cheese bubbles.

▲ Garnish with chopped lettuce and tomatoes.

▲ Yield: 10 servings.

Approx Per Serving: Cal 654; Prot 23 g; Carbo 34 g; T Fat 48 g; 66% Calories from Fat; Chol 48 mg; Fiber 2 g; Sod 1377 mg

> *Kay P. Crocker, Broker/Owner, Heart N Home Realty*
> *Franklin, Indiana*

Arizona Hash

1 *pound ground beef*
2 *onions, chopped*
1 *green bell pepper, chopped*
¹/₂ *cup uncooked rice*
1 *(8-ounce) can tomato sauce*
2 *teaspoons chili powder*

▲ Preheat the oven to 350 degrees.

▲ Line a glass casserole with paper towels. Place the ground beef in the casserole; cover with paper towels.

▲ Microwave on High for 5 minutes. Drain and crumble the ground beef. Microwave the onion and green pepper in a small glass bowl, covered tightly, for 3 minutes or until tender.

▲ Combine the vegetables with the cooked ground beef, rice, tomato sauce and chili powder in a baking dish. Bake for 30 minutes.

▲ May substitute ground turkey for the ground beef.

▲ Yield: 6 servings.

Approx Per Serving: Cal 250; Prot 19 g; Carbo 19 g; T Fat 39 g; 39% Calories from Fat; Chol 56 mg; Fiber 2 g; Sod 271 mg

Cheeseburger Pie

1   pound ground beef
1   cup chopped onion
1/2   teaspoon salt
1   cup shredded Cheddar cheese
1   cup milk
1/2   cup baking mix
2   eggs

▲ Preheat the oven to 400 degrees.

▲ Brown the ground beef with the onion in a skillet, stirring until crumbly and drain. Stir in the salt.

▲ Spread the mixture in a greased 9-inch pie plate. Sprinkle with the cheese.

▲ Combine the milk, baking mix and eggs in a bowl and mix well. Pour over the cheese layer.

▲ Bake for 25 minutes or until a knife inserted in the center comes out clean.

▲ Yield: 8 servings.

Approx Per Serving: Cal 256; Prot 19 g; Carbo 8 g; T Fat 16 g; 57% Calories from Fat; Chol 114 mg; Fiber <1 g; Sod 373 mg

Barbara Adrian, 1993 Top Ten Business Woman of ABWA
President, CEO, First Medical Equipment
Burlington, Iowa

Meats

Shepherd's Pie

1	*pound ground beef*
¹/₂	*medium onion, chopped*
	Garlic pepper seasoning to taste
1	*(16-ounce) can creamed corn*
5	*medium potatoes, peeled, chopped*
2	*tablespoons milk*
	Salt to taste
¹/₄	*cup butter*

▲ Preheat the oven to 350 degrees.

▲ Brown the ground beef with the onion in a skillet sprayed with non-stick cooking spray, stirring until the ground beef is crumbly; drain. Stir in the pepper seasoning.

▲ Spoon into a greased 2-quart baking dish. Add the creamed corn.

▲ Cook the potatoes in enough water to cover in a saucepan until tender, stirring occasionally. Drain and pour into a mixer bowl.

▲ Beat the potatoes until mashed, adding the milk, salt and butter. Spoon the potatoes over the corn.

▲ Bake for 15 minutes or until heated through.

▲ Yield: 4 servings.

Approx Per Serving: Cal 583; Prot 31 g; Carbo 55 g; T Fat 28 g; 42% Calories from Fat; Chol 116 mg; Fiber 4 g; Sod 512 mg

Adele Mariani, Realtor, Weichert Realtors
Horsham, Pennsylvania

Spaghetti Pie

8	ounces ground beef
1	(15-ounce) jar spaghetti sauce
6	ounces spaghetti, cooked
1	tablespoon butter, softened
1/3	cup grated Parmesan cheese
2	eggs
1	cup ricotta cheese
1	cup shredded mozzarella cheese

▲ Preheat the oven to 350 degrees.

▲ Brown the ground beef in a skillet, stirring until crumbly; drain. Add the spaghetti sauce and mix well.

▲ Combine the spaghetti, butter, Parmesan cheese and eggs in a bowl and mix well. Press onto the bottom and up side of a greased 10-inch pie plate.

▲ Combine the ricotta cheese and 1/2 cup of the mozzarella cheese in a bowl and mix well.

▲ Layer the cheese mixture and the ground beef mixture over the spaghetti. Cover loosely with greased foil.

▲ Bake for 20 minutes. Sprinkle with the remaining 1/2 cup mozzarella cheese.

▲ Bake, uncovered, for 8 to 10 minutes longer or until the cheese is melted.

▲ Let stand for 5 to 10 minutes before serving.

▲ Yield: 4 servings.

Approx Per Serving: Cal 587; Prot 36 g; Carbo 32 g; T Fat 35 g; 54% Calories from Fat; Chol 216 mg; Fiber 2 g; Sod 930 mg

Patti L. McLaughlin, Customer Service Representative
First National Bank of Mifflintown
Elliottsburg, Pennsylvania

Meats

Upside-Down Pizza

2	pounds ground beef
1/2	medium onion, chopped
1/2	green bell pepper, chopped
1	(4-ounce) can chopped black olives, drained
1	(4-ounce) can chopped mushrooms, drained
	Pepper to taste
1	cup sour cream
1	(8-ounce) can pizza sauce
8	ounces Cheddar cheese, shredded
8	ounces mozzarella cheese, shredded
1	(8-count) can crescent dinner rolls
2	tablespoons melted butter
1/4	cup grated Parmesan cheese

▲ Preheat the oven to 375 degrees.

▲ Brown the ground beef with the onion and green pepper in a skillet, stirring until the ground beef is crumbly; drain. Add the olives, mushrooms and pepper.

▲ Layer the ground beef mixture, sour cream, pizza sauce, Cheddar cheese and mozzarella cheese in a greased 9x13-inch baking dish.

▲ Unroll the crescent dinner rolls and place over the pizza.

▲ Drizzle with the butter and sprinkle with the Parmesan cheese.

▲ Bake for 20 minutes.

▲ May substitute sausage for the ground beef or add pepperoni.

▲ Yield: 8 servings.

Approx Per Serving: Cal 667; Prot 43 g; Carbo 20 g; T Fat 46 g; 63% Calories from Fat; Chol 162 mg; Fiber 1 g; Sod 973 mg

Patricia L. Morse, retired Area Manager
Southwestern Bell Telephone Company
Bixby, Oklahoma

Pork Chop Casserole

Meats

4   *to 6 potatoes, thinly sliced*
    Salt and pepper to taste
    Garlic powder to taste
1   *(15-ounce) can cream of mushroom soup*
1   *cup milk*
6   *pork chops*
¼   *cup butter, cut into 6 slices*

▲ Preheat the oven to 350 degrees.

▲ Layer the potato slices in a 16x20-inch baking dish. Sprinkle with salt, pepper and garlic powder.

▲ Combine the mushroom soup and milk in a bowl and mix well. Pour over the potatoes.

▲ Sprinkle the pork chops with salt and pepper and place in the baking dish. Add a slice of butter to each pork chop.

▲ Bake, covered with foil, for 1 hour and 15 minutes. Remove the foil.

▲ Bake for 15 minutes longer or until cooked through and brown.

▲ Yield: 6 servings.

Approx Per Serving: Cal 479; Prot 35 g; Carbo 32 g; T Fat 23 g; 44% Calories
    from Fat; Chol 121 mg; Fiber 2 g; Sod 591 mg

Pamela Bratton, 1985 ABWA National Secretary-Treasurer
1984 ABWA District Vice President
Chief Operations Officer, Austin Temporary Services
Dripping Springs, Texas

Meats

Grilled Butterflied Pork Chops

2 tablespoons butter or margarine
4 green onions, chopped
1/2 cup sliced fresh mushrooms
2 cloves of garlic, crushed
1/2 teaspoon ginger
2 tablespoons white cooking wine
1 1/2 cups imitation crab meat
1/2 cup shredded Swiss cheese
1/2 cup shredded sharp Cheddar cheese
1/4 cup whole cashews
4 (1-inch thick) butterflied pork chops

▲ Melt the butter in a large skillet. Add the green onions, mushrooms, garlic, ginger and wine.

▲ Cook until the green onions are tender. Add the imitation crab meat and mix well. Add the Swiss cheese and Cheddar cheese.

▲ Cook over low heat until the cheese is melted, stirring frequently. Remove from heat.

▲ Stir in the cashews. Stuff the mixture into the pork chops.

▲ Preheat the grill.

▲ Grill over hot coals until cooked through.

▲ Yield: 4 servings.

Approx Per Serving: Cal 429; Prot 38 g; Carbo 9 g; T Fat 26 g; 55% Calories from Fat; Chol 122 mg; Fiber 1 g; Sod 614 mg

On-a-Budget Pork Chops

Meats

    8   medium pork chops
    1   large white onion, sliced
    2   lemons, sliced
  1/2   cup packed brown sugar
    1   cup catsup

▲ Preheat the oven to 375 degrees.

▲ Arrange the pork chops in a 9x13-inch baking dish.

▲ Layer 1 onion slice, 1 lemon slice, 1 tablespoon brown sugar and
  2 tablespoons catsup on each pork chop.

▲ Bake, covered with foil, for 30 to 45 minutes or until cooked through.

▲ Yield: 8 servings.

Approx Per Serving: Cal 252; Prot 24 g; Carbo 23 g; T Fat 8 g; 27% Calories
    from Fat; Chol 71 mg; Fiber 1 g; Sod 424 mg

Judy Degginger, Credit Manager, Able Hands Construction
Kansas City, Missouri

Oriental Grilled Pork Chops

  1/2   cup teriyaki sauce
  1/4   cup minced green onions with tops
  1/4   cup lemon juice
    2   tablespoons peanut oil
    4   cloves of garlic, minced
    2   teaspoons crushed red pepper
    4   (3/4-inch) pork chops, trimmed

▲ Mix the teriyaki sauce, green onions, lemon juice, peanut oil, garlic
  and red pepper in a bowl. Arrange the pork chops in a shallow dish.
  Pour the marinade over the pork chops.

▲ Marinate, covered, in the refrigerator for 4 hours or longer, turning
  occasionally. Drain, reserving the marinade.

▲ Preheat the grill.

▲ Grill the pork chops 6 to 8 inches from hot coals for 30 to 45 minutes
  or until cooked through, turning and basting frequently with the
  reserved marinade.

▲ Yield: 4 servings.

Approx Per Serving: Cal 265; Prot 25 g; Carbo 9 g; T Fat 15 g; 49% Calories
    from Fat; Chol 70 mg; Fiber <1 g; Sod 1435 mg.

Meats

Peach-Glazed Pork Chops

 1   *(16-ounce) can sliced peaches*
²/₃   *cup hot water*
¹/₄   *cup margarine*
 1   *(18-ounce) package stuffing mix*
10   *thick pork chops, boned, trimmed*
¹/₂   *cup peach preserves*
1¹/₂   *tablespoons Dijon mustard*

▲ Preheat the oven to 350 degrees.

▲ Drain the peaches, reserving the syrup. Chop the peaches finely.

▲ Mix the hot water and margarine in a bowl. Stir in the stuffing mix, peaches and the reserved syrup. Arrange the chops in a 9x13-inch baking pan. Combine the preserves and mustard in a bowl; mix well. Brush over the chops.

▲ Cover the chops with the stuffing mixture.

▲ Bake for 45 minutes or until the chops are tender.

▲ Yield: 10 servings.

Approx Per Serving: Cal 472; Prot 29 g; Carbo 58 g; T Fat 14 g; 27% Calories from Fat; Chol 71 mg; Fiber 1 g; Sod 990 mg

Easy Pork Chops with Stuffing

10   *(1-inch thick) pork chops*
 2   *cups chicken bouillon*
 1   *small onion, chopped*
¹/₃   *cup melted butter*
 4   *slices bread, crumbled*
 4   *ounces herb-seasoned stuffing mix*
 1   *teaspoon parsley flakes*

▲ Preheat the oven to 325 degrees.

▲ Trim the pork chops. Arrange in a baking pan. Add ¹/₄ cup of the bouillon to the pan. Combine the remaining bouillon, onion, butter, bread, stuffing mix and parsley flakes in a bowl; mix well. Spread over the pork chops.

▲ Bake, uncovered, at 325 degrees for 1 hour or until tender.

▲ Yield: 10 servings.

Approx Per Serving: Cal 388; Prot 31 g; Carbo 14 g; T Fat 22 g; 41% Calories from Fat; Chol 111 mg; Fiber 1 g; Sod 538 mg

Quick-to-Fix Pork Chops and Apples

  4   pork chops
  2   tablespoons butter or margarine
  1   cup chopped apple
  1/4 cup packed light brown sugar
  1/4 teaspoon cinnamon
  4   lemon slices

▲ Cook the pork chops in the butter in a skillet over medium heat for 2 minutes on each side.

▲ Spoon 1/4 cup chopped apple onto each pork chop.

▲ Cook, covered, over low heat for 20 minutes or until the apple is tender and the pork chops are cooked through.

▲ Mix the brown sugar and cinnamon in a bowl. Sprinkle on the pork chops and top with a slice of lemon.

▲ Cook, covered, for 5 minutes longer or until the brown sugar is melted.

▲ Yield: 4 servings.

Approx Per Serving: Cal 280; Prot 23 g; Carbo 17 g; T Fat 13 g; 43% Calories from Fat; Chol 86 mg; Fiber 1 g; Sod 119 mg

Meats

Chinese Pork Pita Sandwiches

¹/₂   pound lean pork shoulder, cut into thin strips
2   cloves of garlic, crushed
1   tablespoon vegetable oil
3   tablespoons soy sauce
¹/₂   teaspoon sugar
¹/₄   teaspoon salt
1¹/₂   cups thinly sliced celery
¹/₂   cup sliced green onions
¹/₂   cup sliced green bell pepper
¹/₂   cup sliced water chestnuts
1   tablespoon cornstarch
¹/₂   cup cold water
2   pita rounds, cut into halves

▲ Stir-fry the pork strips with the garlic in hot oil in a large skillet or wok for 3 minutes or until cooked through.

▲ Combine the soy sauce, sugar and salt in a small bowl. Stir into the skillet. Add the celery, green onions, green pepper and water chestnuts.

▲ Stir-fry over high heat for 3 minutes.

▲ Stir in a mixture of cornstarch and water.

▲ Cook until the sauce thickens and the vegetables are coated, stirring constantly.

▲ Spoon into pita halves.

▲ Yield: 2 servings.

Approx Per Serving: Cal 484; Prot 31 g; Carbo 52 g; T Fat 16 g; 31% Calories from Fat; Chol 80 mg; Fiber 4 g; Sod 2287 mg

Chow Mein

1/4	cup chopped onion
2	ribs celery, diagonally sliced
1	tablespoon vegetable oil
2	cups cooked pork, coarsely chopped
1	(8-ounce) can sliced water chestnuts, drained
1	(8-ounce) can bamboo shoots, drained
1	(16-ounce) can bean sprouts, drained
1	(4-ounce) can sliced mushrooms, drained
1	bouillon cube
1	cup warm water
3	tablespoons soy sauce
1	tablespoon cornstarch
1	(5-ounce) can chow mein noodles, warmed

▲ Stir-fry the onion and celery in hot oil in a wok just until tender-crisp. Add the pork.

▲ Stir-fry until the pork is heated through. Add the vegetables.

▲ Stir-fry until heated through.

▲ Dissolve the bouillon cube in warm water in a bowl. Add the soy sauce and cornstarch and mix well. Add to the mixture in the wok.

▲ Cook until the sauce is thickened, stirring constantly. Cook, covered, until of serving temperature.

▲ Serve over warmed chow mein noodles.

▲ May also serve over rice and add additional soy sauce.

▲ Yield: 4 servings.

Approx Per Serving: Cal 454; Prot 28 g; Carbo 38 g; T Fat 22 g; 43% Calories from Fat; Chol 67 mg; Fiber 6 g; Sod 1564 mg

Carol Stearns, Owner/Interior Decorator, Decorating Den
Fort Walton Beach, Florida

Meats

Stromboli

8	ounces bulk sausage
1	(16-ounce) package frozen bread dough, thawed
1	tablespoon melted butter
2	tablespoons prepared mustard
16	ounces mozzarella cheese, shredded
4	ounces deli-thin sliced cooked ham
4	ounces Colby cheese, shredded
4	ounces sliced pepperoni

▲ Preheat the oven to 350 degrees.

▲ Brown the sausage in a skillet, stirring until crumbly and drain.

▲ Roll the thawed bread dough into a rectangle on a lightly floured surface. Spread the butter and mustard over the dough.

▲ Layer the sausage, half the mozzarella cheese, ham, Colby cheese, pepperoni and remaining mozzarella cheese on the bread dough.

▲ Roll as for a jelly roll to enclose the filling, sealing the edges. Place on a nonstick baking pan. Cover with foil to prevent overbrowning.

▲ Bake for 55 minutes. Remove the foil.

▲ Bake for 5 minutes longer.

▲ Yield: 8 servings.

Approx Per Serving: Cal 508; Prot 28 g; Carbo 30 g; T Fat 30 g; 54% Calories from Fat; Chol 88 mg; Fiber 2 g; Sod 1209 mg

I. "Chris" Christopherson, retired Bookkeeper-Office Manager
Home and Auto Super Mart
Rapid City, South Dakota

City "Chicken"

Meats

1	*pound ground veal*
1/2	*pound ground pork*
1	*egg*
3/4	*cup bread crumbs*
1/2	*cup chopped onion*
	Salt and pepper to taste

▲ Preheat the oven to 350 degrees.

▲ Combine the veal, pork, egg, bread crumbs, onion, salt and pepper in a bowl and mix well.

▲ Shape the mixture into oval shapes around a wooden pick. Brown in a nonstick skillet on all sides. Place in a baking pan.

▲ Roast for 45 minutes.

▲ May also be cooked in a pressure cooker for 15 minutes.

▲ May be coated in additional bread crumbs before browning.

▲ Yield: 4 servings.

Approx Per Serving: Cal 373; Prot 36 g; Carbo 16 g; T Fat 18 g; 44% Calories
   from Fat; Chol 181 mg; Fiber 1 g; Sod 280 mg

Marianne Cobarrubias, Corporate Communications Assistant
The Timberland Company
West Newbury, Maine

Meats

Veal Scallopini with Marsala

1   *pound sliced veal*
1   *cup flour*
     Vegetable oil for frying
     Salt and pepper to taste
1/3 *cup marsala or dry white wine*

▲ Remove any fat from the veal and discard. Pound the veal with a meat mallet until very thin. Coat the veal with the flour on both sides.

▲ Pour enough oil into a skillet to cover the bottom. Heat the oil.

▲ Fry the veal in the hot oil until brown on both sides and done to taste.

▲ Add the salt and pepper. Pour in the wine.

▲ Simmer for 2 minutes. Remove to a serving platter.

▲ Yield: 2 servings.

Approx Per Serving: Cal 667; Prot 47 g; Carbo 52 g; T Fat 24 g; 33% Calories from Fat; Chol 158 mg; Fiber 2 g; Sod 112 mg
     Nutritional information does not include oil for frying.

Adriana Cantelli, Secretary, Cantelli Block and Brick
Sandusky, Ohio

Poultry

Toot Your Volunteer Horn

When Hazel Blackmore visited an old high school friend in Alaska four years ago, it changed her life. "The mountains called my name," she says. "I thought, 'This is where I'm supposed to be.' " So Hazel quit her job in Kansas City, Missouri, and two days later moved herself and her teen-age daughter to Anchorage.

Besides her work experience and education, Hazel detailed her volunteer leadership positions on her resume. In job interviews, she talked about her supervisory experience, even though she'd never been a manager. As president of a Kansas City American Business Women's Association chapter, Hazel helped the group win regional and national awards. "Employers were impressed," says Hazel, an adjunct faculty member and director of the multicultural student program at Alaska Pacific University in Anchorage. "Even though I wasn't supervising anyone at the time, it showed that I knew how to be a leader."

Volunteer experience is the most overlooked training to list on your resume. Describe your volunteer responsibilities the same way you list paid work experience. List your accomplishments and responsibilities in business terms. Detail the number of volunteers you supervised, how much money an event raised and your leadership skills.

Poultry

Sunshine Barbecued Chicken

2	tablespoons flour
1	cup barbecue sauce
$^1/_4$	cup orange juice
8	skinless chicken pieces

▲ Preheat the oven to 350 degrees.

▲ Place the flour in a 14x20-inch baking bag. Shake to coat the bag and place in a baking pan. Add the barbecue sauce and the orange juice, squeezing the bag gently to mix the liquids.

▲ Rinse the chicken and pat dry. Place the chicken in the baking bag, turning the bag to coat the chicken with the sauce.

▲ Arrange the chicken in 1 layer and close the bag with the enclosed tie. Cut six $^1/_2$-inch vents in the top of the bag.

▲ Bake for 45 to 50 minutes or until the chicken is tender.

▲ Place the chicken on a serving platter. Stir the sauce and spoon over the chicken.

▲ Yield: 4 servings.

Approx Per Serving: Cal 413; Prot 54 g; Carbo 13 g; T Fat 15 g; 33% Calories from Fat; Chol 161 mg; Fiber 1 g; Sod 665 mg

Marilyn McCauley, 1990 Top Ten Business Woman of ABWA
1981 ABWA District Vice President
Program Control Manager, Federal Aviation Administration
Arlington, Virginia

Chicken Pizzaioli

1	(3- to 4-pound) chicken fryer, cut into serving pieces
3	to 4 pounds russet potatoes, peeled
1	(28-ounce) can peeled tomatoes
1/2	cup coarsely chopped fresh parsley
2	large cloves of garlic, chopped
1	tablespoon dried oregano
1/2	cup grated Romano cheese
	Salt and pepper to taste
1/4	cup olive oil

▲ Preheat the oven to 400 degrees.

▲ Rinse the chicken and pat dry. Arrange in a 9x13-inch baking dish.

▲ Cut the potatoes into large wedges as for French fries. Arrange around the chicken.

▲ Pour the undrained tomatoes over the top, breaking up the tomatoes and spreading over all. Sprinkle with the parsley, garlic, oregano and cheese. Add the salt and pepper. Drizzle with the olive oil.

▲ Bake, covered with foil, for 1 hour. Remove the foil. Bake for 15 minutes longer or until the chicken is tender.

▲ Yield: 6 servings.

Approx Per Serving: Cal 709; Prot 54 g; Carbo 72 g; T Fat 23 g; 29% Calories from Fat; Chol 143 mg; Fiber 7 g; Sod 463 mg

Grace T. Cadmus
Tustin, California

Poultry

Chicken Cacciatore

6   chicken breasts or thighs
1/2   cup vegetable oil
1/2   cup margarine
2   cups chopped onion
1   green bell pepper, chopped
2   cloves of garlic, chopped
1/2   teaspoon basil
1   teaspoon Italian seasoning
1   cup Dawn mushroom sauce
2   (8-ounce) cans tomato sauce
    Salt and pepper to taste
1/4   cup red wine
8   ounces noodles, cooked

▲ Rinse the chicken and pat dry. Fry the chicken in the oil and margarine for 10 minutes or until brown on both sides.

▲ Add the chopped onion, green pepper, garlic, basil, Italian seasoning and mushroom sauce. Simmer for 5 minutes, stirring occasionally.

▲ Add the tomato sauce. Simmer for 20 minutes, stirring occasionally.

▲ Add salt, pepper and wine. Simmer for 10 minutes, stirring occasionally.

▲ Spoon over the hot noodles.

▲ Yield: 6 servings.

Approx Per Serving: Cal 556; Prot 31 g; Carbo 23 g; T Fat 38 g; 61% Calories from Fat; Chol 86 mg; Fiber 3 g; Sod 885 mg

Mary Lou Jessup, retired CPA
Salem, Oregon

Microwave Chicken Breasts Cacciatore

Poultry

   1   (16-ounce) can whole tomatoes
  1/2   medium green bell pepper, cut into strips
   1   medium onion, sliced into rings
  1/4   cup dry white wine
 1 1/2 teaspoons Italian seasoning
   4   boneless skinless chicken breasts
   7   ounces vermicelli, cooked
   2   tablespoons grated Romano cheese

▲ Drain and chop the tomatoes.

▲ Combine the tomatoes, green pepper, onion, wine and Italian seasoning in a glass bowl.

▲ Microwave, covered, on High for 5 to 7 minutes, stirring once.

▲ Rinse the chicken and pat dry. Arrange the chicken in a 2-quart glass dish with the meatier portions toward the outer edge. Pour the sauce over the top.

▲ Microwave for 14 to 18 minutes or until the chicken is cooked through, spooning the sauce over the chicken once.

▲ Toss the vermicelli with the Romano cheese.

▲ Serve chicken and sauce over vermicelli.

▲ Yield: 4 servings.

Approx Per Serving: Cal 382; Prot 36 g; Carbo 45 g; T Fat 5 g; 12% Calories from Fat; Chol 76 mg; Fiber 3 g; Sod 291 mg

Oven Chicken and Linguini

2   tablespoons margarine
2   cups thinly sliced onion
2   cloves of garlic, minced
1   tablespoon basil
1/2   teaspoon crushed red pepper
8   chicken breasts or thighs
8   ounces linguini
2   (10-ounce) packages frozen chopped spinach, thawed
2   ounces freshly grated Parmesan cheese
1/4   teaspoon salt
1   small orange, cut into quarters

▲ Preheat the oven to 400 degrees.

▲ Melt the margarine in a 10x15-inch baking dish in the oven. Remove from the oven.

▲ Add the onion, garlic, basil and red pepper, stirring to mix with the margarine.

▲ Rinse the chicken and pat dry. Place the chicken in the baking dish, turning to coat with the margarine mixture.

▲ Bake, uncovered, for 45 minutes or until the chicken is tender.

▲ Cook the linguini using package directions until just tender and drain. Drain the spinach.

▲ Remove the chicken from the baking dish and keep warm on a warm platter.

▲ Add the spinach to the baking dish and stir to mix with the chicken drippings.

▲ Add the linguini, Parmesan cheese and salt, tossing gently to mix.

▲ Place 1 1/2 cups of the linguini mixture on each serving plate. Arrange 2 pieces of chicken beside the mixture. Add an unpeeled orange quarter to each plate and squeeze orange juice over all before eating.

▲ Yield: 4 servings.

Approx Per Serving: Cal 677; Prot 72 g; Carbo 57 g; T Fat 18 g; 24% Calories from Fat; Chol 157 mg; Fiber 6 g; Sod 702 mg

Joanne Streiffert, Administrator, E and E Services
Lenoir City, Tennessee

Best-Choice-Ever Baked Chicken Supreme

1	cup fat-free sour cream
4¹/₂	tablespoons lemon juice
1¹/₂	teaspoons celery salt
¹/₄	teaspoon paprika
2	teaspoons Worcestershire sauce
	Salt and pepper to taste
8	whole boneless skinless chicken breasts
3	cups Italian bread crumbs
¹/₂	cup margarine, melted

▲ Preheat the oven to 350 degrees.

▲ Combine the sour cream, lemon juice, celery salt, paprika, Worcestershire sauce, salt and pepper in a large bowl; mix well.

▲ Rinse the chicken and pat dry. Place in the sour cream mixture, turning to coat. Chill, covered, in the refrigerator for 8 to 10 hours.

▲ Roll each chicken breast in the bread crumbs. Place the chicken in a 9x13-inch baking dish. Spoon the margarine over the chicken.

▲ Bake for 1¹/₄ hours or until the chicken is tender.

▲ Yield: 8 servings.

Approx Per Serving: Cal 543; Prot 61 g; Carbo 31 g; T Fat 19 g; 31% Calories from Fat; Chol 147 mg; Fiber <1 g; Sod 1570 mg

Poultry

Chicken Aloha

1 boneless skinless chicken breast
1 cup ¹/₂-inch pieces fresh green beans
¹/₂ cup cubed fresh pineapple
2 tablespoons vinegar
1 package sugar substitute

▲ Rinse the chicken.

▲ Combine the chicken and green beans in a saucepan with a small amount of water. Cook until the chicken is just barely tender, stirring occasionally.

▲ Drain the chicken and green beans. Chop the chicken coarsely.

▲ Stir-fry the chicken and green beans in a wok or skillet coated with nonstick cooking spray until the chicken is tender.

▲ Add the pineapple, vinegar and sugar substitute.

▲ Stir-fry until mixed and heated to serving temperature.

▲ Yield: 1 serving.

Approx Per Serving: Cal 221; Prot 29 g; Carbo 20 g; T Fat 4 g; 14% Calories from Fat; Chol 73 mg; Fiber 4 g; Sod 75 mg

Vivian Gardner, 1978 Top Ten Business Woman of ABWA
1973 ABWA National President, 1971 ABWA District Vice President
Broker-Realtor, Century 21 Brock-Mills Group
Wilmington, North Carolina

Buttermilk-Pecan Chicken

1/3	cup butter
1	cup flour
1	cup pecans, ground
1/4	cup sesame seeds
1	tablespoon paprika
1 1/2	teaspoons salt
1/8	teaspoon pepper
1	egg, beaten
1	cup buttermilk
8	boneless skinless chicken breast halves
1/4	cup coarsely chopped pecans

▲ Preheat the oven to 350 degrees.

▲ Melt the butter in a 9x13-inch baking dish in the oven. Remove from the oven.

▲ Combine the flour, ground pecans, sesame seeds, paprika, salt and pepper in a shallow bowl and mix well.

▲ Combine the egg and buttermilk in a shallow bowl and mix well.

▲ Rinse the chicken and pat dry. Dip the chicken in egg mixture to coat and dredge in the flour mixture. Place in the baking dish, turning to coat with the butter. Sprinkle with the chopped pecans.

▲ Bake for 30 minutes or until cooked through.

▲ Yield: 8 servings.

Approx Per Serving: Cal 441; Prot 33 g; Carbo 18 g; T Fat 27 g; 55% Calories from Fat; Chol 121 mg; Fiber 2 g; Sod 584 mg

Connie Loesch Cargin, 1989 Top Ten Business Woman of ABWA
Vice President of Finance/Administration
Kingswood Manor
Kansas City, Missouri

Poultry

Chicken Breasts Diane

4   boneless skinless chicken breasts
1/2 teaspoon salt
1/4 to 1/2 teaspoon pepper
2   tablespoons vegetable oil
2   tablespoons margarine
3   tablespoons chopped green onions
    Juice of 1/2 lemon
3   tablespoons chopped parsley
2   teaspoons Dijon mustard
1/4 cup chicken broth

▲ Rinse the chicken and pat dry. Flatten the chicken between pieces of waxed paper with a meat mallet. Sprinkle with salt and pepper.

▲ Heat 1 tablespoon each of oil and margarine in a skillet. Cook the chicken in hot oil mixture for 4 minutes on each side over high heat. Do not overcook. Remove the chicken to a warm platter.

▲ Add the green onions, lemon juice, parsley and mustard to the skillet. Cook for 15 seconds, stirring constantly.

▲ Add the broth. Cook until heated through, stirring constantly.

▲ Add remaining 1 tablespoon each oil and margarine. Cook until of serving temperature, stirring frequently. Pour over the chicken.

▲ Yield: 4 servings.

Approx Per Serving: Cal 263; Prot 27 g; Carbo 1 g; T Fat 16 g; 56% Calories from Fat; Chol 73 mg; Fiber <1 g; Sod 515 mg

Chicken Breasts Oriental

1   (4-ounce) jar sweet and sour sauce
1   envelope dry onion soup mix
1   (16-ounce) can whole cranberry sauce
8   chicken breast fillets

▲ Preheat the oven to 325 degrees.

▲ Mix the sweet and sour sauce, onion soup mix and cranberry sauce in a bowl. Rinse the chicken and pat dry. Place in a 7x11-inch baking dish.

▲ Bake, covered, for 30 minutes. Bake, uncovered, for 30 minutes longer.

▲ Yield: 8 servings.

Approx Per Serving: Cal 254; Prot 27 g; Carbo 29 g; T Fat 3 g; 12% Calories from Fat; Chol 73 mg; Fiber 1 g; Sod 210 mg

Chicken Breasts Wellington

  2   large whole chicken breasts
  1   (8-count) can crescent dinner rolls
  4   slices pepper cheese
       Grey Poupon mustard to taste
  1   egg, beaten
  1   tablespoon dark brown sugar
  2   tablespoons red wine vinegar
 1/8   cup corn oil
 1/2   teaspoon dry mustard

▲ Preheat the oven to 350 degrees.

▲ Rinse the chicken and place in a heavy saucepan. Add enough water to cover. Simmer for 30 minutes and drain.

▲ Let the chicken cool; remove skin and bones. Cut chicken breasts into halves.

▲ Unroll the crescent roll dough on a pastry board. Make 4 squares by pressing the perforations to seal. Place 1 chicken breast half on each square. Top with pepper cheese and Grey Poupon mustard. Wrap dough to enclose filling. Brush with egg. Place on a baking sheet.

▲ Bake for 20 to 25 minutes or until light brown.

▲ Combine the brown sugar, vinegar, oil and dry mustard in a saucepan. Simmer for 5 minutes, stirring vigorously.

▲ Serve over the chicken.

▲ Yield: 4 servings.

Approx Per Serving: Cal 505; Prot 42 g; Carbo 31 g; T Fat 23 g; 42% Calories from Fat; Chol 163 mg; Fiber 0 g; Sod 845 mg

Poultry

Creamy Baked Chicken Breasts

8   boneless skinless chicken breasts
8   (4-inch) slices Swiss cheese
1   (10-ounce) can cream of chicken soup
1/4   cup dry white wine
1   cup crushed herb-seasoned stuffing mix
1/4   cup melted butter

▲ Preheat the oven to 350 degrees.

▲ Rinse the chicken and pat dry. Arrange in a lightly greased 9x13-inch baking dish and top with the Swiss cheese.

▲ Combine the chicken soup and white wine in a bowl and mix well. Spoon over the chicken.

▲ Sprinkle with the crushed stuffing mix and drizzle with the melted butter.

▲ Bake for 45 to 55 minutes or until cooked through.

▲ Yield: 8 servings.

Approx Per Serving: Cal 370; Prot 37 g; Carbo 11 g; T Fat 19 g; 47% Calories from Fat; Chol 118 mg; Fiber <1 g; Sod 635 mg

Debbie Everman, Executive Secretary
Navistar International
Indianapolis, Indiana

Chicken Can-Can

- 10   boneless skinless chicken breasts
      Salt and pepper to taste
- 1   (4-ounce) can mushroom caps, drained
- 1   (14-ounce) can artichoke hearts, drained, cut into quarters
- 1   (7-ounce) jar hearts of palm, cut into thirds
- 1   (8-ounce) can sliced water chestnuts, drained
- 1   (10-ounce) can cream of mushroom soup or cream of asparagus soup
- 1/2   cup sherry or dry white wine
- 1   cup sour cream
      Paprika to taste

▲ Preheat the oven to 350 degrees.

▲ Rinse the chicken and pat dry. Arrange in a shallow 9x13-inch baking dish. Season with the salt and pepper.

▲ Layer the mushrooms, artichokes, hearts of palm and water chestnuts over the chicken.

▲ Combine the soup, sherry and sour cream in a bowl and mix well. Pour the soup mixture over the layers. Sprinkle with paprika.

▲ Bake, covered, for 30 minutes. Remove the cover. Bake for 30 minutes longer or until the chicken is tender.

▲ Yield: 8 servings.

Approx Per Serving: Cal 324; Prot 37 g; Carbo 12 g; T Fat 13 g; 37% Calories from Fat; Chol 105 mg; Fiber 1 g; Sod 755 mg

Orange Chicken

4   *boneless skinless chicken breast halves*
1   *cup orange juice*
1/4 *cup orange marmalade*
1   *tablespoon vinegar*
1   *tablespoon brown sugar*
1/2 *cup mandarin oranges, drained*

▲ Rinse the chicken and pat dry.

▲ Arrange the chicken in a baking dish.

▲ Combine the orange juice, marmalade, vinegar and brown sugar in a bowl and mix well.

▲ Spoon the mixture over the chicken. Arrange the mandarin oranges over the top.

▲ Bake for 30 minutes or until tender.

▲ Yield: 4 servings.

Approx Per Serving: Cal 246; Prot 27 g; Carbo 27 g; T Fat 3 g; 12% Calories from Fat; Chol 73 mg; Fiber <1 g; Sod 78 mg

> *Beverly A. Trimble, 1992 ABWA District Vice President*
> *General Administrative Manager, Power-Draulics, Inc.*
> *Lancaster, Pennsylvania*

Microwave Honey-Glazed Chicken

6	boneless skinless chicken breasts
2	tablespoons melted margarine
1 1/2	cups chicken broth
1/4	cup finely chopped onion
2/3	cup honey
1/2	cup lemon juice
1/3	cup soy sauce

▲ Rinse the chicken and pat dry. Brown the chicken on all sides in the margarine in a skillet.

▲ Combine the broth, onion, honey, lemon juice and soy sauce in a 4-cup glass bowl; mix well.

▲ Microwave on High until the mixture boils.

▲ Place the chicken in a microwave-safe dish. Pour the sauce over the chicken. Microwave, covered, on Medium until the chicken is tender, basting 3 or 4 times.

▲ Yield: 6 servings.

Approx Per Serving: Cal 315; Prot 29 g; Carbo 35 g; T Fat 7 g; 20% Calories from Fat; Chol 73 mg; Fiber <1 g; Sod 1216 mg

Taco Chicken Nuggets

1/4	cup cornmeal
2 1/2	tablespoons taco seasoning mix
6	boneless skinless chicken breasts

▲ Combine the cornmeal and taco seasoning in a sealable plastic bag; mix well.

▲ Rinse the chicken and pat dry. Cut into 1-inch pieces. Shake the chicken in the cornmeal mixture to coat.

▲ Arrange the chicken pieces in a 7x12-inch glass baking dish; cover with a paper towel.

▲ Microwave on High for 5 to 7 minutes or until the chicken is tender, turning once.

▲ May serve with picante sauce or other favorite sauce as an appetizer.

▲ Yield: 6 servings.

Approx Per Serving: Cal 181; Prot 28 g; Carbo 8 g; T Fat 3 g; 17% Calories from Fat; Chol 73 mg; Fiber <1 g; Sod 473 mg

Poultry

Santa Fe Chicken for One

1	*boneless skinless chicken breast*
1	*teaspoon melted butter*
1	*tablespoon lime juice*
1/4	*teaspoon chili powder*
1/8	*teaspoon garlic powder*
1	*tablespoon chopped cilantro*
3	*lime slices*

▲ Rinse the chicken and pat dry.

▲ Pound the chicken flat between plastic wrap. Peel off plastic wrap carefully. Place the chicken on a microwave-safe plate.

▲ Blend the butter and lime juice together. Spread over the chicken. Sprinkle with chili powder, garlic powder and cilantro. Arrange the lime slices over the top.

▲ Microwave, covered with plastic wrap, on High for 1 minute and 45 seconds.

▲ Let stand for several minutes before serving.

▲ Yield: 1 serving.

Approx Per Serving: Cal 142; Prot 20 g; Carbo 5 g; T Fat 5 g; 32% Calories from Fat; Chol 59 mg; Fiber 1 g; Sod 89 mg

Raspberry Chicken

8   boneless skinless chicken breast halves
5   ounces low-sugar raspberry preserves
1/2   cup thawed pineapple juice concentrate
1/4   cup low-sodium soy sauce
2   tablespoons rice vinegar
1/2   teaspoon chili powder
1/2   teaspoon pressed fresh garlic
1/2   cup chopped fresh basil
1/2   cup fresh raspberries

▲ Rinse the chicken and pat dry.

▲ Arrange in a 9x13-inch baking dish.

▲ Combine the preserves, pineapple juice concentrate, soy sauce, vinegar, chili powder, garlic and basil in a bowl and mix well. Pour over the chicken.

▲ Marinate, covered, in the refrigerator for 8 to 10 hours.

▲ Preheat the oven to 350 degrees.

▲ Bake in the marinade for 30 minutes or until cooked through.

▲ Remove the chicken to a serving platter. Top with the marinade and fresh raspberries.

▲ Yield: 8 servings.

Approx Per Serving: Cal 209; Prot 28 g; Carbo 17 g; T Fat 3 g; 14% Calories from Fat; Chol 73 mg; Fiber 1 g; Sod 93 mg

Phony Abalone

2   boneless skinless chicken breast halves
1   bottle clam juice
1   cup seasoned bread crumbs
¹/₂   cup margarine

▲ Rinse the chicken and pat dry. Flatten with a meat mallet and place in a shallow bowl. Pour the clam juice over the chicken.

▲ Marinate, covered, in the refrigerator for 8 to 10 hours and drain.

▲ Roll the chicken in the bread crumbs to coat.

▲ Fry in the margarine in a skillet over medium or low heat until brown and cooked through.

▲ Yield: 2 servings.

Approx Per Serving: Cal 735; Prot 35 g; Carbo 36 g; T Fat 50 g; 61% Calories from Fat; Chol 78 mg; Fiber 0 g; Sod 2168 mg

Marianne Cobarrubias, Corporate Communications Assistant
The Timberland Company
West Newbury, Maine

Rosemary Chicken

4   chicken breast fillets
1   teaspoon rosemary
1   (10-ounce) can cream of chicken soup

▲ Preheat the oven to 350 degrees.

▲ Rinse the chicken and pat dry. Cut into strips and place in a 2-quart baking dish. Sprinkle with rosemary. Pour the chicken soup over the chicken.

▲ Bake for 25 to 30 minutes or until cooked through.

▲ May be served with baked potatoes, rice or noodles.

▲ Yield: 4 servings.

Approx Per Serving: Cal 212; Prot 29 g; Carbo 6 g; T Fat 8 g; 33% Calories from Fat; Chol 79 mg; Fiber <1 g; Sod 663 mg

Lois Gowler, Owner, Gowler's Painting and Wallcovering
Lincoln, Nebraska

Reuben Chicken

4   boneless chicken breasts
8   slices Swiss cheese
1   (16-ounce) jar sauerkraut, drained
1   (8-ounce) bottle Russian dressing

▲ Preheat the oven to 400 degrees.

▲ Rinse the chicken and pat dry. Arrange in a baking dish sprayed with nonstick cooking spray.

▲ Layer the Swiss cheese and sauerkraut over the chicken and cover with Russian dressing.

▲ Bake for 25 to 30 minutes or until cooked through.

▲ Yield: 4 servings.

Approx Per Serving: Cal 654; Prot 45 g; Carbo 13 g; T Fat 48 g; 65% Calories from Fat; Chol 135 mg; Fiber 3 g; Sod 1452 mg

Connie Alexander, 1984 American Business Woman of ABWA
Administrator, Employee Assistance Program, NASA Johnson Space Center
Houston, Texas

Quick Chicken and Macaroni with Vegetables

1	pound boneless skinless chicken breast halves
1/2	cup chopped green bell pepper
1/4	cup chopped onion
1/4	cup chopped celery
1/4	cup vegetable oil
1	(10-ounce) package frozen mixed vegetables
1	(10-ounce) can chicken soup
1	soup can water
2	cups cooked macaroni
1/4	cup shredded Colby/Monterey Jack cheese

▲ Rinse the chicken and pat dry.

▲ Sauté the green pepper, onion, celery and chicken in the oil in a large skillet until the chicken is cooked through.

▲ Add the mixed vegetables, chicken soup and water. Simmer for 5 minutes and stir. Simmer for 15 minutes longer, stirring occasionally.

▲ Stir in the macaroni and cheese. Heat for 5 minutes, stirring occasionally. Spoon into a serving bowl.

▲ Yield: 6 servings.

Approx Per Serving: Cal 320; Prot 24 g; Carbo 24 g; T Fat 14 g; 40% Calories from Fat; Chol 56 mg; Fiber 3 g; Sod 472 mg

Nellie E. Dorsey, Executive Secretary/Librarian
Saint Therese Medical Center
Waukegan, Illinois

Tomato Lover's Chicken

6   boneless skinless chicken breast halves
1/2 cup flour
1/2 teaspoon salt
1/4 teaspoon pepper
3   tablespoons vegetable oil
8   ounces fresh mushrooms, sliced
1   cup white wine
2   large tomatoes, cut into 1/2-inch chunks
3   cups cooked rice

▲ Rinse the chicken and pat dry. Flatten the chicken with a meat mallet.

▲ Combine the flour, salt and pepper in a shallow bowl and mix well.
Dredge the chicken in the flour mixture to lightly coat.

▲ Brown the chicken in the hot oil in a skillet for about 5 minutes on
each side. Remove to a warm platter.

▲ Add the mushrooms to the skillet. Sauté for 4 to 5 minutes. Remove to
the warm platter.

▲ Blot any oil remaining in skillet with paper towels but leave any
sediment. Stir in wine and deglaze skillet.

▲ Add the chicken and mushrooms. Reduce the heat. Simmer, covered,
for 10 minutes, checking occasionally to see if more wine is needed to
prevent boiling dry.

▲ Add the tomatoes. Cook for 2 to 3 minutes longer or just until the
tomatoes are heated through. Serve over cooked rice.

▲ Yield: 6 servings.

Approx Per Serving: Cal 421; Prot 32 g; Carbo 42 g; T Fat 11 g; 23% Calories
from Fat; Chol 73 mg; Fiber 2 g; Sod 251 mg

Sara Connor, 1995 American Business Woman of ABWA
Assistant to the Vice President, Armstrong State College
Thunderbolt, Georgia

Chicken and Linguini Stir-Fry

 1   (16-ounce) package fresh linguini
 2   tablespoons olive oil
 2   cloves of garlic, finely minced
     Ginger to taste
 1   pound chicken breast fillets, cut into strips
 2   carrots, peeled, thinly sliced
 2   cups broccoli florets
 2   cups cauliflowerets
 1   small red bell pepper, julienned
 2   tablespoons olive oil
 4   cups fresh spinach
 1/2 cup chopped green onions
 1   cup red wine vinegar
 1/4 cup soy sauce
 2   tablespoons olive oil

▲ Cook the linguini using package directions and drain.

▲ Heat 2 tablespoons olive oil in a large skillet or wok over medium-high heat. Add the garlic and ginger. Sauté for 1 minute.

▲ Add the chicken strips. Sauté for 5 minutes.

▲ Add the carrots, broccoli, cauliflowerets and red pepper. Sauté for 5 minutes, adding the 2 tablespoons olive oil 1 tablespoon at a time as needed.

▲ Add the spinach and green onions. Sauté for 2 minutes. Remove to a large bowl. Add the linguini to the bowl and mix well.

▲ Combine the vinegar, soy sauce and 2 tablespoons olive oil in the same skillet. Simmer for 1 minute, stirring occasionally. Add the vinegar sauce to the linguini mixture and toss to mix.

▲ Yield: 8 servings.

Approx Per Serving: Cal 409; Prot 23 g; Carbo 51 g; T Fat 13 g; 28% Calories from Fat; Chol 36 mg; Fiber 4 g; Sod 592 mg

Green Enchilada and Chicken Casserole

2	(10-ounce) cans green enchilada sauce
2	(10-ounce) cans cream of chicken soup
18	corn tortillas
1	(2-pound) chicken, cooked, shredded
1¹/₂	cups shredded Monterey Jack or Cheddar cheese
	Garlic powder and pepper to taste
¹/₂	cup chopped green onions
1	(4-ounce) can chopped green chiles

▲ Preheat the oven to 350 degrees.

▲ Combine the enchilada sauce and the chicken soup in a saucepan. Heat over medium heat until bubbly around the edge, stirring frequently.

▲ Dip 6 tortillas into the sauce and layer in a 9x13-inch baking dish.

▲ Add layers of ¹/₃ of the chicken, cheese, garlic powder, pepper, green onions and green chiles.

▲ Repeat the layers 2 times.

▲ Spoon the remaining sauce over the top.

▲ Bake for 30 minutes.

▲ Let stand for 5 to 10 minutes before serving.

▲ Yield: 10 servings.

Approx Per Serving: Cal 373; Prot 23 g; Carbo 35 g; T Fat 16 g; 38% Calories from Fat; Chol 69 mg; Fiber 4 g; Sod 918 mg

Linda Todd, Administrative Secretary, Superintendents Office
Tucson Unified School District
Tucson, Arizona

Poultry

Impossible Chicken and Broccoli Pie

1	*(10-ounce) package frozen chopped broccoli, thawed*
1¹/₂	*cups coarsely chopped cooked chicken*
²/₃	*cup chopped onions*
3	*cups shredded Cheddar cheese*
1¹/₃	*cups milk*
3	*eggs*
³/₄	*cup baking mix*
	Salt and pepper to taste

▲ Preheat the oven to 400 degrees.

▲ Combine the broccoli, chicken, onions and 2 cups of the cheese in a bowl and mix well. Spoon into a baking dish.

▲ Mix the milk, eggs, baking mix, salt and pepper together in a bowl. Pour over the broccoli mixture.

▲ Bake for 30 minutes. Top with the remaining 1 cup cheese. Bake for 1 to 2 minutes longer or until the cheese melts.

▲ Yield: 6 servings.

Approx Per Serving: Cal 444; Prot 32 g; Carbo 17 g; T Fat 28 g; 56% Calories from Fat; Chol 204 mg; Fiber 2 g; Sod 631 mg

Thelma M. Chisholm, Quality Control, retired
General Electric
Daytona Beach, Florida

Leftover Chicken Pie

1/4   cup butter or margarine
1/4   cup flour
      Salt and pepper to taste
2   cups chicken broth
2/3   cup cream
2   cups chopped cooked chicken
1   (10-count) can biscuits

▲ Preheat the oven to 375 degrees.

▲ Melt the butter in a saucepan. Stir in the flour, salt and pepper. Add the broth and cream. Cook over medium heat until the sauce is thickened, stirring constantly. Stir in the chicken.

▲ Pour into a 9x13-inch baking dish. Place the biscuits on top.

▲ Bake for 10 to 12 minutes or until the biscuits are brown.

▲ May substitute cooked turkey or beef for the chicken, beef broth for the chicken broth and half-and-half for the cream.

▲ Yield: 4 servings.

Approx Per Serving: Cal 620; Prot 30 g; Carbo 38 g; T Fat 42 g; 59% Calories from Fat; Chol 147 mg; Fiber <1 g; Sod 1330 mg

> *Jeneva W. Gibson, 1972 ABWA National Secretary-Treasurer*
> *retired Accountant, Federal Mogul Corporation*
> *Independence, Missouri*

Poultry

Chicken Strata

6	slices white bread, torn
4	cups chopped cooked chicken
1/2	cup chopped celery
1/2	cup chopped onion
1/2	cup chopped green bell pepper
1/2	cup mayonnaise
1	(10-ounce) can mushroom soup
2	eggs
2	cups milk
1/2	cup shredded Cheddar cheese

▲ Combine the bread, chicken, celery, onion, green pepper and mayonnaise in a bowl and mix well. Spoon into a 9x13-inch baking dish. Chill, covered tightly, in the refrigerator for 8 to 10 hours.

▲ Preheat the oven to 350 degrees.

▲ Spread the soup over the top of the mixture.

▲ Beat the eggs and milk together in a bowl. Pour over the soup layer. Top with the cheese.

▲ Bake for 1 hour.

▲ Yield: 12 servings.

Approx Per Serving: Cal 281; Prot 19 g; Carbo 12 g; T Fat 17 g; 54% Calories from Fat; Chol 95 mg; Fiber 1 g; Sod 424 mg

Ruth McKamey, 1971 ABWA National President, 1970 ABWA Vice President
1969 ABWA District Vice President
Executive Assistant, Blossom Chevrolet Geo Inc.
Indianapolis, Indiana

Chicken Roll-Ups

1   (10-ounce) can white chicken
4   ounces Colby/Monterey Jack cheese, shredded
3   tablespoons chopped onion
1   tablespoon dried parsley
1   clove of garlic, minced
1/2 teaspoon pepper
2   (8-count) cans crescent rolls
8   ounces cream cheese, softened
2   (10-ounce) cans cream of chicken soup
4   ounces Colby/Monterey Jack cheese, shredded
     Paprika to taste

▲ Preheat the oven to 350 degrees.

▲ Combine the chicken, 4 ounces cheese, onion, parsley, garlic and pepper in a bowl and mix well.

▲ Unroll the crescent roll dough; separate into triangles. Place 2 to 3 tablespoons of the chicken mixture in center of each triangle. Fold in sides of the dough and roll up to enclose the filling.

▲ Combine the cream cheese and soup in a bowl and mix well. Spoon 2/3 of the mixture into a 9x13-inch baking dish. Place the chicken rolls in the mixture, turning in the ends to shape into crescents. Top with the remaining soup mixture and sprinkle with remaining 4 ounces of cheese and paprika.

▲ Bake for 45 to 60 minutes or until golden brown.

▲ Yield: 8 servings.

Approx Per Serving: Cal 483; Prot 22 g; Carbo 33 g; T Fat 29 g; 55% Calories
    from Fat; Chol 89 mg; Fiber <1 g; Sod 1498 mg

Melanie Mayberry, Brokerage Services Coordinator
Commodity Services, Inc.
West Des Moines, Iowa

Poultry

Shake and Bake for Chicken

1   *(18-ounce) package cornflakes, finely crushed*
1   *cup each flour and yellow cornmeal*
1   *tablespoon paprika*
1   *tablespoon meat tenderizer*
2   *teaspoons onion salt*
1   *teaspoon pepper*
1   *tablespoon poultry seasoning*
2   *teaspoons salt*
1   *cup melted margarine*

▲ Combine all the ingredients in a bowl and mix well.

▲ Store, tightly covered, in the freezer until needed. Use to coat chicken or other meats before baking.

▲ Yield: 24 servings.

Approx Per Serving: Cal 192; Prot 3 g; Carbo 27 g; T Fat 8 g; 37% Calories from Fat; Chol 0 mg; Fiber 2 g; Sod 837 mg

Gina L. Plummer, Teacher-Director
Wee Shipmates Preschool
Sidney, Iowa

15-Minute Chili

1   *pound ground turkey*
1   *cup fresh or frozen chopped onion*
1   *(28-ounce) can chopped stewed tomatoes*
1   *tablespoon chili powder*
1   *tablespoon cumin*
1/2 *cup salsa*
1   *(16-ounce) can pinto beans, drained, rinsed*
1   *(16-ounce) can kidney beans, drained, rinsed*

▲ Brown the turkey with the onion in a large saucepan, stirring frequently. Add the tomatoes, chili powder, cumin and salsa. Stir in the pinto beans and kidney beans. Cook over medium heat until of serving temperature, stirring frequently.

▲ Yield: 10 servings.

Approx Per Serving: Cal 189; Prot 15 g; Carbo 22 g; T Fat 5 g; 24% Calories from Fat; Chol 35 mg; Fiber 5 g; Sod 647 mg

Mary Ann McElroy, Executive Secretary
Union Central Insurance Company
Cincinnati, Ohio

Grilled Turkey Breast

- *³/₄   cup red cooking wine*
- *¹/₄   cup soy sauce*
- *¹/₂   teaspoon garlic powder*
- *¹/₂   teaspoon crushed basil*
- *1   tablespoon olive oil*
- *1   pound turkey scallops*

▲ Combine the wine, soy sauce, garlic, basil and oil in a shallow bowl; mix well.

▲ Rinse the turkey and pat dry. Marinate the turkey in the wine mixture in the refrigerator for several hours. Drain, reserving the marinade.

▲ Grill the turkey over hot coals for 10 minutes or until tender, basting occasionally with the reserved marinade.

▲ Yield: 6 servings.

Approx Per Serving: Cal 157; Prot 17 g; Carbo 2 g; T Fat 7 g; 39% Calories
from Fat; Chol 41 mg; Fiber 0 g; Sod 719 mg
Nutritional information includes the entire amount of marinade.

Turkey Sautéed with Pears and Pecans

- *1   pound turkey breast slices*
- *2   cloves of garlic, chopped*
- *1   tablespoon olive oil*
- *1   teaspoon cracked peppercorns*
- *¹/₃   cup apple juice*
- *2   tablespoons light cream*
- *2   pears, sliced ¹/₄ inch thick*
- *¹/₄   to ¹/₂ cup pecan halves, toasted*

▲ Rinse the turkey and pat dry. Sauté the turkey and garlic in the hot oil in a skillet for 1 to 2 minutes or until brown; reduce heat.

▲ Stir in the peppercorns, apple juice, cream and pears. Cook for 1 to 2 minutes or until the sauce is heated through.

▲ Arrange the turkey slices on a serving platter. Sprinkle with the toasted pecans.

▲ Serve the turkey with sauce over hot cooked rice.

▲ Yield: 6 servings.

Approx Per Serving: Cal 245; Prot 17 g; Carbo 12 g; T Fat 15 g; 53% Calories
from Fat; Chol 46 mg; Fiber 2 g; Sod 35 mg

Poultry

Presto Potpies

2   (6-ounce) cans chunk turkey
1   (16-ounce) can each peas, whole kernel corn, sliced carrots
      and sliced potatoes
2   (10-ounce) cans cream of mushroom soup
      Salt and pepper to taste
2   frozen unbaked (9-inch) deep-dish pie shells
2   unbaked all-ready pie pastries

▲ Preheat the oven to 425 degrees.

▲ Drain the turkey and canned vegetables.

▲ Combine in a large saucepan. Add the soup and salt and pepper;
   mix well.

▲ Cook until heated through. Spoon into the frozen pie shells.

▲ Top with the pie pastries. Moisten each pie shell edge with a little
   milk or water. Seal the edges; flute decoratively and cut vents.

▲ Bake for 30 minutes or until golden brown.

▲ Yield: 16 servings.

Approx Per Serving: Cal 384; Prot 10 g; Carbo 40 g; T Fat 21 g; 48% Calories
   from Fat; Chol 22 mg; Fiber 3 g; Sod 994 mg

Seafood

Finding a Business Coach

Professional organizations are powerful networks where business owners can share their expertise, find new customers and have a circle of friends who cheer them on. When business owners connect through the American Business Women's Association, they form business adviser relationships. That's a welcome resource to entrepreneurs like Jackie Whitaker.

As owner of Castrol GTX 10-Minute Oil Change in Canton, Ohio, Jackie is the only woman in a six-man shop. Each month, she has lunch with ABWA members who own trucking and fabricating businesses. "Only someone else in business understands what it's like to be in business for yourself," says Jackie. "It's not like a 40-hour-a-week job because your business never leaves your mind. You wake up each morning and face different problems."

Jackie brainstorms solutions to tax and employee problems with other business owners, and shares the funny side of entrepreneurship. "We laugh together and lighten up over the serious issues of business," she says.

Seafood

Sweet Mustard-Sauced Fish

1¹/₂   *pounds cod fillets*
¹/₂   *cup salsa*
2   *tablespoons mayonnaise*
2   *to 3 tablespoons honey*
2   *tablespoons prepared mustard*

▲ Preheat the oven to 450 degrees.

▲ Cut the fish into 6 servings. Arrange in a 9x13-inch baking dish.

▲ Bake for 4 to 6 minutes or until the fish flakes easily.

▲ Drain the fish.

▲ Combine the salsa, mayonnaise, honey and mustard in a bowl and mix well. Pour over the fish.

▲ Bake for 2 to 3 minutes longer or until the sauce is heated through.

▲ Remove to serving plates; spoon the sauce over the fish.

▲ Yield: 6 servings.

Approx Per Serving: Cal 171; Prot 21 g; Carbo 11 g; T Fat 5 g; 25% Calories from Fat; Chol 53 mg; Fiber <1 g; Sod 256 mg

Halibut and Sour Cream Bake

Seafood

2	(8-ounce) halibut steaks, 1 inch thick
1/4	cup sour cream
1/4	cup mayonnaise
1/4	cup sliced green onions
1	teaspoon lemon juice
1/4	teaspoon salt
	Red pepper to taste
1/4	cup shredded Cheddar cheese

▲ Preheat the oven to 450 degrees.

▲ Cut the halibut steaks into halves and arrange in a 6x10-inch baking dish.

▲ Bake for 12 to 15 minutes or until the fish flakes easily.

▲ Combine the sour cream, mayonnaise, green onions, lemon juice, salt and pepper in a bowl and mix well.

▲ Spoon over the fish and sprinkle with the cheese.

▲ Bake for 3 to 4 minutes longer or until the sauce is heated through.

▲ Yield: 4 servings.

Approx Per Serving: Cal 287; Prot 27 g; Carbo 2 g; T Fat 19 g; 60% Calories from Fat; Chol 59 mg; Fiber <1 g; Sod 327 mg

Seafood

Turbot with Grapefruit Butter

1	*fresh turbot fillet*
	Juice of 1/2 (or less) lemon
	Salt and pepper to taste
1/4	*cup unsalted butter*
	Juice of 1/2 lemon
1	*teaspoon chopped shallot*
2	*tablespoons white wine*
2	*ounces fresh grapefruit juice*
10	*1/2-inch sprigs of dill*
6	*tablespoons unsalted butter*

▲ Sprinkle the fillet with the juice of 1/2 lemon, salt and pepper.

▲ Sauté in 1/4 cup butter in a saucepan until nearly done to taste.

▲ Remove to a warm plate. The fish will continue to cook in the hot juices.

▲ Combine the juice of 1/2 lemon, shallot, wine, grapefruit juice, salt and pepper in small saucepan.

▲ Cook over medium heat until reduced to 2 tablespoons. Remove from heat.

▲ Add dill and 6 tablespoons butter. Swirl pan until well mixed.

▲ Pour onto a warm plate, pushing the dill sprigs to the outer edge and the fish fillets to the center.

▲ Yield: 1 serving.

Approx Per Serving: Cal 1461; Prot 67 g; Carbo 10 g; T Fat 127 g; 78% Calories from Fat; Chol 508 mg; Fiber <1 g; Sod 628 mg

Tunaburgers

1   *(6-ounce) can water-pack light tuna*
2   *slices whole grain bread, crumbled*
1/2   *cup chopped celery*
1   *tablespoon onion flakes*
1/4   *cup low-fat cottage cheese*
1   *teaspoon chili powder*
1   *teaspoon lemon juice*
1/4   *teaspoon pepper*
1/2   *teaspoon salt*
1/4   *cup skim milk*

▲ Combine the tuna, bread crumbs, celery and onion flakes in a bowl.
Add the cottage cheese, chili powder, lemon juice, pepper, salt and
enough milk to moisten and blend; mix well.

▲ Shape into 2 patties; place in a 10-inch foil pie plate.

▲ Broil for 8 to 10 minutes or until golden brown on both sides.
Serve hot.

▲ Yield: 2 servings.

Approx Per Serving: Cal 210; Prot 15 g; Carbo 28 g; T Fat 5 g; 20% Calories
from Fat; Chol 20 mg; Fiber 3 g; Sod 1138 mg

Seafood

Open-Face Tuna Sandwiches

1   *(6-ounce) can water-pack tuna, drained*
¼   *cup chopped celery*
1   *hard-cooked egg, chopped*
2   *tablespoons mayonnaise*
6   *slices whole wheat bread*
1   *tablespoon butter, softened*
6   *slices low-fat sharp cheese*

▲ Preheat the broiler.

▲ Combine the tuna, celery, egg and mayonnaise in a bowl; mix well.

▲ Toast the bread on one side. Spread the untoasted side of the bread with the butter; spread with the tuna mixture. Add the cheese slices.

▲ Broil for 5 minutes or until light brown.

▲ Yield: 6 servings.

Approx Per Serving: Cal 252; Prot 20 g; Carbo 18 g; T Fat 12 g; 42% Calories from Fat; Chol 67 mg; Fiber 3 g; Sod 560 mg

Tuna Casserole

1	(10-ounce) can cream of celery soup
1/2	cup milk
1/2	cup almonds, toasted
1	cup shredded Cheddar cheese
5	ounces cooked noodles
1	(9-ounce) can tuna
1/2	cup mayonnaise
1	cup sliced celery
1/3	cup chopped onion
1/4	cup chopped green bell pepper
1/4	cup chopped pimento
1	teaspoon salt
1/2	cup crushed cornflakes

▲ Preheat the oven to 425 degrees.

▲ Combine the celery soup, milk, almonds and cheese in a saucepan. Heat over medium heat until the cheese is melted, stirring frequently. Remove from the heat.

▲ Add the noodles, tuna, mayonnaise, celery, onion, green pepper, pimento and salt and mix well. Spoon into a greased baking dish. Sprinkle the cornflakes over the top.

▲ Bake for 20 minutes.

▲ Yield: 6 servings.

Approx Per Serving: Cal 442; Prot 22 g; Carbo 22 g; T Fat 31 g; 62% Calories from Fat; Chol 60 mg; Fiber 3 g; Sod 1201 mg

Susie M. Dye, CHHA, St. Vincent Home Care
Indianapolis, Indiana

Seafood

Baked Broccoli and Tuna

1	*(16-ounce) package frozen chopped broccoli*
1	*(10-ounce) can cream of mushroom soup*
2/3	*cup skim milk*
1/3	*cup lemon juice*
2	*(7-ounce) cans water-pack tuna*
2	*tablespoons seasoned bread crumbs*

▲ Preheat the oven to 450 degrees.

▲ Cook the broccoli using package directions for half the time indicated or until tender-crisp; drain.

▲ Add the soup, milk, lemon juice and tuna; mix well.

▲ Spoon into a 2-quart baking dish. Sprinkle with the bread crumbs.

▲ Bake until bubbly and golden brown.

▲ Yield: 6 servings.

Approx Per Serving: Cal 207; Prot 27 g; Carbo 17 g; T Fat 5 g; 22% Calories from Fat; Chol 38 mg; Fiber 6 g; Sod 699 mg

Impossible Tuna Pie

1	(7-ounce) can tuna, drained
1/2	cup shredded Cheddar cheese
3	ounces cream cheese, chopped
1/4	cup sliced green onions
3/4	cup baking mix
1 1/2	cups skim milk
3	eggs
1/4	teaspoon salt

Seafood

▲ Preheat the oven to 400 degrees.

▲ Layer the tuna, Cheddar cheese, cream cheese and green onions in a greased 9-inch pie plate.

▲ Combine the baking mix, milk, eggs and salt in a bowl; mix well.

▲ Pour over the layers.

▲ Bake for 40 minutes or until brown.

▲ Let stand for 5 minutes before cutting.

▲ Yield: 6 servings.

Approx Per Serving: Cal 246; Prot 18 g; Carbo 13 g; T Fat 13 g; 49% Calories from Fat; Chol 143 mg; Fiber <1 g; Sod 545 mg

Seafood

Tuna Pasta Sauce

1   *clove of garlic, finely chopped*
2   *teaspoons vegetable oil*
1   *(6-ounce) can water-pack tuna*
1   *(6-ounce) can tomato sauce*
2   *tablespoons tomato paste*
1   *teaspoon chopped parsley*
1/2   *cup water*

▲ Sauté the garlic in the oil in a skillet until golden brown.

▲ Add the tuna and cook over medium heat for 5 minutes, stirring frequently.

▲ Add the tomato sauce, tomato paste, parsley and water.

▲ Cook for 20 minutes, stirring frequently.

▲ Serve over cooked pasta.

▲ Yield: 2 servings.

Approx Per Serving: Cal 180; Prot 24 g; Carbo 10 g; T Fat 6 g; 27% Calories from Fat; Chol 26 mg; Fiber 2 g; Sod 932 mg

Adriana Cantelli, Secretary, Cantelli Block and Brick
Sandusky, Ohio

Tuna Noodle Casserole

1   (8-ounce) package wide noodles, cooked
1   (9-ounce) can tuna
3/4 cup black olives
1   (10-ounce) can cream of mushroom soup
1   cup milk

▲ Preheat the oven to 300 degrees.

▲ Layer 1/2 of the noodles, all the tuna and olives and remaining 1/2 of the noodles in a buttered baking dish. Combine the soup and milk in a bowl and mix well. Pour over the layers.

▲ Bake, covered, for 20 minutes. Remove the cover. Bake for 10 minutes longer.

▲ Yield: 6 servings.

Approx Per Serving: Cal 143; Prot 19 g; Carbo 33 g; T Fat 8 g; 27% Calories from Fat; Chol 89 mg; Fiber <1 g; Sod 631 mg

Mary Lou Minton
Nashville, Tennessee

Healthy Quickie

1   (10-ounce) can cream of mushroom soup
1   (6-ounce) can tuna, drained
2   slices bread, toasted

▲ Heat the soup in a saucepan over medium heat until bubbly around the edge, stirring frequently.

▲ Add the tuna. Heat for 2 to 3 minutes or until of serving temperature, stirring to break up chunks of tuna. Spoon the mixture over the hot toast.

▲ Yield: 2 servings.

Approx Per Serving: Cal 341; Prot 30 g; Carbo 26 g; T Fat 13 g; 34% Calories from Fat; Chol 39 mg; Fiber 1 g; Sod 1609 mg

Dorothy J. Cissel, 1980 Top Ten Business Woman of ABWA, retired Supervisor
Dade County Public School System
Miami, Florida

Seafood

Crab Cakes

2	pounds fresh crab meat
1	cup each finely chopped onion and celery
1	cup finely chopped green and red bell pepper
1¹/₂	cups light mayonnaise
1	teaspoon dry mustard
	Cayenne, salt and pepper to taste
1	egg, lightly beaten
1¹/₃	cups cracker crumbs
2	tablespoons unsalted butter
	Remoulade Sauce

▲ Combine the crab meat, onion, celery, green and red pepper in a bowl; mix well.

▲ Mix the next 3 ingredients in a small bowl. Add to the crab meat mixture. Add the salt and pepper and mix well. Fold in the egg and ¹/₃ cup of the cracker crumbs. Shape into cakes, coating with the remaining 1 cup cracker crumbs. Place on a plate.

▲ Chill, wrapped securely, in the refrigerator for 30 minutes.

▲ Brown the crab cakes in the butter in a skillet, turning to brown both sides. Serve with the Remoulade Sauce.

Remoulade Sauce

1	cup mayonnaise
1	tablespoon lemon juice
2	tablespoons chopped sweet gherkin pickles
2	teaspoons Dijon mustard
1	teaspoon minced parsley
2	teaspoons chopped chives
³/₄	teaspoon anchovy paste
1	small red bell pepper, finely chopped
	Peel of 1 small lemon
2	tablespoons hot sauce
1	tablespoon each horseradish and capers

▲ Combine all the ingredients in a bowl and mix well. Chill, covered, in the refrigerator until serving time.

▲ Yield: 6 servings.

Approx Per Serving: Cal 974; Prot 36 g; Carbo 23 g; T Fat 84 g; 76% Calories from Fat; Chol 251 mg; Fiber 2 g; Sod 1355 mg

Diane Cullen, Community Volunteer, retired
Beaverton, Oregon

Basic Shrimp Creole

1/4   cup chopped green bell pepper
1/2   cup chopped onion
  2   ribs celery, chopped
  1   clove of garlic, chopped
  2   tablespoons butter
  1   (20-ounce) can tomatoes
  1   teaspoon (heaping) chili powder
1/2   teaspoon sugar
  1   bay leaf
1/4   teaspoon thyme
  1   pound peeled cooked shrimp

▲ Sauté the green pepper, onion, celery and garlic in the butter in a large skillet.

▲ Add the undrained tomatoes, chili powder, sugar, bay leaf and thyme.

▲ Simmer for 35 minutes, stirring occasionally.

▲ Add the shrimp.

▲ Cook for 10 minutes longer, stirring occasionally.

▲ Remove the bay leaf.

▲ Serve over rice.

▲ Yield: 4 servings.

Approx Per Serving: Cal 207; Prot 26 g; Carbo 10 g; T Fat 7 g; 32% Calories from Fat; Chol 237 mg; Fiber 3 g; Sod 562 mg

Carolyn B. Elman, Executive Director, American Business Women's Association
Kansas City, Missouri

Seafood

Shrimp and Chicken Kabobs

3/4   *cup jalapeño jelly*

2   *tablespoons fresh lemon juice*

1¹/₂   *chicken breast fillets*

1   *pineapple*

36   *peeled fresh jumbo shrimp with tails*

Salt and pepper to taste

▲ Soak 6 wooden skewers in water for 30 minutes and drain.

▲ Combine the jalapeño jelly and lemon juice in a small saucepan. Heat over medium heat until the jelly melts, stirring to mix well.

▲ Cut the chicken into ³/₄-inch pieces. Cut the pineapple into ³/₄-inch pieces.

▲ Thread the shrimp, chicken and pineapple onto the skewers.

▲ Place a few at a time in boiling salted water in a deep saucepan.

▲ Cook for 6 minutes; drain well.

▲ Brush with the jelly mixture; season with salt and pepper.

▲ Grill 5 to 6 inches above hot coals for 1 to 2 minutes or until golden brown, turning frequently.

▲ Yield: 6 servings.

Approx Per Serving: Cal 217; Prot 17 g; Carbo 36 g; T Fat 2 g; 7% Calories from Fat; Chol 106 mg; Fiber 1 g; Sod 130 mg

Egg & Pasta Dishes

Moonlighting to a New Business

After 5 p.m. weekdays, plus all weekend, Suzi Berman runs Design Ink., a desktop publishing business, from her bedroom. She designs brochures, logos and business cards, and plans advertising campaigns for small-business owners.

Design Ink. is important to Suzi—she might lose her day job as public information and media specialist for the Dallas County Health Department in a downsizing. Suzi's clients know her job situation and have bombarded her with work. Her biggest challenge: Keeping pace with her night job. Suzi's advice to wanna-be entrepreneurs: Research the business and possible obstacles and have a support system—morally and financially. She gets support from her husband, clients and American Business Women's Association members.

Egg Dishes

Anytime Super Quiche

¹/₂	*cup chopped onion*
1	*tablespoon margarine*
2	*tablespoons sherry*
2	*unbaked (9-inch) pie shells*
1	*tablespoon melted margarine*
2	*eggs, beaten*
2	*cartons egg substitute*
1	*envelope leek soup mix*
2	*ups buttermilk*
¹/₂	*cup shredded Monterey Jack cheese*
¹/₂	*cup bacon bits*

▲ Preheat the oven to 375 degrees.

▲ Sauté the onion in 1 tablespoon margarine in a skillet. Stir in the sherry.

▲ Brush the pie shells with 1 tablespoon melted margarine. Spoon the sautéed onion into the pie shells.

▲ Combine the eggs, egg substitute, soup mix, buttermilk and cheese in a bowl; mix well.

▲ Pour over the onion. Top with the bacon bits.

▲ Bake for 40 minutes or until set.

▲ Let stand for several minutes before serving.

▲ Yield: 12 servings.

Approx Per Serving: Cal 294; Prot 13 g; Carbo 21 g; T Fat 17 g; 53% Calories from Fat; Chol 42 mg; Fiber 1 g; Sod 636 mg.

Breakfast Tacos

2   *eggs*
1   *(10-ounce) package tortillas*
1   *cup chopped ham*
1   *cup sliced mushrooms*
¹/₂   *cup shredded cheese*

▲ Scramble the eggs as desired in a skillet. Spoon onto the tortillas. Sprinkle with the ham, mushrooms and cheese and roll to enclose the filling.

▲ Place the tacos in a microwave-safe dish. Microwave for 30 seconds or until the cheese is melted.

▲ Yield: 10 servings.

Approx Per Serving: Cal 153; Prot 9 g; Carbo 16 g; T Fat 6 g; 34% Calories from Fat; Chol 56 mg; Fiber 1 g; Sod 369 mg

Easy Eggs Benedict

1   *(10-ounce) can golden mushroom soup*
1   *soup can milk*
4   *small slices ham*
2   *English muffins, split, toasted*
4   *eggs, poached*

▲ Mix the soup and milk in a saucepan. Heat until bubbly.

▲ Place the ham on a microwave-safe dish. Microwave on Medium just until heated through.

▲ Place the toasted muffins on 4 serving plates. Top each with 1 slice of ham and 1 egg.

▲ Spoon the soup over the top. Garnish with paprika and parsley.

▲ Yield: 4 servings.

Approx Per Serving: Cal 296; Prot 17 g; Carbo 23 g; T Fat 15 g; 45% Calories from Fat; Chol 233 mg; Fiber 1 g; Sod 1127 mg

Fran Kudray, Real Estate Broker, Realty Executives
Phoenix, Arizona

Garden Eggs

¹/₂ cup chopped ham
1 clove of garlic, chopped
¹/₂ cup chopped onion
¹/₃ cup chopped green bell pepper
¹/₄ cup olive oil
¹/₄ cup small green peas
4 eggs
¹/₂ cup grated Parmesan cheese
2 teaspoons cracker meal

▲ Preheat the oven to 350 degrees.

▲ Sauté the ham, garlic, onion and green pepper in the olive oil in a saucepan until the onion is translucent.

▲ Remove from the heat and stir in the peas.

▲ Spread half the ham mixture in a 1¹/₂-quart baking dish.

▲ Break the eggs gently onto the top. Spread the remaining ham mixture over the eggs.

▲ Sprinkle with the cheese and cracker meal.

▲ Bake for 15 minutes or until the eggs are done to taste.

▲ Garnish with pimento strips.

▲ Serve over wild rice with a Spanish avocado salad.

▲ Yield: 2 servings.

Approx Per Serving: Cal 601; Prot 34 g; Carbo 12 g; T Fat 47 g; 70% Calories from Fat; Chol 463 mg; Fiber 2 g; Sod 1058 mg

Carmen Castillo, Public Relations Coordinator
Greater Greenspoint Management District
Houston, Texas

Cheesy Bacon and Egg Pie

1   recipe (2-crust) pie pastry
8   ounces Cheddar cheese, cut into cubes
6   slices crisp-fried bacon, crumbled
4   hard-cooked eggs, sliced
1   tablespoon milk

▲ Preheat the oven to 400 degrees.

▲ Line an 8-inch pie plate with 1 pastry.

▲ Layer the cheese, bacon and eggs in the prepared plate.

▲ Top with the remaining pastry. Trim the edges and cut vents. Brush with the milk.

▲ Bake for 30 to 35 minutes or until the crust is golden brown.

▲ Cool slightly before serving.

▲ May substitute Colby cheese for Cheddar, cubed canned ham for bacon and use whole hard-cooked eggs.

▲ Yield: 6 servings.

Approx Per Serving: Cal 521; Prot 19 g; Carbo 26 g; T Fat 38 g; 65% Calories from Fat; Chol 187 mg; Fiber 1 g; Sod 666 mg

Marilyn S. Stallard
Tuscon, Arizona

Egg Dishes

Creamed Eggs on Toast

1/4 cup butter
3   to 4 tablespoons flour
2   cups milk
6   hard-cooked eggs, sliced
6   slices bread, toasted

▲ Melt the butter in a skillet. Stir in the flour. Cook over medium heat for several minutes, stirring constantly. Add the milk gradually. Cook until the sauce is thickened, stirring constantly with a wire whisk. Fold in the egg slices.

▲ Serve over toasted bread.

▲ Yield: 6 servings.

Approx Per Serving: Cal 290; Prot 12 g; Carbo 23 g; T Fat 17 g; 52% Calories from Fat; Chol 245 mg; Fiber 1 g; Sod 323 mg

Pam Sultzman, Senior Inventory Control Analyst
Greenpoint Mortgage
Charlotte, North Carolina

Chiles Rellenos Casserole

2   (7-ounce) cans chopped green chiles
1 1/2 pounds Monterey Jack cheese, shredded
4   eggs, beaten
1/2   cup milk
1   teaspoon salt
1/4   teaspoon pepper

▲ Preheat the oven to 350 degrees.

▲ Layer the green chiles and cheese 1/2 at a time in a greased 8x12-inch baking dish.

▲ Combine the eggs, milk, salt and pepper in a small bowl and mix well. Pour over the layers.

▲ Bake for 30 minutes or until light brown and set.

▲ Cool for 5 minutes before cutting into squares.

▲ Yield: 8 servings.

Approx Per Serving: Cal 376; Prot 25 g; Carbo 5 g; T Fat 29 g; 69% Calories from Fat; Chol 184 mg; Fiber 1 g; Sod 1342 mg

Judith Martin, Office Manager, St. Anthony's Family Medicare
St. Petersburg, Florida

Deli Veggie Sandwiches

Meatless Dish

1	cup mayonnaise-type salad dressing
1/2	cup vinegar
1/4	cup sugar
1/2	teaspoon celery seeds
1	small head cabbage, shredded
4	carrots, shredded
16	slices dark pumpernickel rye bread
4	green bell peppers, cut into 1/4-inch strips
4	tomatoes, sliced
8	slices provolone cheese

▲ Combine the salad dressing, vinegar, sugar and celery seeds in a large bowl and mix until smooth.

▲ Add the cabbage and carrots, tossing to coat.

▲ Chill the coleslaw, covered, in the refrigerator until just before serving time.

▲ Layer 1 slice bread, 4 green pepper strips, 3 tomato slices, 1 slice cheese, 2 tablespoons coleslaw and 1 slice bread on a glass plate.

▲ Repeat the process until all the ingredients are used.

▲ Microwave on High for 1 minute.

▲ Serve with tortilla chips and sliced fruit.

▲ Yield: 8 servings.

Approx Per Serving: Cal 460; Prot 16 g; Carbo 59 g; T Fat 20 g; 38% Calories from Fat; Chol 27 mg; Fiber 8 g; Sod 921 mg

Sue Harper, Regional Manager, Electronic Data Systems
Plano, Texas

Pasta Dishes

Pasta con Broccoli

12	ounces pasta shells
1	bunch fresh broccoli, chopped
1	cup half-and-half
1/4	cup butter, softened
1	(8-ounce) can tomato sauce
2	tablespoons fresh crushed garlic
1	teaspoon salt
1/2	teaspoon pepper
2	cups chopped fresh mushrooms
2	cups grated Parmesan cheese

▲ Cook the pasta using the package directions; drain.

▲ Cook the broccoli in a small amount of water in a saucepan for 5 minutes or just until tender-crisp; drain.

▲ Combine the half-and-half, butter, tomato sauce, garlic, salt and pepper in a saucepan. Bring to a boil, stirring occasionally.

▲ Reduce the heat and add the mushrooms.

▲ Simmer for 3 minutes, stirring occasionally.

▲ Remove from the heat and stir in the cheese.

▲ Combine the pasta, broccoli and sauce in a serving dish.

▲ Yield: 6 servings.

Approx Per Serving: Cal 520; Prot 25 g; Carbo 53 g; T Fat 24 g; 40% Calories from Fat; Chol 62 mg; Fiber 4 g; Sod 1320 mg

Melanie Mayberry, Brokerage Services Coordinator
Community Services, Inc.
West Des Moines, Iowa

Pasta Frittata

1/2   cup chopped onion
3/4   cup chopped green bell pepper
3/4   cup chopped red bell pepper
2   tablespoons margarine
3   cups cooked spaghetti
1 1/2   cups shredded mozzarella cheese
5   eggs
1/3   cup milk
1/4   cup grated Parmesan cheese
1   tablespoon basil
1   teaspoon oregano
1   teaspoon salt
1/2   teaspoon pepper

▲ Preheat the oven to 400 degrees.

▲ Sauté the onion, green pepper and red pepper in the margarine in a 10-inch ovenproof skillet over medium heat for 5 minutes.

▲ Add the spaghetti and toss to mix.

▲ Reduce the heat and add the mozzarella cheese.

▲ Beat the eggs, milk, Parmesan cheese, basil, oregano, salt and pepper in a bowl. Add to the spaghetti and cook until almost set.

▲ Bake for 8 minutes or until the eggs are set.

▲ Yield: 4 servings.

Approx Per Serving: Cal 473; Prot 25 g; Carbo 38 g; T Fat 25 g; 47% Calories from Fat; Chol 306 mg; Fiber 3 g; Sod 964 mg

Marilyn Dial, Administration Manager
Fort Walton Machining, Inc.
Fort Walton Beach, Florida

Pasta Dishes

Italian Veggie Pasta

2	*(5-ounce) zucchini, cut into ¹/₄-inch strips*
1	*(12-ounce) eggplant, cut into cubes*
1	*medium green, red or yellow bell pepper, cut into slices*
¹/₂	*cup thinly sliced onion*
2	*tablespoons plus 2 teaspoons margarine*
12	*cherry tomatoes, cut into halves*
8	*pimento-stuffed olives, cut into halves*
1	*teaspoon salt*
¹/₂	*teaspoon oregano*
¹/₈	*teaspoon garlic powder*
¹/₈	*teaspoon pepper*

▲ Sauté the zucchini, eggplant, bell pepper and onion in the margarine in a large skillet for 2 to 3 minutes or until the vegetables are softened.

▲ Add the tomatoes, olives, salt, oregano, garlic powder and pepper; mix well.

▲ Reduce the heat to medium. Cook, covered, until the vegetables are tender-crisp, stirring occasionally.

▲ Serve as a side dish or over pasta with grated Parmesan cheese.

▲ For a variation, add 10 sliced mushrooms to the vegetables.

▲ Yield: 6 servings.

Approx Per Serving: Cal 86; Prot 2 g; Carbo 8 g; T Fat 6 g; 57% Calories from Fat; Chol 0 mg; Fiber 3 g; Sod 532 mg

Sharen Hausmann, Associate Director, University of Georgia
Lawrenceville, Georgia

Lemon Pasta

1 (16-ounce) package linguini
2 cloves of garlic, chopped
1/4 cup olive oil
2 large tomatoes, chopped
1/3 cup fresh lemon juice
2 tablespoons dill
1 teaspoon oregano
4 ounces feta cheese, crumbled

▲ Cook the linguini using the package directions and drain.

▲ Sauté the garlic in the olive oil in a medium skillet for 2 to 3 minutes.

▲ Add the tomatoes. Simmer for 1 minute, stirring occasionally.

▲ Add the lemon juice. Simmer for 2 minutes, stirring occasionally.

▲ Stir in the dill and oregano.

▲ Spoon the linguini into a large serving bowl. Pour the lemon sauce over the pasta and toss well to mix. Sprinkle feta cheese on top of each serving.

▲ May substitute one 16-ounce can chopped tomatoes for the fresh tomatoes.

▲ Yield: 4 servings.

Approx Per Serving: Cal 644; Prot 20 g; Carbo 93 g; T Fat 22 g; 30% Calories from Fat; Chol 25 mg; Fiber 4 g; Sod 335 mg

Jeannie Teasley, Therapist
Raleigh, North Carolina

Pasta Dishes

Baked Macaroni and Cheese

1 (8-ounce) package small macaroni shells
1 (16-ounce) can tomatoes, chopped
8 ounces Velveeta cheese, cut into cubes
2 tablespoons plus 2 teaspoons margarine, sliced

▲ Preheat the oven to 350 degrees.

▲ Cook the macaroni using the package directions and drain.

▲ Place in a 2-quart baking dish. Add the tomatoes and cheese, tossing to mix. Top with margarine slices.

▲ Bake for 30 minutes or until the top is crunchy and the cheese is melted.

▲ Yield: 4 servings.

Approx Per Serving: Cal 512; Prot 21 g; Carbo 48 g; T Fat 27 g; 46% Calories from Fat; Chol 52 mg; Fiber 3 g; Sod 1077 mg

Bobbi Economy, 1995 ABWA District Vice President
Executive Secretary, Florida Power and Light Company
Jupiter, Florida

Microwave Macaroni and Ham Dish

1/4 cup margarine, sliced
6 ounces grated Parmesan cheese
1 (1*1/2*-pound) ham, slivered
2 cups shredded Swiss cheese
5 cups cooked macaroni
3 cups shredded mozzarella cheese
   Pepper to taste

▲ Place the margarine slices in a 2-quart glass baking dish. Layer the Parmesan cheese, ham, Swiss cheese, macaroni, mozzarella cheese and pepper 1/3 at a time in the prepared baking dish. Cover with plastic wrap.

▲ Microwave on High for 20 minutes.

▲ Yield: 10 servings.

Approx Per Serving: Cal 499; Prot 40 g; Carbo 22 g; T Fat 27 g; 49% Calories from Fat; Chol 97 mg; Fiber 1 g; Sod 1454 mg

Macaroni Relleno

Pasta Dishes

1	*(7-ounce) package elbow macaroni*
1	*egg, beaten*
1/2	*cup skim milk*
1/4	*teaspoon cumin*
1	*(4-ounce) can chopped green chiles, drained*
1	*(4-ounce) can chopped pimentos*
1	*(15-ounce) can pinto beans, heated, drained*
1	*cup shredded Monterey Jack cheese*
1	*medium tomato, chopped*
1	*medium green bell pepper, chopped*
1/4	*cup sliced green onions*

▲ Cook the macaroni using the package directions and drain.

▲ Combine the egg, milk and cumin in a large bowl and mix well. Add the hot cooked macaroni, chiles and pimentos and mix well.

▲ Heat a nonstick 9-inch skillet sprayed with nonstick cooking spray.

▲ Add the macaroni mixture.

▲ Cook, covered, over low heat for 15 minutes or until the mixture is set.

▲ Loosen the edge with a spatula and invert onto a warm serving platter.

▲ Spread the hot beans over the top and sprinkle with the tomato, green pepper and green onions.

▲ Let stand for 2 minutes before cutting.

▲ Yield: 8 servings.

Approx Per Serving: Cal 214; Prot 11 g; Carbo 30 g; T Fat 6 g; 23% Calories from Fat; Chol 39 mg; Fiber 2 g; Sod 484 mg

Sara Root, Accounting Utility Clerk
North Star Steel Texas
Beaumont, Texas

Pasta Dishes

Tomato Garlic Pasta

1	(12-ounce) package rotelle pasta
3	cloves of garlic, pressed
1	teaspoon olive oil
1/4	teaspoon crushed red pepper
1	(15-ounce) can chopped tomatoes
	Salt and pepper to taste

▲ Cook the pasta using the package directions and drain.

▲ Sauté the garlic in the olive oil in a skillet over medium heat. Add the red pepper, tomatoes, salt and pepper. Simmer for 5 to 10 minutes.

▲ Place the pasta in a serving bowl. Pour the tomato sauce over the pasta.

▲ Garnish with fresh Parmesan cheese.

▲ Yield: 4 servings.

Approx Per Serving: Cal 350; Prot 12 g; Carbo 69 g; T Fat 3 g; 7% Calories from Fat; Chol 0 mg; Fiber 4 g; Sod 180 mg

Sue Lane, Independent Sales Director, The Pampered Chef
Alpine, California

Garlic Oil for Pasta

1/4	cup butter
1/4	cup olive oil
4	cloves of garlic, chopped
1	teaspoon salt
	Pepper to taste

▲ Melt the butter with the olive oil in a skillet. Add the garlic, salt and pepper.

▲ Cook over medium heat until the garlic turns medium brown. Toss with cooked pasta. Serve with grated Parmesan cheese.

▲ Yield: 2 servings.

Approx Per Serving: Cal 451; Prot 1 g; Carbo 2 g; T Fat 50 g; 98% Calories from Fat; Chol 62 mg; Fiber <1 g; Sod 1301 mg

Adriana Cantelli, Secretary, Cantelli Brick and Block
Sandusky, Ohio

The Working Woman's Quick Cookbook

Vegetables & Side Dishes

Surviving the Job Jungle

Diane Walter's storybook career was about to reach its zenith. She had risen to upper management at her hospital, was named a 1994 Top Ten Business Woman of ABWA and finished her master's degree in organizational management.

Then she stepped into a career trap. In August 1994, her hospital reorganized its nurse-management staff and Diane's job disappeared. That's why lifelong learning and support networks like the American Business Women's Association are survival tools for today's working women.

Savvy employees replace job security with "employability security." You may get a paycheck from a company, but you're actually working for yourself. Lifetime employability means you seek growth, make an ongoing effort to improve your skills and can adapt and synthesize your skills into other positions and industries. "No one is responsible for your career but you," says Diane, who now works as a nurse manager at University Medical Center in Tucson, Arizona.

Vegetables

Navigating Your Career Path

When the gas company where Evelyn Sorenson had worked for 12 years was sold, she turned the chaotic situation into an opportunity to chase her career dream. Rather than wait for her turn in the "I'm-sorry-but-we're-eliminating-your-position" line, Evelyn solicited a severance package and started her job search. "It wasn't hard—but it wasn't easy either," she says. "It wasn't hard because I prepared for it. The day I left was a loss because 12 years of my career path were turning another angle. But I was in control of my career and made the decision to leave."

She took her 12 years of experience as a supervisor of customer advisors and benefit analyst and transferred it to a new career in health care. Now an executive assistant at Blue Cross Blue Shield in Kansas City, Missouri, Evelyn is one of three team members who assists the CEO in developing a new subsidiary to match health care's changing needs.

Evelyn navigated her new career path through careful goal setting and planning. "My goals give me a guide or map to where I'm heading," she says. "There's something magical about writing goals down. Once you write it, it happens."

Vegetables

Broccoli Casserole

1	(10-ounce) package frozen broccoli pieces
1	(10-ounce) can cream of mushroom soup
1/4	cup mayonnaise
2	tablespoons lemon juice
1	cup crushed butter crackers
1	cup shredded Cheddar cheese

▲ Preheat the oven to 350 degrees.

▲ Cook the broccoli using the package directions; drain.

▲ Mix the soup, mayonnaise and lemon juice in a medium bowl. Add the broccoli and mix well. Spoon into a 9x13-inch baking dish.

▲ Mix the cracker crumbs and cheese in a bowl. Sprinkle over the broccoli mixture.

▲ Bake for 25 minutes or until the cheese is melted.

▲ Yield: 4 servings.

Approx Per Serving: Cal 403; Prot 12 g; Carbo 22 g; T Fat 31 g; 67% Calories
   from Fat; Chol 39 mg; Fiber 3 g; Sod 1041 mg

Marianne Cobarrubias, Corporate Communications Assistant
The Timberland Company
West Newbury, Massachusetts

Stir-Fry Cabbage

3	slices bacon, chopped
3	eggs
1/2	head cabbage, shredded
	Minced garlic to taste
	Salt and pepper to taste

▲ Fry the bacon in a skillet until browned. Add the eggs and mix well. Stir in the cabbage.

▲ Season with the garlic, salt and pepper.

▲ Yield: 6 servings.

Approx Per Serving: Cal 74; Prot 5 g; Carbo 4 g; T Fat 4 g; 50% Calories
   from Fat; Chol 109 mg; Fiber 1 g; Sod 96 mg

Marianne Cobarrubias, Corporate Communications Assistant
The Timberland Company
West Newbury, Massachusetts

Vegetables

Baked Corn Casserole

¹/₂	cup melted margarine
2	eggs, beaten
1	(8-ounce) package corn muffin mix
1	(15-ounce) can whole kernel corn, drained
1	(15-ounce) can cream-style corn
1	cup sour cream

▲ Preheat the oven to 350 degrees.

▲ Combine the margarine, eggs, muffin mix, corn and sour cream in a bowl; mix well.

▲ Pour into a greased 9x13-inch casserole.

▲ Bake for 45 to 60 minutes or until bubbly and heated through.

▲ Yield: 15 servings.

Approx Per Serving: Cal 197; Prot 3 g; Carbo 22 g; T Fat 11 g; 50% Calories from Fat; Chol 35 mg; Fiber 1 g; Sod 358 mg

Susan Stout, Teacher, Metropolitan School District Decatur Township
Indianapolis, Indiana

Cheese-Scalloped Onions

      3   large onions, cut into 1/2-inch slices
          Salt to taste
      4   slices toast
      1   tablespoon margarine, softened
      8   ounces sharp Cheddar cheese, cut into cubes
    1/4   cup margarine
    1/4   cup flour
      2   cups milk
    1/2   teaspoon salt
    1/4   teaspoon pepper
      2   eggs

▲ Combine the onions, salt to taste and water to cover in a saucepan.
Cook for 10 to 15 minutes or until the onions are tender.

▲ Spread the toast with 1 tablespoon margarine. Cut the toast into 1/2-inch cubes.

▲ Drain the onions. Layer half the onions, half the cheese, half the toast,
remaining onions and remaining cheese in an 8x8-inch casserole.

▲ Melt 1/4 cup margarine in a saucepan. Blend in the flour.

▲ Stir in the milk gradually. Cook until thickened, stirring constantly.
Add 1/2 teaspoon salt and pepper.

▲ Beat the eggs in a bowl.

▲ Stir a small amount of the hot mixture into the eggs; stir the eggs into
the hot mixture. Pour over the layers.

▲ Top with the remaining toast.

▲ Preheat the oven to 350 degrees.

▲ Bake for 30 minutes.

▲ Yield: 8 servings.

Approx Per Serving: Cal 307; Prot 13 g; Carbo 18 g; T Fat 20 g; 59% Calories
from Fat; Chol 92 mg; Fiber 1 g; Sod 511 mg

Jane Wilkin, Human Resources Consultant
Munith, Michigan

Vegetables

Baked Potatoes and Toppings

$^{1}/_{2}$ cup butter or margarine, softened
$^{1}/_{4}$ to $^{1}/_{2}$ cup crumbled crisp-fried bacon
1   teaspoon Dijon mustard
$^{1}/_{2}$ teaspoon horseradish or horsey sauce
1   teaspoon parsley
2   potatoes, baked

▲ Mix the butter, bacon, Dijon mustard, horseradish and parsley in a bowl.

▲ Slice open the potatoes. Top with the bacon mixture.

▲ For additional toppings, combine any of the following mixtures with $^{1}/_{2}$ cup softened butter or margarine:

　▲ 2 tablespoons finely chopped pepperoni or salami and 1$^{1}/_{2}$ teaspoons Italian herbs

　▲ $^{1}/_{2}$ to $^{3}/_{4}$ cup shredded Cheddar cheese, $^{1}/_{2}$ teaspoon dillweed and 1 tablespoon chopped green onions

　▲ $^{1}/_{4}$ cup shredded Swiss cheese, 1 teaspoon fresh or dried chives and $^{1}/_{2}$ teaspoon Dijon or prepared mustard

　▲ $^{1}/_{4}$ cup crumbled bleu cheese, 1 teaspoon chopped green onions and $^{1}/_{4}$ teaspoon horseradish or horsey sauce.

▲ Yield: 2 servings.

Approx Per Serving: Cal 565; Prot 6 g; Carbo 31 g; T Fat 48 g; 74% Calories from Fat; Chol 130 mg; Fiber 3 g; Sod 728 mg

Janet M. Priewe, Legal Secretary, Curran Law Office
La Valle, Wisconsin

Quick Scalloped Potatoes

 2   large potatoes, peeled, cut into quarters
 1   onion, chopped
 1   rib celery, chopped
 2   tablespoons melted butter or margarine
 2   tablespoons flour
 1/2   teaspoon salt
 1   cup milk
 1/2   cup shredded Cheddar cheese
 1   ounce Cheddar cheese, thinly sliced
     Paprika to taste

▲ Cut the potatoes into 1/4-inch slices.

▲ Combine the potatoes, onion and celery with water to cover in a large saucepan. Boil for 10 minutes or until tender.

▲ Combine the butter, flour and salt in a medium saucepan. Cook for 2 minutes, stirring constantly.

▲ Add the milk. Cook until thickened, stirring constantly.

▲ Stir in the shredded cheese.

▲ Drain the potato mixture and pour the sauce into the potato mixture.

▲ Cook until thickened, stirring gently. Pour into a baking dish. Cover with the sliced cheese. Sprinkle with paprika.

▲ Preheat the broiler.

▲ Broil just until the cheese melts over the potatoes.

▲ May add chopped ham or bacon to the sauce.

▲ Yield: 4 servings.

Approx Per Serving: Cal 285; Prot 10 g; Carbo 29 g; T Fat 15 g; 47% Calories from Fat; Chol 46 mg; Fiber 2 g; Sod 501 mg

Yvonne Long, Controller, Able Home Health Service Inc.
Lewiston, Idaho

Potato Casserole Supreme

8   large potatoes, cooked, mashed
8   ounces cream cheese, softened
1   cup sour cream
    Minced chives to taste
    Garlic salt, salt and pepper to taste
1   tablespoon butter
    Paprika to taste

▲ Preheat the oven to 350 degrees.

▲ Combine the potatoes, cream cheese and sour cream in a mixer bowl. Beat until fluffy. Stir in the chives. Season with the garlic salt, salt and pepper.

▲ Spoon into a 2-quart casserole.

▲ Dot with the butter; sprinkle with paprika.

▲ Bake until the casserole is heated through and the top is browned.

▲ Freezes well.

▲ Yield: 8 servings.

Approx Per Serving: Cal 344; Prot 7 g; Carbo 42 g; T Fat 18 g; 45% Calories from Fat; Chol 48 mg; Fiber 3 g; Sod 123 mg

Janae Herman, Radiologic Technologist/Office Manager
Ahrlin, Orthopedic, LTD
Rapid City, South Dakota

Hash Brown Potato Bake

2	pounds frozen hash brown potatoes, thawed
1	cup sour cream
1	(10-ounce) can cream of chicken soup
1/4	cup butter, softened
10	ounces Cheddar cheese, shredded
1/4	cup melted butter
2	cups cornflakes

▲ Preheat the oven to 350 degrees.

▲ Mix the potatoes, sour cream, soup, 1/4 cup butter and cheese in a bowl. Spoon into a 9x13-inch baking dish. Mix the melted butter and cornflakes in a bowl. Spread over the potato mixture.

▲ Bake for 1 hour.

▲ Yield: 8 servings.

Approx Per Serving: Cal 458; Prot 14 g; Carbo 30 g; T Fat 32 g; 62% Calories from Fat; Chol 84 mg; Fiber <1 g; Sod 741 mg

Bernice M. Piwowarczyk, Senior Secretary
Commerce Bank
St. Louis, Missouri

Spinach Casserole

2	(10-ounce) packages frozen chopped spinach, thawed, drained
1	(10-ounce) can cream of potato soup
1/4	cup grated Parmesan cheese
1	cup sour cream
1/2	cup shredded Monterey Jack cheese

▲ Preheat the oven to 350 degrees.

▲ Squeeze the spinach dry. Mix the spinach, potato soup, Parmesan cheese and sour cream in a bowl. Spoon into a 9x13-inch baking dish. Top with the Monterey Jack cheese.

▲ Bake for 20 minutes.

▲ Yield: 4 servings.

Approx Per Serving: Cal 283; Prot 13 g; Carbo 15 g; T Fat 20 g; 61% Calories from Fat; Chol 47 mg; Fiber 3 g; Sod 934 mg

Marianne Cobarrubias, Corporate Communications Assistant
The Timberland Company
West Newbury, Massachusetts

Vegetables

Easy Cheesy Squash Casserole

3	pounds yellow squash, cut into $^1/_2$-inch slices
1	cup chopped onion
8	ounces Cheddar cheese, shredded
$^1/_2$	cup Italian bread crumbs
$^3/_4$	cup milk
2	eggs, beaten
$^1/_2$	teaspoon salt, or to taste
$^1/_4$	teaspoon pepper

▲ Preheat the oven to 350 degrees.

▲ Boil the squash and onion in water to cover in a saucepan just until tender.

▲ Drain in a colander; mash with a fork while in the colander.

▲ Combine the squash mixture, cheese, bread crumbs, milk and eggs in a bowl and mix well. Season with the salt and pepper.

▲ Spoon into a 9x13-inch glass baking dish sprayed with nonstick cooking spray.

▲ Bake for 30 minutes.

▲ Yield: 10 servings.

Approx Per Serving: Cal 169; Prot 10 g; Carbo 12 g; T Fat 10 g; 49% Calories from Fat; Chol 69 mg; Fiber 2 g; Sod 404 mg

Sara Connor, 1995 American Business Woman of ABWA
Assistant to the Vice President, Armstrong State College
Thunderbolt, Georgia

Squash or Zucchini on-the-Run

    3   medium yellow squash or zucchini
         Red pepper or Cajun seasoning to taste
         Chopped green onion tops to taste
    3   tablespoons grated Parmesan cheese

▲ Cut the squash or zucchini lengthwise into slices. Sprinkle the cut sides with seasoning; place in a microwave-safe dish.

▲ Sprinkle with the green onion tops and Parmesan cheese.

▲ Microwave on High for 3 to 5 minutes or until tender-crisp.

▲ Yield: 6 servings.

Approx Per Serving: Cal 40; Prot 3 g; Carbo 6 g; T Fat 1 g; 24% Calories from Fat; Chol 2 mg; Fiber 2 g; Sod 61 mg

Vegetable Casserole

    2   medium yellow squash, sliced
    1   large onion, sliced
    2   cups thinly sliced potatoes
    1   (10-ounce) can cream of chicken soup
    1/2 soup can water

▲ Preheat the oven to 350 degrees.

▲ Layer the squash, onion and potatoes in a 9x9-inch baking dish.

▲ Mix the soup with the water; pour over the layers.

▲ Bake for 45 minutes.

▲ May sprinkle shredded cheese over the hot casserole.

▲ Yield: 6 servings.

Approx Per Serving: Cal 112; Prot 4 g; Carbo 18 g; T Fat 3 g; 25% Calories from Fat; Chol 4 mg; Fiber 2 g; Sod 404 mg

Carolyn L. Beane, retired Social Worker
Randolph County Department of Social Services
Asheboro, North Carolina

Vegetables

Sweet Potato Casserole

5	pounds sweet potatoes, peeled, cooked
1	egg yolk
1	cup applesauce
1	teaspoon cinnamon
1	teaspoon vanilla extract
2	egg whites
1/2	cup packed brown sugar
1	teaspoon butter
1	teaspoon flour

▲ Preheat the oven to 350 degrees.

▲ Cut the sweet potatoes into cubes.

▲ Combine the sweet potatoes, egg yolk, applesauce, cinnamon and vanilla in a food processor container. Process until mixed.

▲ Beat the egg whites in a mixer bowl until stiff peaks form. Fold into the sweet potato mixture. Spoon into a greased casserole.

▲ Mix the brown sugar, butter and flour in a bowl. Sprinkle over the sweet potato mixture.

▲ Bake for 35 minutes.

▲ Yield: 15 servings.

Approx Per Serving: Cal 204; Prot 3 g; Carbo 46 g; T Fat 1 g; 5% Calories from Fat; Chol 15 mg; Fiber 5 g; Sod 33 mg

Barbara Conklin, 1993 ABWA District Vice President
Supervisor, Time Warner
Clearwater, Florida

Sweet Potatoes au Gratin

- 3 cups mashed cooked sweet potatoes
- 1 cup sugar
- 1/4 cup milk
- 2 eggs
- 1 teaspoon vanilla extract
- 1/2 cup margarine or butter
- 1 cup flaked coconut
- 1/2 cup melted margarine or butter
- 1 cup packed brown sugar
- 1 cup chopped pecans
- 1/2 cup flour

▲ Preheat the oven to 350 degrees.

▲ Combine the sweet potatoes, sugar, milk, eggs, vanilla, 1/2 cup margarine and coconut in a bowl and mix well. Spoon into a 10x10-inch casserole.

▲ Mix 1/2 cup margarine, brown sugar, pecans and flour in a bowl. Sprinkle over the sweet potato mixture.

▲ Bake for 20 minutes.

▲ Yield: 12 servings.

Approx Per Serving: Cal 439; Prot 4 g; Carbo 52 g; T Fat 25 g; 50% Calories from Fat; Chol 36 mg; Fiber 3 g; Sod 206 mg

Sara Ratliff Davis, 1990 Top Ten Business Woman of ABWA
Human Services Surveyor Specialist, State of Florida
Orlando, Florida

Vegetables

Scalloped Tomatoes

1/4   cup chopped onion
1   tablespoon butter
3   slices bacon, crisp-fried, crumbled
2   cups toasted bread crumbs
2   (14-ounce) cans stewed tomatoes
1   tablespoon chopped basil
2   tablespoons brown sugar
      Pepper to taste

▲ Preheat the oven to 350 degrees.

▲ Sauté the onion in the butter in a skillet.

▲ Mix the onion, bacon and bread crumbs in a small bowl.

▲ Mix the tomatoes, basil, brown sugar and pepper in a medium bowl.

▲ Alternate layers of the tomato mixture and the bacon mixture in a greased 1-quart casserole, ending with the bacon mixture.

▲ Bake for 20 minutes.

▲ Yield: 6 servings.

Approx Per Serving: Cal 215; Prot 6 g; Carbo 36 g; T Fat 5 g; 22% Calories from Fat; Chol 8 mg; Fiber 4 g; Sod 695 mg

Betty Cole, Realtor, Edina Realty
Minneapolis, Minnesota

Zucchini Casserole

Vegetables

1	*large zucchini, chopped, cooked*
1	*cup sour cream*
1	*(10-ounce) can cream of chicken soup*
1	*cup carrots*
1	*small onion, chopped*
1	*(6-ounce) package stuffing mix*
2	*to 3 tablespoons butter*

▲ Preheat the oven to 350 degrees.

▲ Mix the zucchini, sour cream, soup, carrots and onion in a 9x13-inch casserole.

▲ Stir in the contents of the stuffing mix seasoning packet and half the stuffing mix crumbs.

▲ Mix the remaining stuffing mix crumbs with the butter in a bowl. Spread over the zucchini mixture.

▲ Bake for 30 minutes.

▲ May add other vegetables.

▲ Yield: 8 servings.

Approx Per Serving: Cal 227; Prot 5 g; Carbo 23 g; T Fat 13 g; 52% Calories
from Fat; Chol 28 mg; Fiber 1 g; Sod 702 mg

Judy Howe, Secretary, UAW Local 651
Flint, Michigan

Vegetables

Fresh Zucchini Bake

4	zucchini, chopped
1	large tomato, chopped
1	(7-ounce) can sliced mushrooms, drained
1	small onion, chopped
3	cloves of garlic, minced
2	tablespoons grated Parmesan cheese
1/2	teaspoon salt
1/2	teaspoon pepper
1/4	cup shredded mixed Italian cheeses

▲ Combine the zucchini, tomato, mushrooms, onion, garlic, Parmesan cheese, salt and pepper in a 2-quart microwave-safe casserole; mix gently.

▲ Top with the mixed cheeses.

▲ Microwave, covered, on High for 15 minutes.

▲ Let stand for 5 minutes.

▲ Yield: 4 servings.

Approx Per Serving: Cal 107; Prot 8 g; Carbo 15 g; T Fat 3 g; 26% Calories from Fat; Chol 9 mg; Fiber 5 g; Sod 565 mg

Debi DeBenedetto, General Manager
Best Western Naples Inn & Suites
Naples, Florida

Zucchini Patties

4	*eggs*
1	*medium onion, minced*
2	*cups crushed crackers*
1	*cup shredded Cheddar cheese*
4	*cups grated fresh zucchini*
1	*envelope onion-mushroom soup mix*
¹/₂	*cup chopped pecans*
	Vegetable oil for frying
1	*(10-ounce) can cream of mushroom soup*
1	*cup milk*

▲ Preheat the oven to 350 degrees.

▲ Mix the eggs, onion, cracker crumbs, cheese, zucchini, soup mix and pecans in a bowl. Shape into patties.

▲ Cook the patties in the oil in a skillet until browned. Place in a 9x13-inch casserole.

▲ Mix the soup and milk in a bowl. Pour over the patties.

▲ Bake for 30 minutes.

▲ Patties may be prepared 1 day ahead and stored in the refrigerator until baking time; prepare the soup mixture at baking time.

▲ Yield: 8 servings.

Approx Per Serving: Cal 303; Prot 14 g; Carbo 26 g; T Fat 17 g; 49% Calories from Fat; Chol 127 mg; Fiber 3 g; Sod 786 mg
Nutritional profile does not include vegetable oil for frying.

Criss Kramer, Owner, HMK Insurance
Bellingham, Washington

Vegetables

Zucchini Boats

3   medium zucchini
1   tablespoon butter
1   tablespoon dried parsley
1   tablespoon olive oil
1   tablespoon dried minced onion
1   clove of garlic, minced
1   large tomato, chopped
$^1/_2$ cup fine dry bread crumbs
2   tablespoons grated Parmesan cheese
     Salt, pepper and cayenne to taste
$^1/_2$ cup shredded mozzarella cheese

▲ Cut the zucchini into halves lengthwise; scoop out and chop the pulp, leaving 1/4-inch shells.

▲ Place the shells in a 6x10-inch microwave-safe dish.

▲ Combine the butter, parsley, olive oil, onion and garlic in a small microwave-safe bowl. Microwave on High until the butter is melted.

▲ Stir in the tomato, bread crumbs, Parmesan cheese, zucchini pulp and seasonings.

▲ Spoon into the zucchini shells.

▲ Microwave, covered with waxed paper, on High for 5 minutes. Sprinkle with mozzarella cheese.

▲ Microwave on High for 1 minute longer or until the cheese is melted.

▲ Yield: 6 servings.

Approx Per Serving: Cal 133; Prot 6 g; Carbo 12 g; T Fat 8 g; 49% Calories from Fat; Chol 14 mg; Fiber 2 g; Sod 172 mg.

Side Dishes
& Breads

Opening the Window of Opportunity

Sometimes assuming more responsibility can open doors in your career. Barbara Pevoto is learning this firsthand in her position as director of the Arapahoe-Douglas Area Vocational School and vocational director of Arapahoe Community College in Littleton, Colorado.

As director, Barbara's responsibilities already included planning the curriculum and budgets for 21 programs and 50 faculty and staff, as well as supervising five school districts. But when school executives reorganized the ranks and eliminated several administrators, Barbara agreed to take on extra responsibilities as dean—with no salary increase.

"I've always been willing to assume more responsibility, and maybe that's a weakness, but I truly believe hard work still pays off," says the 1996 Top Ten Business Woman of ABWA. "The dean position will allow me to grow in several disciplines where I've had little experience. To succeed at an opportunity, you must be able to see the bigger picture."

Side Dishes

Robert's Dressing

3 to 4 cups seasoned bread cubes
1 (6-ounce) package wild rice, cooked
  Giblets of 1 turkey, cooked, chopped
1 medium onion, minced
1¹/₂ cups chopped mushrooms
1¹/₂ cups chopped walnuts
2 cups chopped celery
  Soy sauce to taste
  Pepper to taste
1 cup (about) warm water

▲ Combine the bread cubes, rice, giblets, onion, mushrooms, walnuts, celery and soy sauce in a bowl and mix well. Season with pepper. Add enough of the warm water to just moisten the dressing.

▲ Stuff the turkey.

▲ Will bake while the turkey is roasting.

▲ Do not stuff the turkey until just before baking.

▲ Yield: 12 servings.

Approx Per Serving: Cal 214; Prot 8 g; Carbo 22 g; T Fat 12 g; 47% Calories from Fat; Chol 30 mg; Fiber 2 g; Sod 148 mg

Marianne Cobarrubias, Corporate Communications Assistant
The Timberland Company
West Newbury, Massachusetts

Dumplings

1   egg, beaten
1   cup chicken broth
1   tablespoon melted butter
1¹/₂   cups (about) flour
¹/₈   teaspoon baking powder
    Salt and pepper to taste
    Chicken broth

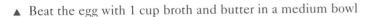

▲ Beat the egg with 1 cup broth and butter in a medium bowl

▲ Mix the flour, baking powder, salt and pepper together.

▲ Add to the egg mixture; mix well. Add enough additional flour if necessary to make a stiff dough.

▲ Bring the desired amount of broth to a boil in a large saucepan.

▲ Break off small pieces of the dough; drop into the boiling broth. Reduce the heat.

▲ Simmer, uncovered, for 10 minutes, stirring occasionally. Simmer, covered, for 10 minutes longer or until the dumplings are cooked through.

▲ Yield: 6 servings.

Approx Per Serving: Cal 188; Prot 6 g; Carbo 32 g; T Fat 3 g; 17% Calories
    from Fat; Chol 41 mg; Fiber 1 g; Sod 167 mg
    Nutritional information does not include the broth for cooking dumplings.

Bernice M. Piwowarczyk, Senior Secretary
Commerce Bank
St. Louis, Missouri

Hominy Harmony

1	(30-ounce) can white hominy
2	cups broccoli florets
1/2	cup chopped onion
1/2	cup chopped green bell pepper
1	(4-ounce) can chopped green chiles
1	(2-ounce) jar chopped pimento
1	cup chopped cooked ham, chicken or turkey
8	ounces Velveeta cheese, cut into small pieces
1	(10-ounce) can cream of mushroom soup
1/4	cup plain yogurt
2	eggs or equivalent egg substitute, beaten
	Salt and pepper to taste

▲ Preheat the oven to 350 degrees.

▲ Combine the hominy, broccoli, onion, green pepper, green chiles, pimento and ham in a bowl. Add the cheese, soup, yogurt, eggs, salt and pepper and mix well.

▲ Spoon into a lightly greased 2-quart glass baking dish.

▲ Bake for 35 minutes.

▲ Yield: 8 servings.

Approx Per Serving: Cal 289; Prot 16 g; Carbo 23 g; T Fat 15 g; 47% Calories from Fat; Chol 91 mg; Fiber 2 g; Sod 1362 mg

Nita Gooch, Real Estate Broker
Katy, Texas

Rice Casserole

2   cups uncooked rice
1/2   cup butter or margarine, cut into small pieces
1   (10-ounce) can cream of mushroom soup
1   (10-ounce) can onion soup
1   soup can water

▲ Preheat the oven to 350 degrees.

▲ Combine the rice, butter, mushroom soup, onion soup and water in a bowl and mix well. Spoon into a baking dish.

▲ Bake for 1 hour.

▲ Yield: 4 servings.

Approx Per Serving: Cal 654; Prot 10 g; Carbo 84 g; T Fat 30 g; 42% Calories from Fat; Chol 63 mg; Fiber 1 g; Sod 1497 mg

> *Pamela Bratton, 1985 ABWA National Secretary-Treasurer*
> *1984 ABWA District Vice President, Chief Operations Officer*
> *Austin Temporary Services, Inc.*
> *Dripping Springs, Texas*

French Rice

1   (4-ounce) jar sliced mushrooms
1   (8-ounce) can sliced water chestnuts
1   (10-ounce) can French onion soup
1/2   cup melted butter or margarine
1   cup uncooked rice

▲ Preheat the oven to 350 degrees.

▲ Drain the mushrooms and water chestnuts, reserving the liquids. Add enough water to the reserved liquids to measure 1 1/3 cups.

▲ Mix the soup and butter in a large bowl. Add the mushrooms, water chestnuts, reserved liquids and rice and mix well. Spoon into a lightly greased 6x10-inch baking dish.

▲ Bake, covered, for 1 hour.

▲ Yield: 8 servings.

Approx Per Serving: Cal 221; Prot 3 g; Carbo 25 g; T Fat 12 g; 49% Calories from Fat; Chol 31 mg; Fiber 1 g; Sod 501 mg

> *Debbie Everman, Executive Secretary, Navistar International*
> *Indianapolis, Indiana*

Green Rice Casserole

$^1\!/_2$ cup chopped onion
$^1\!/_2$ cup chopped celery
  1 tablespoon margarine
$1^1\!/_2$ cups uncooked rice
  1 (10-ounce) package frozen chopped broccoli
  1 (8-ounce) jar Cheez Whiz
  1 (10-ounce) can cream of mushroom soup

▲ Preheat the oven to 350 degrees.

▲ Sauté the onion and celery in the margarine in a skillet.

▲ Cook the rice and the broccoli using the package directions. Drain the broccoli.

▲ Stir the Cheez Whiz into the rice in a large bowl. Stir in the hot broccoli, sautéed vegetables and soup. Spoon into a 2-quart baking dish.

▲ Bake for 30 minutes or until bubbly and heated through.

▲ Yield: 8 servings.

Approx Per Serving: Cal 276; Prot 9 g; Carbo 36 g; T Fat 11 g; 35% Calories from Fat; Chol 16 mg; Fiber 2 g; Sod 723 mg

Carolyn E. Rogers, Customer Service Manager
Hecht Department Store/May Co.
Raleigh, North Carolina

Louisiana Puddin'

2	eggs
2	cups cooked long grain rice
1	cup shredded Cheddar cheese
1	(17-ounce) can cream-style corn
1	small onion, minced
1	medium green bell pepper, chopped
1¹/₂	teaspoons salt, or to taste
¹/₈	teaspoon pepper

Side Dishes

▲ Preheat the oven to 350 degrees.

▲ Beat the eggs in a bowl. Add the rice, cheese, corn, onion and bell pepper and mix well. Season with the salt and pepper. Spoon into a baking dish.

▲ Bake for 45 minutes.

▲ Yield: 6 servings.

Approx Per Serving: Cal 255; Prot 10 g; Carbo 36 g; T Fat 8 g; 29% Calories from Fat; Chol 91 mg; Fiber 2 g; Sod 901 mg

Gladys V. Makerewich, 1961 ABWA National Secretary-Treasurer, retired
Las Vegas, Nevada

Side Dishes

Best-Ever Microwave Pickles

1	cup sugar
1/2	cup vinegar
1/4	teaspoon mustard seeds
1/4	teaspoon celery seeds
1/4	teaspoon turmeric
1/2	teaspoon salt
3/4	cup sliced onion, separated into rings
1	quart unpeeled cucumbers, thinly sliced

▲ Combine the sugar, vinegar, mustard seeds, celery seeds, turmeric and salt in a large microwave-safe bowl and mix well. Add the onion and cucumbers, stirring to coat.

▲ Microwave for 10 minutes, stirring every 5 minutes.

▲ Let cool. Store in a jar or plastic container in the refrigerator.

▲ Will keep for many weeks.

▲ Yield: 1 quart.

Approx Per Serving: Cal 917; Prot 6 g; Carbo 234 g; T Fat 1 g; 1% Calories from Fat; Chol 0 mg; Fiber 8 g; Sod 1086 mg

Sharon K. Anderson, retired Pharmaceutical Assistant
Sterling Drug Company
Smolan, Kansas

Fried Biscuits

2²/₃   *envelopes dry yeast*
1   *cup warm water*
1   *quart milk*
¹/₄   *cup sugar*
¹/₂   *cup lard or shortening*
2   *tablespoons salt*
7   *to 9 cups flour*
     Vegetable oil for frying

Breads

▲ Dissolve the yeast in the warm water.

▲ Combine the milk, sugar, lard and salt in a large bowl and mix well. Cool to lukewarm. Stir in the yeast. Add enough of the flour to make a soft dough. Let the dough rise in a warm place.

▲ Roll the dough on a lightly floured surface. Cut with a biscuit cutter.

▲ Heat the oil to 350 degrees in a skillet. Drop in several biscuits at a time. Cook until browned. Drain on paper towels. If the oil is too hot, the centers of the biscuits will be soggy.

▲ Biscuits may be frozen individually and stored in sealable plastic bags.

▲ Yield: 84 servings.

Approx Per Serving: Cal 70; Prot 2 g; Carbo 11 g; T Fat 2 g; 23% Calories
     from Fat; Chol 3 mg; Fiber <1 g; Sod 158 mg
     Nutritional profile does not include vegetable oil for frying.

Patricia Harding, 1975 Top Ten Business Woman of ABWA
Office Manager, Indiana Basketball Hall of Fame
New Castle, Indiana

Breads

Sour Cream Coffee Cake

1	(2-layer) package yellow cake mix
1	(4-ounce) package vanilla instant pudding mix
4	eggs
1/2	cup vegetable oil
1	cup sour cream
1	cup chopped pecans
2/3	cup sugar
4	teaspoons cinnamon

▲ Preheat the oven to 350 degrees.

▲ Combine the cake mix, pudding mix, eggs, oil and sour cream in a mixer bowl. Beat for 10 minutes.

▲ Mix the pecans, sugar and cinnamon in a bowl.

▲ Layer the batter and pecan mixture 1/3 at a time in a greased and floured bundt pan, ending with the pecan mixture.

▲ Bake for 1 hour. Cool in the pan for 30 minutes.

▲ Yield: 8 servings.

Approx Per Serving: Cal 707; Prot 8 g; Carbo 83 g; T Fat 40 g; 50% Calories from Fat; Chol 120 mg; Fiber 2 g; Sod 645 mg

Marianne Cobarrubias, Corporate Communications Assistant
The Timberland Company
West Newbury, Massachusetts

Breads

Corn Bread Cake

2   (7-ounce) packages corn muffin mix
1   (1-layer) package yellow cake mix
2/3 cup milk
1/2 cup cold water
3   eggs

▲ Preheat the oven to 350 degrees.

▲ Combine the muffin mix and cake mix in a bowl. Add the milk, cold water and eggs and mix well; the batter will be slightly lumpy.

▲ Let the batter stand for 3 to 4 minutes. Pour into a greased 9x13-inch baking pan.

▲ Bake for 20 to 25 minutes or until the top is golden brown and the sides leave the pan.

▲ May top with honey butter.

▲ Yield: 15 servings.

Approx Per Serving: Cal 267; Prot 4 g; Carbo 46 g; T Fat 7 g; 24% Calories from Fat; Chol 45 mg; Fiber <1 g; Sod 414 mg

Lois Gowler, Owner, Gowler's Painting & Wallcovering
Lincoln, Nebraska

Beer Bread

3   cups self-rising flour
1   cup beer
3   tablespoons sugar

▲ Preheat the oven to 350 degrees.

▲ Mix the flour, beer and sugar in a bowl. Pour into a greased loaf pan.

▲ Bake for 55 minutes or until the loaf tests done.

▲ Slice the partially cooled loaf with an electric knife.

▲ Yield: 6 servings.

Approx Per Serving: Cal 262; Prot 6 g; Carbo 54 g; T Fat 1 g; 2% Calories from Fat; Chol 0 mg; Fiber 2 g; Sod 795 mg

Marianne Cobarrubias, Corporate Communications Assistant
The Timberland Company
West Newbury, Massachusetts

Breads

Spoon Rolls

1	*envelope dry yeast*
2	*cups warm water*
1/2	*cup melted margarine*
1/4	*cup sugar*
1	*egg, beaten*
4	*cups self-rising flour*

▲ Preheat the oven to 400 degrees.

▲ Dissolve the yeast in the warm water in a large bowl. Add the margarine, sugar and egg; mix well.

▲ Stir in the self-rising flour; the batter may be slightly lumpy. Fill greased muffin cups 1/2 full.

▲ Bake for 15 minutes or until golden brown.

▲ May store the dough in the refrigerator and use as needed.

▲ These rolls do not have to rise before baking.

▲ Yield: 24 servings.

Approx Per Serving: Cal 120; Prot 2 g; Carbo 18 g; T Fat 4 g; 32% Calories from Fat; Chol 9 mg; Fiber 1 g; Sod 312 mg

The Working Woman's Quick Cookbook

Desserts &
Cookies

Work for Success, Not Failures

Helen Guillette Vassallo's career is a testament to lifelong learning. Although Helen has bachelor's, master's and doctoral degrees in biology and pharmacology, she wanted a broader understanding of the industry's business side. After nearly 40 years in the pharmaceutical field, Helen returned to school at age 50 to get an MBA. Besides the degree, she's gained a new career.

She chose the Worcester Polytechnic Institute, which needed new instructors to bring real-life experiences to the classroom. After graduating, Helen joined the faculty as an associate professor of management and rose to department head and tenured professor, the position she holds today. She is also an adjunct professor of biology and lectures on pharmacology. "It was exciting changing careers and starting all over," says Helen, a 1996 Top Ten Business Woman of ABWA and 1981 American Business Woman of ABWA. "Teaching young people what I learned in the industry was an opportunity for me to make a difference and be a role model. And when opportunities arise, I don't think, 'What if I fail?' I just take a deep breath and think, 'Whatever happens, I'll handle it.' I work for success, not failures."

Desserts

Setting Her Own Rules

Laying everything on the line came naturally to Linda Frechette on her journey to entrepreneurhood. After graduating with a doctorate in optometry in 1980, Linda joined the small practice of a soon-to-be-retiring doctor in Franklin, Indiana. Although the job paid a mere $6 an hour, Linda eagerly accepted it for the chance to buy the practice when the doctor retired. Plus, she was told that she'd get a raise after her 60-day evaluation. Linda's 60 days came and went, and no raise appeared.

To supplement her income, Linda cleaned the office on weekends—at $8 an hour. When the situation didn't improve after a year, she left to start her own practice. Now, 14 years later, Linda employs three other doctors—all women who job-share so they can care for their children. For Linda, setting her own rules is the No. 1 perk of owning a business. "You have to take risks to get above a certain level," advises the 1996 Top Ten Business Woman of ABWA. "A risk is a plan or a goal—it doesn't mean instant gratification. You have to look at what you're willing to do to get there."

Apricot Ice

1   (20-ounce) can apricots
     Juice of 1 lemon
1¹/₂ *cups (scant) sugar*
2   *cups milk*

▲ Mash the undrained apricots in a bowl. Add the lemon juice, sugar and
milk; mix well. Pour into an ice cream freezer container. Freeze using
the manufacturer's directions.

▲ Yield: 8 servings.

Approx Per Serving: Cal 243; Prot 2 g; Carbo 56 g; T Fat 2 g; 8% Calories
   from Fat; Chol 8 mg; Fiber 1 g; Sod 33 mg

Carla S. Lallatin, 1978 Top Ten Business Woman of ABWA
President, Lallatin and Associates
Rego Park, New York

Sugar-Free Banana Ice Cream

3   *bananas*
1   *cup (or more) milk*

▲ Peel the bananas; place in a freezer container and seal securely. Freeze
the bananas until just before serving time.

▲ Cut the frozen bananas into ¹/₂-inch slices; place in a food processor or
blender container.

▲ Process until puréed, adding just enough milk to achieve a thick
consistency. Do not add too much milk or you will make a milk shake.
Serve immediately.

▲ Allow ¹/₂ banana per person when making this recipe.

▲ Yield: 6 servings.

Approx Per Serving: Cal 77; Prot 2 g; Carbo 15 g; T Fat 2 g; 18% Calories
   from Fat; Chol 6 mg; Fiber 1 g; Sod 20 mg

Bernice M. Piwowarczyk, Senior Secretary
Commerce Bank
St. Louis, Missouri

Shari's Cheesecake

1¹/₂	cups fine graham cracker crumbs
1	teaspoon cinnamon
¹/₄	cup sugar
¹/₄	cup melted margarine
	Cream Cheese Filling
1	(21-ounce) can cherry pie filling

▲ Combine the graham cracker crumbs, cinnamon, sugar and margarine in a bowl; mix well. Press the mixture over the bottom and up the sides of a buttered 9x13-inch dish. Chill in the refrigerator until set.

▲ Spoon the Cream Cheese Filling into the pie shell. Top with the pie filling. Chill until serving time.

▲ The cream cheese filling may also be topped with blueberries, pineapple or strawberries. If strawberries are used, add a jar of strawberry glaze.

Cream Cheese Filling

8	ounces cream cheese, softened
1	(14-ounce) can sweetened condensed milk
¹/₃	cup lemon juice
1	teaspoon vanilla extract
12	ounces whipped topping

▲ Cream the cream cheese in a mixer bowl. Add the sweetened condensed milk; beat well. Add the lemon juice and vanilla; mix well. Fold in the whipped topping.

▲ Yield: 36 servings.

Approx Per Serving: Cal 145; Prot 2 g; Carbo 19 g; T Fat 7 g; 45% Calories from Fat; Chol 11 mg; Fiber <1 g; Sod 89 mg

Shari Todd, Nail Technician
Chez Josef Hair & Nail Salon
Tucson, Arizona

Chocopea Dip

1¹/₂   *cups Choco Fudge Frosting*
¹/₂   *cup peanut butter*
¹/₄   *cup milk*
4   *cups animal crackers*

▲ Combine the frosting, peanut butter and milk in a bowl; mix well.
Spoon into a serving bowl. Serve with the animal crackers to dip.

▲ May substitute vanilla wafers or teddy bear crackers for the animal
crackers.

▲ Yield: 16 servings.

Approx Per Serving: Cal 224; Prot 4 g; Carbo 30 g; T Fat 11 g; 42% Calories
from Fat; Chol 1 mg; Fiber 1 g; Sod 155 mg

Jana High, Owner, Paralegal Services Plus
Plano, Texas

Peach Crisp

1   *(29-ounce) can sliced peaches, drained*
1   *cup rolled oats*
¹/₂   *cup packed brown sugar*
¹/₃   *cup flour*
¹/₂   *teaspoon cinnamon*
¹/₄   *teaspoon nutmeg*
¹/₃   *cup melted butter*

▲ Preheat the oven to 375 degrees.

▲ Arrange the peach slices in a buttered 8x8-inch baking pan.

▲ Combine the oats, brown sugar, flour, cinnamon, nutmeg and butter in
a bowl; mix until crumbly. Sprinkle over the peaches.

▲ Bake for 30 minutes.

▲ May serve warm or cold, plain or with ice cream or whipped cream.
Other fruits may be substituted for peaches.

▲ Yield: 8 servings.

Approx Per Serving: Cal 225; Prot 3 g; Carbo 36 g; T Fat 9 g; 36% Calories
from Fat; Chol 21 mg; Fiber 3 g; Sod 87 mg

Gina L. Plummer, Teacher-Director
Wee Shipmates Preschool
Sidney, Iowa

Easy Peach Cobbler

¹/₂	*cup butter or margarine*
1	*cup flour*
1	*cup sugar*
	Salt to taste
1	*tablespoon baking powder*
1	*cup milk*
1	*teaspoon vanilla extract*
1	*(29-ounce) can sliced peaches*
	Cinnamon to taste

▲ Preheat the oven to 350 degrees.

▲ Melt the butter in a 9x13-inch baking dish.

▲ Sift the flour, sugar, salt and baking powder in a bowl. Add the milk and vanilla; mix well. Pour over the melted butter.

▲ Pour in the undrained peaches. Do not stir. Sprinkle lightly with the cinnamon.

▲ Bake for 30 to 40 minutes or until brown.

▲ Yield: 15 servings.

Approx Per Serving: Cal 188; Prot 2 g; Carbo 32 g; T Fat 7 g; 32% Calories from Fat; Chol 19 mg; Fiber 1 g; Sod 140 mg

Pamela Bratton, 1985 ABWA National Secretary-Treasurer
1984 ABWA District Vice President, Chief Operations Officer
Austin Temporary Services, Inc.
Dripping Springs, Texas

Harvest Pumpkin Dessert

1 medium pumpkin
2 cups sliced apples
1 cup raisins
1 cup walnuts
   Cinnamon to taste
   Nutmeg to taste
1 cup (or less) packed brown sugar
   Lemon juice to taste
2 quarts vanilla ice cream

▲ Preheat the oven to 350 degrees.

▲ Slice the top off the pumpkin and reserve. Scoop the seeds from the pumpkin and discard, leaving the pumpkin intact.

▲ Combine the apple slices, raisins, walnuts, cinnamon, nutmeg, brown sugar and lemon juice in a bowl; toss to mix.

▲ Spoon the mixture into the pumpkin; replace the top. Place the pumpkin on a baking sheet.

▲ Bake for 40 minutes to 1¹/₂ hours or until the pumpkin is tender.

▲ Place the pumpkin on a serving dish; garnish with ivy leaves.

▲ Let guests scoop out the mixture and place on their servings of ice cream. This brings on lots of raves.

▲ Yield: 12 servings.

Approx Per Serving: Cal 452; Prot 9 g; Carbo 76 g; T Fat 16 g; 30% Calories from Fat; Chol 39 mg; Fiber 10 g; Sod 84 mg

Louise Spicer, 1992 ABWA National President
1991 ABWA National Vice President, 1990 ABWA District Vice President
Co-owner, Spicers Boat City
Houghton Lake, Michigan

Desserts

Pumpkin Ice Cream Dessert

1¹/₂   cups graham cracker crumbs
¹/₄   cup melted butter
¹/₄   cup sugar
¹/₂   cup chopped pecans
1¹/₂   cups mashed cooked pumpkin
¹/₂   cup packed brown sugar
¹/₂   teaspoon salt
1   teaspoon cinnamon
¹/₄   teaspoon ginger
¹/₈   teaspoon cloves
1   quart vanilla ice cream, softened

▲ Preheat the oven to 375 degrees.

▲ Combine the graham cracker crumbs, butter, sugar and pecans in a bowl; mix well. Press the mixture over the bottom and up the sides of a 9x13-inch baking dish.

▲ Bake for 8 minutes.

▲ Combine the pumpkin, brown sugar, salt, cinnamon, ginger and cloves in a bowl; mix well. Fold in the ice cream. Spoon over the baked crust.

▲ Freeze, covered, until 20 minutes before serving time.

▲ Soften in the refrigerator for 20 minutes. Cut into servings.

▲ Yield: 16 servings.

Approx Per Serving: Cal 202; Prot 2 g; Carbo 27 g; T Fat 10 g; 44% Calories from Fat; Chol 22 mg; Fiber 1 g; Sod 193 mg

Sue Alberti, Administrative Assistant
Missouri Union Presbytery
Jefferson City, Missouri

Fat-Free Trifle

  4   cups skim milk
  2   (3-ounce) packages sugar-free vanilla instant pudding mix
  1   (12-ounce) angel food cake
  1   (16-ounce) package individually frozen strawberries
  1   (10-ounce) package individually frozen raspberries
  1   (16-ounce) package individually frozen blackberries
  4   ounces light whipped topping

▲ Process the milk and pudding mix in a blender until mixed.

▲ Break the cake into large bite-sized pieces.

▲ Reserve 1 strawberry for garnish.

▲ Layer ⅓ of the cake pieces and ⅓ of the pudding in a 9x13-inch dish.
   Add the strawberries.

▲ Add layers of half the remaining cake and half the pudding. Add
   the raspberries.

▲ Layer the remaining cake, pudding and the blackberries in the dish.

▲ Top the layers with whipped topping.

▲ Garnish with the reserved strawberry.

▲ Chill in the refrigerator for 8 to 10 hours.

▲ The berries will thaw slowly while the trifle flavors meld.

▲ Yield: 15 servings.

Approx Per Serving: Cal 152; Prot 4 g; Carbo 32 g; T Fat 1 g; 8% Calories
    from Fat; Chol 1 mg; Fiber 3 g; Sod 276 mg

Vickie Chunn, Owner, Scruples International Hair Salon
Englewood, Florida

Desserts

Strawberry Angel Food Delight

 1   *(6-ounce) package strawberry gelatin*
2¹/₂ *cups boiling water*
 2   *(10-ounce) packages frozen sliced strawberries*
 8   *ounces whipped topping*
 1   *(12-ounce) angel food cake*

▲ Dissolve the strawberry gelatin in the boiling water in a bowl. Add the strawberries, stirring until separated.

▲ Chill in the refrigerator until partially set.

▲ Fold in the whipped topping.

▲ Break the cake into large bite-sized pieces.

▲ Layer the cake and gelatin mixture ¹/₂ at a time in a 9x13-inch. Chill until set.

▲ Cut into squares. Garnish with sliced fresh strawberries.

▲ Yield: 15 servings.

Approx Per Serving: Cal 163; Prot 3 g; Carbo 30 g; T Fat 4 g; 22% Calories
   from Fat; Chol 0 mg; Fiber 1 g; Sod 203 mg

Karen M. Panko, 1996 Top Ten Business Woman of ABWA
Broker Associate, Re/Max Southern Shores
North Myrtle Beach, South Carolina

Cookies

Go Outside the Gates

When Eileen Heyn accepted a new job assignment, what she discovered about herself changed her life. In 18 years with Boeing Co., Eileen worked her way up through 11 positions from entry-level clerk to technical manager.

Then in 1990, she was "loaned" to the local United Way as part of Boeing's executive training program. "Going outside the gates of Boeing gave me a sense of freedom," says the Seattle businesswoman. "It was a big turning point for me."

The move exposed Eileen to people whose personal struggles struck a chord deep inside her. She began to relive her foster home upbringing and to reflect on the thin line of suffering that separated her from the people she met through United Way. Eileen knew their pain, and it touched her.

Two years later, she's re-evaluated her secure career with Boeing and stepped outside its gates for the last time to begin work on a master's degree in grief and loss counseling at Seattle Pacific University. Now completing her therapy internship at Seattle Counseling Service, Eileen used the winds of change to launch her career in a new direction.

"Change happens," says Eileen. "It's how you deal with it that determines the outcome."

Cookies

Buckeyes

1   (18-ounce) jar peanut butter
10   tablespoons plus 2 teaspoons melted butter
1   (1-pound) package confectioners' sugar
1   pound chocolate bark

▲ Combine the peanut butter and melted butter in a bowl; mix well. Add the confectioners' sugar; mix until smooth. Shape into bite-sized balls; place in a shallow pan.

▲ Chill in the refrigerator for 30 minutes.

▲ Microwave the chocolate bark in a small deep microwave-safe bowl until melted.

▲ Dip each ball partially into the melted chocolate, leaving a small circle without chocolate. Place in a shallow pan; let stand until the chocolate is set.

▲ Yield: 125 servings.

Approx Per Serving: Cal 66; Prot 1 g; Carbo 7 g; T Fat 4 g; 53% Calories from Fat; Chol 3 mg; Fiber <1 g; Sod 29 mg

Pam Martin, 1995 ABWA District Vice President
Senior Systems Engineer, BDM Federal, Inc.
Fairborn, Ohio

Microwave Fudge

1   (1-pound) package confectioners' sugar
1/2   cup baking cocoa
1/2   cup butter
1/4   cup milk
1   tablespoon vanilla extract

▲ Combine the confectioners' sugar and cocoa in a microwave-safe bowl. Add the butter and milk but do not mix.

▲ Microwave for 2 minutes. Add the vanilla; mix well. Pour into a buttered 8x8-inch pan. Chill in the refrigerator until set.

▲ Yield: 24 servings.

Approx Per Serving: Cal 115; Prot <1 g; Carbo 20 g; T Fat 4 g; 31% Calories from Fat; Chol 11 mg; Fiber 1 g; Sod 41 mg

Patty Allen, Cashier, Lumber Jack Building Centers
Algonac, Michigan

Cake Mix Cookies

  1   *(2-layer) package devil's food cake mix*
  ¹/₂ *cup vegetable oil*
  2   *eggs*

▲ Preheat the oven to 350 degrees.

▲ Combine the cake mix, oil and eggs in a mixer bowl; mix well. Drop by teaspoonfuls onto a nonstick cookie sheet.

▲ Bake for 10 to 12 minutes or until the cookies are brown around the edges. Cool in the pan for several minutes; remove to a wire rack to cool completely.

▲ May add chocolate chips and nuts to the mixture if desired. May use lemon cake mix or cake mix in any flavor.

▲ Yield: 48 servings.

Approx Per Serving: Cal 69; Prot 1 g; Carbo 9 g; T Fat 3 g; 45% Calories
    from Fat; Chol 9 mg; Fiber 0 g; Sod 90 mg

Sandy Reed, Payroll Supervisor, Inland Container
Martinsville, Indiana

Chew Bread

  ¹/₂ *cup melted butter*
  1   *(1-pound) package light brown sugar*
  3   *eggs*
  2   *cups self-rising flour*
  1   *teaspoon vanilla extract*
  ¹/₂ *cup chopped pecans*

▲ Preheat the oven to 325 degrees.

▲ Combine the butter and brown sugar in a large bowl; mix well. Beat in the eggs one at a time, mixing well after each addition. Add the flour and vanilla; mix well. Stir in the pecans. Spoon into a 9x11-inch baking dish sprayed with nonstick baking spray.

▲ Bake for 45 minutes or until a wooden pick inserted comes out clean. Cool in the baking dish. Cut into squares.

▲ Yield: 48 servings.

Approx Per Serving: Cal 84; Prot 1 g; Carbo 13 g; T Fat 3 g; 33% Calories
    from Fat; Chol 18 mg; Fiber <1 g; Sod 93 mg

Sandra Stanfield, Revenue Officer, IRS
Lakeland, Florida

Cookies

408-Calorie Cookies

1   *cup butter, softened*
1   *cup packed brown sugar*
1   *cup sugar*
2   *eggs*
1   *cup peanut butter*
3   *cups flour*
1   *teaspoon baking soda*
1   *teaspoon baking powder*
1/4   *teaspoon salt*
1   *cup large chocolate chips*
1/2   *cup peanut butter chips*

▲ Preheat the oven to 350 degrees.

▲ Cream the butter, brown sugar and sugar in a mixer bowl. Beat in the eggs one at a time, mixing well after each addition. Add the peanut butter; beat well.

▲ Mix the flour, baking soda, baking powder and salt together. Add to the creamed mixture; mix well. Stir in the chocolate chips and peanut butter chips.

▲ Drop the batter by 1/4 cupfuls 2 inches apart onto a lightly greased cookie sheet.

▲ Bake for 14 to 16 minutes or until golden brown.

▲ Cool on the cookie sheet for several minutes; remove to a wire rack to cool completely.

▲ Yield: 18 servings.

Approx Per Serving: Cal 408; Prot 8 g; Carbo 48 g; T Fat 22 g; 47% Calories from Fat; Chol 51 mg; Fiber 2 g; Sod 290 mg

Mary Kristensen, Vice President, Kristensen Insurance Inc.
Council Bluffs, Iowa

Chocolate Raspberry Truffle Cookies

 1/4 cup nonfat margarine, softened
 1/4 cup nonfat cream cheese, softened
 1/3 cup sugar
 1/2 cup packed brown sugar
   1 teaspoon vanilla extract
   1 cup flour
 1/2 cup baking coc
 1/4 teaspoon salt
 3/4 cup Hershey's raspberry chips

▲ Preheat the oven to 350 degrees.

▲ Cream the margarine, cream cheese, sugar, brown sugar and vanilla in
   a large mixer bowl.

▲ Sift the flour, cocoa and salt together. Add to the creamed mixture;
   mix well. Stir in the raspberry chips.

▲ Shape by tablespoonfuls into balls; place on a nonstick cookie sheet
   sprayed with nonstick cooking spray. Flatten the balls into 2-inch
   rounds with the bottom of a glass.

▲ Bake for 8 to 10 minutes or until slightly puffed and soft to the touch.

▲ Cool on the cookie sheet for 1 minute; remove to a wire rack to
   cool completely.

▲ Yield: 32 servings.

Approx Per Serving: Cal 61; Prot 1 g; Carbo 11 g; T Fat 1 g; 20% Calories
   from Fat; Chol 1 mg; Fiber 1 g; Sod 54 mg

Wendy S. Myers, Editor in Chief, Women in Business *magazine*
American Business Women's Association
Kansas City, Missouri

Cookies

Lemon Angel Bars

1   *(1-pound) package one-step angel food cake mix*
1   *(21-ounce) can lemon pie filling*
1/3 *cup margarine, softened*
2   *cups confectioners' sugar*
1   *tablespoon lemon juice*

▲ Preheat the oven to 350 degrees.

▲ Mix the cake mix and lemon pie filling in a bowl. Pour into a greased 12x18-inch baking pan. Bake for 15 minutes or until firm.

▲ Mix the margarine, confectioners' sugar and lemon juice in a mixer bowl. Spread over the hot layer. Cut into bars to serve.

▲ Yield: 24 servings.

Approx Per Serving: Cal 218; Prot 3 g; Carbo 43 g; T Fat 4 g; 17% Calories from Fat; Chol 33 mg; Fiber <1 g; Sod 189 mg

I. "Chris" Christopherson, retired Bookkeeper-Office Manager
Home and Auto Super Mart
Rapid City, South Dakota

O'Henry Bars

1   *cup each sugar and light corn syrup*
1¹/₂ *cups peanut butter*
6   *cups puffed rice cereal*
1   *cup each chocolate chips and butterscotch chips*

▲ Mix the sugar and corn syrup in a saucepan. Bring to a boil over medium heat, stirring frequently. Remove from the heat. Stir in the peanut butter and cereal. Spread the mixture in a greased 9x13-inch pan.

▲ Combine the chocolate chips and butterscotch chips in a saucepan. Heat over medium heat until the chips are melted, stirring frequently. Spread over the cereal layer.

▲ Chill in the refrigerator until set. Cut into bars. Store in the refrigerator.

▲ Yield: 16 servings.

Approx Per Serving: Cal 374; Prot 7 g; Carbo 52 g; T Fat 18 g; 41% Calories from Fat; Chol <1 mg; Fiber 2 g; Sod 150 mg

Melanie Mayberry, Brokerage Services Coordinator
Commodity Services, Inc.
West Des Moines, Iowa

Quick Pudding Cookies

Cookies

1   *(3-ounce) package any flavor instant pudding mix*
1   *cup baking mix*
1/4   *cup vegetable oil*
1   *egg, slightly beaten*
3   *tablespoons water*

▲ Preheat the oven to 375 degrees.

▲ Combine the pudding mix and baking mix in a bowl; mix well. Add the oil, egg and water; mix well.

▲ Drop by teaspoonfuls onto a nonstick cookie sheet.

▲ Bake for 10 to 12 minutes or until light brown.

▲ Cool on the baking sheet for several minutes; remove to a wire rack to cool completely.

▲ May stir 1/2 cup chocolate chips into the mixture before baking for quick chocolate chip cookies.

▲ Yield: 20 servings.

Approx Per Serving: Cal 70; Prot 1 g; Carbo 8 g; T Fat 4 g; 49% Calories
from Fat; Chol 11 mg; Fiber <1 g; Sod 147 mg

Janae Herman, Office Manager/Radiologic Technologist
Ahrlin Orthopedic, LTD
Rapid City, South Dakota

Cookies

Texas Pecan Tassies

3	ounces cream cheese, softened
1/2	cup margarine, softened
1	cup flour
1/4	cup finely chopped pecans
2/3	cup packed light brown sugar
1	cup finely chopped pecans
1	egg
1	teaspoon vanilla extract
1/8	teaspoon salt
1	tablespoon melted margarine

▲ Preheat the oven to 350 degrees.

▲ Combine the cream cheese, margarine and flour in a bowl; mix well. Stir in 1/4 cup pecans.

▲ Shape the mixture into 24 small balls. Press over bottoms and up sides of greased muffin cups, forming a shell.

▲ Combine the brown sugar, 1 cup pecans, egg, vanilla, salt and margarine in a bowl; mix well. Spoon into the cream cheese shells, filling each 2/3 full.

▲ Bake for 20 minutes or until the filling is set.

▲ Cool in the pans for 5 minutes; remove to a wire rack to cool completely.

▲ Store in an airtight container.

▲ Yield: 24 servings.

Approx Per Serving: Cal 133; Prot 2 g; Carbo 10 g; T Fat 10 g; 66% Calories from Fat; Chol 13 mg; Fiber 1 g; Sod 77 mg

Myrleen Knott, 1992 ABWA National Secretary-Treasurer
1991 ABWA District Vice President, Vice President/Controller
Buffalo Flange, Inc.
Houston, Texas

Pumpkin Cheesecake Bars

1	cup flour
1/3	cup packed light brown sugar
5	tablespoons butter, softened
1/2	cup chopped walnuts
8	ounces cream cheese, softened
3/4	cup sugar
1/2	cup solid-pack pumpkin
2	eggs, lightly beaten
1 1/2	teaspoons cinnamon
1	teaspoon allspice
1	teaspoon vanilla extract

▲ Preheat the oven to 350 degrees.

▲ Combine the flour and brown sugar in a bowl. Cut in the butter until crumbly. Stir in the walnuts. Reserve 3/4 cup of the mixture for topping.

▲ Press the remaining mixture onto the bottom of a nonstick 8x8-inch baking pan.

▲ Bake for 15 minutes. Cool slightly.

▲ Combine the cream cheese, sugar, pumpkin, eggs, cinnamon, allspice and vanilla in a bowl; mix well. Pour over the baked crust. Sprinkle with the reserved topping.

▲ Bake for 30 to 35 minutes or until light brown. Cool for several minutes. Cut into bars.

▲ May substitute pecans for walnuts.

▲ Yield: 32 servings.

Approx Per Serving: Cal 98; Prot 2 g; Carbo 10 g; T Fat 6 g; 52% Calories from Fat; Chol 26 mg; Fiber <1 g; Sod 44 mg

Lucille Farrar, retired Secretary/Bookkeeper
Salina, Kansas

Cookies

Whole Grain Snack Cookies

3/4	cup margarine, softened
1	cup packed brown sugar
1	egg
1/4	cup milk
1	teaspoon vanilla extract
1	cup (about) flour
1/2	teaspoon salt
1/2	teaspoon baking soda
2 1/2	cups rolled oats
3/4	cup wheat germ
1/2	cup chopped pecans
3/4	cup chocolate chips

▲ Preheat the oven to 375 degrees.

▲ Combine the margarine, brown sugar, egg, milk and vanilla in a mixer bowl; beat until smooth.

▲ Mix the flour, salt and baking soda together. Add to the brown sugar mixture; mix well. Stir in the oats, wheat germ, pecans and chocolate chips.

▲ Drop by rounded teaspoonfuls onto a greased cookie sheet.

▲ Bake for 8 to 10 minutes or until light brown around the edges.

▲ Cool on the cookie sheet for 1 minute. Remove to a wire rack to cool completely.

▲ May add chopped dates, dried apricots or prunes.

▲ Yield: 60 servings.

Approx Per Serving: Cal 78; Prot 2 g; Carbo 10 g; T Fat 4 g; 45% Calories from Fat; Chol 4 mg; Fiber 1 g; Sod 51 mg

Cakes & Pies

Persistence Pays

Lynne Powell finally got the chance to go to college in her mid-30s. While working full time and caring for her three children, Lynne took night classes and completed her nursing degree in 10 years. At the Milford-Whitinsville Regional Hospital in Milford, Massachusetts, she worked as a staff nurse for five years before moving into a management position.

"I think it's important to take advantage of opportunities, and I've been given a chance to grow with the hospital," says the 1996 Top Ten Business Woman of ABWA. "You can't run from change or let yourself stagnate. You must look at change as a chance to succeed, and I hope to take others down that road with me."

Today, Lynne is the director of surgical services and manages the operating room, post-anesthesia care unit, surgical floor and two special medical facilities.

Cakes

Forging New Ground

After only three years in an entry-level position, Barbara Lovette Wright got an opportunity for a management position on the corporate ladder. An African-American woman, then without a college degree, Barbara jumped on the ladder and started climbing.

In 1973, she joined General Motors Corporation's Detroit office as a secretary in the personnel department. During the next few years, the company focused on moving women into traditionally male positions. Barbara accepted a production supervisor job at the company's Atlanta plant, becoming the first African-American and woman to hold the position. She moved from a quiet office environment to a loud, bustling brake assembly line, where she supervised 30 men. "I had men tell me they didn't take orders from their wives or from someone who's wet behind the ears," says the 1996 American Business Woman of ABWA. "I had to figure out a way to use my femininity to my advantage."

Instead of ordering, she empowered employees by asking for their suggestions on how to improve working conditions. She also rewarded good behavior and performance. "I didn't see my job as building cars, but rather as building people," says Barbara. Her strategy worked. Now she's manager of work force diversity and community relations.

Apple Cake

Cakes

1	*cup sugar*
2	*cups thinly sliced apples*
1¹/₂	*cups flour*
1	*teaspoon baking soda*
¹/₂	*teaspoon salt*
¹/₂	*teaspoon cinnamon*
¹/₂	*cup vegetable oil*
1	*egg, beaten*

▲ Preheat the oven to 350 degrees.

▲ Combine the sugar and apple slices in a bowl; toss to mix. Let stand for 10 minutes.

▲ Combine the flour, baking soda, salt and cinnamon in a bowl; mix well.

▲ Add the oil and egg to the apple slices; mix well. Add to the flour mixture; mix well.

▲ Spoon into a greased and floured 8x8-inch cake pan.

▲ Bake for 35 to 40 minutes or until the cake tests done.

▲ Cool in the pan. Garnish with confectioners' sugar.

▲ Yield: 12 servings.

Approx Per Serving: Cal 218; Prot 2 g; Carbo 31 g; T Fat 10 g; 40% Calories from Fat; Chol 18 mg; Fiber 1 g; Sod 163 mg

Dora Mae Reither, Computer Programmer Consultant
Application Design and Development
Omaha, Nebraska

Cakes

Applesauce Carrot Cake

2³/4 cups flour
1 tablespoon baking soda
¹/2 teaspoon salt
1 tablespoon cinnamon
1 teaspoon nutmeg
1 cup egg substitute
¹/2 cup vegetable oil
³/4 cup sugar
1 teaspoon vanilla extract
2 cups applesauce
2¹/4 cups grated carrots
1¹/2 cups raisins

▲ Preheat the oven to 350 degrees.

▲ Combine the flour, baking soda, salt, cinnamon and nutmeg in a bowl; mix well.

▲ Combine the egg substitute, oil, sugar, vanilla, applesauce and carrots in a bowl; mix well. Add the dry ingredients; mix well. Stir in the raisins.

▲ Spoon into a 9x13-inch cake pan sprayed with nonstick cooking spray.

▲ Bake for 25 minutes or until the cake tests done.

▲ Yield: 24 servings.

Approx Per Serving: Cal 177; Prot 3 g; Carbo 31 g; T Fat 5 g; 25% Calories from Fat; Chol <1 mg; Fiber 2 g; Sod 171 mg

Thelma M. Chisholm, Quality Control, retired, General Electric
Daytona Beach, Florida

California Earthquake

1   cup flaked coconut
1   cup pecans, chopped
1   (2-layer) package German chocolate cake mix
1/2   cup melted margarine
8   ounces cream cheese, softened
1   (1-pound) package confectioners' sugar

▲ Preheat the oven to 350 degrees.

▲ Sprinkle the coconut and pecans into a greased and floured 9x13-inch cake pan.

▲ Prepare the cake mix using package directions. Spoon over the coconut and pecans.

▲ Combine the margarine and cream cheese in a bowl; mix well. Add the confectioners' sugar; mix well. Drop by spoonfuls over the cake mix.

▲ Bake for 45 minutes or until the cake tests done.

▲ The top of the cake will look like an earthquake but the taste is earth-shaking.

▲ Yield: 36 servings.

Approx Per Serving: Cal 212; Prot 2 g; Carbo 26 g; T Fat 12 g; 49% Calories from Fat; Chol 25 mg; Fiber <1 g; Sod 189 mg

Caroline Moyer, Business Relations
Efratom Time and Frequency Products, Inc.
Garden Grove, California

Indian Chocolate Cake

2	cups sugar
2	eggs
1/2	cup margarine, softened
1/2	cup cold coffee
2	cups flour
1/2	cup baking cocoa
1	teaspoon baking soda
1/2	teaspoon salt
1	cup boiling water

▲ Preheat the oven to 350 degrees.

▲ Combine the sugar, eggs and margarine in a mixer bowl; beat well. Add the coffee; mix well.

▲ Mix the flour, cocoa, baking soda and salt together. Add to the sugar mixture; beat well. Add the boiling water; mix well.

▲ Spoon into a greased and floured 9x13-inch cake pan.

▲ Bake for 30 minutes or until the cake tests done.

▲ Yield: 36 servings.

Approx Per Serving: Cal 98; Prot 1 g; Carbo 17 g; T Fat 3 g; 27% Calories from Fat; Chol 12 mg; Fiber 1 g; Sod 86 mg

Gina L. Plummer, Teacher-Director
Wee Shipmates Preschool
Sidney, Iowa

Texas Devil Cake

    2   cups sugar
    2   cups flour
    1   teaspoon baking soda
    2   eggs
    1/2 cup sour cream
    1   cup margarine
    1   cup water
    6   tablespoons baking cocoa
        Confectioners' Sugar Icing

▲ Preheat the oven to 350 degrees.

▲ Combine the sugar, flour and baking soda in a bowl; mix well. Add the eggs and sour cream; mix well.

▲ Combine the margarine, water and cocoa in a saucepan. Bring to a boil over medium heat, stirring frequently. Add to the sugar mixture; mix well. The mixture will be thin. Pour into a greased and floured 12x18-inch cake pan.

▲ Bake for 20 to 25 minutes or until the cake tests done.

▲ Spread the Confectioners' Sugar Icing over the hot cake.

Confectioners' Sugar Icing

    6   tablespoons milk
    1/2 cup margarine
    1/4 cup baking cocoa
    1   (1-pound) package confectioners' sugar
    1   teaspoon vanilla extract
    1/2 cup chopped pecans

▲ Combine the milk, margarine and cocoa in a saucepan. Bring to a boil over medium heat, stirring frequently. Remove from the heat. Stir in the confectioners' sugar, vanilla and pecans.

▲ Yield: 35 servings.

Approx Per Serving: Cal 218; Prot 2 g; Carbo 31 g; T Fat 10 g; 41% Calories
    from Fat; Chol 14 mg; Fiber 1 g; Sod 123 mg

Carole J. Smock, Secretary/Bookkeeper
Christine D. Sowders, Inc.
Bowling Green, Kentucky

Cakes

Greek Cake

2   cups sugar
2¹/₂ cups flour
2   teaspoons baking soda
2   eggs, slightly beaten
1   (20-ounce) can crushed pineapple
1   cup chopped walnuts
     Cream Cheese Frosting

▲ Preheat the oven to 350 degrees.

▲ Combine the sugar, flour, baking soda and eggs in a bowl; mix well with a wooden spoon. Add the undrained pineapple; mix well. Stir in the walnuts.

▲ Spoon into a greased 9x13-inch cake pan.

▲ Bake for 30 to 40 minutes or until the cake tests done.

▲ Let stand to partially cool.

▲ Spread the Cream Cheese Frosting over the slightly warm cake.

▲ Chill in the refrigerator for 8 to 10 hours.

Cream Cheese Frosting

8   ounces cream cheese, softened
¹/₂ cup butter, softened
1   teaspoon vanilla extract
2   cups confectioners' sugar

▲ Combine the cream cheese, butter and vanilla in a bowl; mix well. Add the confectioners' sugar; mix until of spreading consistency.

▲ Yield: 36 servings.

Approx Per Serving: Cal 183; Prot 2 g; Carbo 28 g; T Fat 7 g; 35% Calories from Fat; Chol 26 mg; Fiber 1 g; Sod 95 mg

Shirley L. Romberger, Judicial Secretary
Commonwealth Court of Pennsylvania
Millersburg, Pennsylvania

Hummingbird Cake

2	*cups flour*
1	*teaspoon baking soda*
1	*teaspoon salt*
1	*teaspoon cinnamon*
2	*cups sugar*
1¹/₂	*cups vegetable oil*
1	*teaspoon butter flavoring*
2	*eggs*
1	*(8-ounce) can crushed pineapple*
2	*small bananas, chopped*
1	*cup pecans, chopped*
¹/₃	*cup flaked coconut*

▲ Preheat the oven to 350 degrees.

▲ Combine the flour, baking soda, salt, cinnamon and sugar in a bowl;
  mix well with a wooden spoon. Add the oil, butter flavoring, eggs,
  undrained pineapple, bananas, pecans, and coconut; mix well.

▲ Spoon into a greased and floured bundt cake pan.

▲ Bake for 1 hour and 5 minutes or until the cake tests done.

▲ Cool in the pan for several minutes.

▲ Invert onto a cake plate.

▲ Yield: 16 servings.

Approx Per Serving: Cal 416; Prot 3 g; Carbo 44 g; T Fat 26 g; 56% Calories
    from Fat; Chol 27 mg; Fiber 1 g; Sod 194 mg

Sara Root, Accounting/Utility Clerk, North Star Steel Texas
Beaumont, Texas

Cakes

Lemonade Cake

1   (2-layer) package lemon cake mix
1   (3-ounce) package instant lemon pudding mix
1   cup plus 2 teaspoons water
1   cup corn oil
4   eggs
1   (6-ounce) can frozen lemonade concentrate, thawed
2¹/₂ cups confectioners' sugar

▲ Preheat the oven to 350 degrees.

▲ Combine the cake mix, pudding mix, water, corn oil and eggs in a mixer bowl; mix well.

▲ Spoon into a nonstick 9x13-inch cake pan.

▲ Bake for 25 to 30 minutes.

▲ Combine the lemonade concentrate and confectioners' sugar in a bowl; mix well.

▲ Pierce holes in the hot cake. Spread the lemonade mixture over the cake.

▲ Bake for 3 minutes longer.

▲ Yield: 36 servings.

Approx Per Serving: Cal 173; Prot 1 g; Carbo 25 g; T Fat 8 g; 40% Calories from Fat; Chol 24 mg; Fiber <1 g; Sod 133 mg

Nina Fields Jackson, Attorney
Goldsboro, North Carolina

Pineapple Torte

1   (10-ounce) jar apricot jam
1   13-inch diameter 1-inch high round sponge cake
1   (16 ounce) can sliced pineapple, drained
1   (3-ounce) can flaked coconut
1   (4-ounce) jar maraschino cherries, drained

Cakes

▲ Preheat the broiler.

▲ Spread the apricot jam over the top of the cake. Arrange the pineapple slices over the jam; sprinkle the top with the coconut.

▲ Place the cake on a rack in a broiler pan.

▲ Broil under a hot broiler until the coconut is light brown.

▲ Cut the maraschino cherries into halves. Decorate the top of the cake with the cherry halves.

▲ Yield: 12 servings.

Approx Per Serving: Cal 307; Prot 4 g; Carbo 66 g; T Fat 4 g; 12% Calories
    from Fat; Chol 66 mg; Fiber 2 g; Sod 170 mg

Sheila Zia-Gerschler, Director, Transition Resources
Ashland, Oregon

Cakes

Country Shortcake

2	*cups flour*
2	*tablespoons sugar*
1/2	*teaspoon salt*
4	*teaspoons baking powder*
5	*tablespoons melted shortening*
1	*egg, beaten*
1/2	*cup milk*
4	*cups sliced fresh strawberries*

▲ Preheat the oven to 375 degrees.

▲ Sift the flour, sugar, salt and baking powder together 4 times.

▲ Combine the flour mixture, shortening, egg and milk in a bowl; mix just until the dry ingredients are moistened.

▲ Spoon into a 9-inch pie pan sprayed with nonstick baking spray.

▲ Bake for 20 minutes or until the cake tests done.

▲ Cut into wedges. Serve with fresh strawberries.

▲ May split the wedges horizontally into 2 layers and spoon the strawberries between the layers.

▲ May substitute raspberries, blueberries or peaches for strawberries.

▲ Yield: 8 servings.

Approx Per Serving: Cal 243; Prot 5 g; Carbo 34 g; T Fat 10 g; 36% Calories from Fat; Chol 29 mg; Fiber 3 g; Sod 315 mg

Janet M. Priewe, Legal Secretary, Curran Law Office
La Valle, Wisconsin

Pies

Making Connections That Count

Last spring, a group of business owners who belong to an American Business Women's Association chapter in Amherst, New York, started talking about what it means to be an entrepreneur.

"The group started out because we realized that so many people didn't understand what it was like to be an entrepreneur," says Elaine Marsha, who co-owns L.E. Marsha Company, a warehouse facility for printing inks in Buffalo, New York, with her husband. "Nobody pays your bills but you."

Business owners meet for two hours each month to help one another with advertising, marketing and management challenges. They discuss topics such as renting office space, contract labor vs. hiring someone on salary and how to make your one-person business seem bigger.

When you form a business owners networking group, make your objectives clear. Meet with interested entrepreneurs and involve them in establishing the networking group's structure, advises Sue Jan Herber, a licensed professional counselor and vice president of Competitive Resources Inc., a management-consulting firm in The Woodlands, Texas.

Getting members' input on the group's organization will keep them satisfied—and coming back to each networking meeting. "If they keep coming back, then that's a successful meeting," Elaine says.

Pies

Impossible Coconut Pie

4   *eggs*
1/2 *cup (or more) sugar*
1   *cup flaked coconut*
2   *teaspoons vanilla extract*
1/2 *cup melted butter*
1/2 *cup flour*
2   *cups milk*
1/4 *teaspoon salt*

▲ Preheat the oven to 350 degrees.

▲ Combine the eggs, sugar, coconut, vanilla, butter, flour, milk and salt in a blender container.

▲ Process for 1 to 2 minutes or until mixed.

▲ Pour into a buttered 10-inch pie plate.

▲ Bake for 30 to 35 minutes or until golden brown and firm.

▲ Yield: 6 servings.

Approx Per Serving: Cal 394; Prot 9 g; Carbo 34 g; T Fat 26 g; 57% Calories from Fat; Chol 194 mg; Fiber 2 g; Sod 330 mg

Gina L. Plummer, Teacher-Director
Wee Shipmates Preschool
Sidney, Iowa

Toasty Coconut Pie

1	cup sugar
1	(3-ounce) can flaked coconut
1/2	cup milk
1	teaspoon vanilla extract
2	eggs
1/4	cup melted butter
1	unbaked (9-inch) pie shell

▲ Preheat the oven to 350 degrees.

▲ Combine the sugar, coconut, milk, vanilla and eggs in a bowl; mix well. Add the butter; mix well. Pour into the pie shell.

▲ Bake for 1 hour or until golden brown.

▲ Yield: 8 servings.

Approx Per Serving: Cal 341; Prot 4 g; Carbo 41 g; T Fat 19 g; 48% Calories from Fat; Chol 71 mg; Fiber 2 g; Sod 206 mg

Carol L. McDonald, 1990 Top Ten Business Woman of ABWA
President/Owner, McDonald and Associates, Inc.
Omaha, Nebraska

Pies

Minnie-Jean's Pecan Pie

3 *eggs*
1 *cup sugar*
¹/₂ *cup corn syrup*
¹/₄ *cup melted butter or margarine*
¹/₄ *teaspoon vanilla extract*
1 *cup pecans*
1 *unbaked (9-inch) pie shell*

▲ Preheat the oven to 375 degrees.

▲ Beat the eggs slightly in a mixer bowl. Add the sugar, corn syrup, butter and vanilla; mix well. Stir in the pecans.

▲ Pour into the pie shell. Place near the center of the oven.

▲ Bake for 35 to 40 minutes or until the filling is slightly firm. The center of the pie may look soft when the pie is gently shaken but will become firm as the pie cools.

▲ Yield: 8 servings.

Approx Per Serving: Cal 451; Prot 5 g; Carbo 54 g; T Fat 26 g; 49% Calories from Fat; Chol 95 mg; Fiber 1 g; Sod 229 mg

Jean Fulkerson, 1967 ABWA District Vice President
1962 Top Ten Business Woman of ABWA
Administrative Assistant, Accounting
Holderfield Battery Company
Bowling Green, Kentucky

Pecan Pie

1   (3-ounce) package vanilla instant pudding and pie filling mix
3/4 cup evaporated milk
1   egg
1   cup dark corn syrup
1   teaspoon vanilla extract
1   tablespoon melted margarine or butter
1   cup pecan halves
1   unbaked (9-inch) pie shell

▲ Preheat the oven to 375 degrees.

▲ Combine the pudding and pie filling mix, evaporated milk, egg, corn syrup, vanilla and margarine in a bowl; mix well. Stir in the pecans.

▲ Pour the mixture into the pie shell.

▲ Bake for 40 minutes. Cool the pie completely before cutting.

▲ Yield: 12 servings.

Approx Per Serving: Cal 282; Prot 3 g; Carbo 39 g; T Fat 14 g; 43% Calories from Fat; Chol 22 mg; Fiber 1 g; Sod 276 mg

Marvis M. Bedford, Office Manager
Environmental Protection Agency
Atlanta, Georgia

Pies

Pumpkin Pie

2	cups flour
1/2	cup vegetable oil
1/4	cup milk
2/3	cup sugar
2	teaspoons pumpkin pie spice
2	eggs, beaten
1 2/3	cups evaporated milk
1 1/2	cups (or more) mashed cooked pumpkin

▲ Preheat the oven to 375 degrees.

▲ Combine the flour, oil and milk in a bowl; mix well.

▲ Roll out between sheets of waxed paper. Press over the bottom and up the side of a 9-inch pie plate.

▲ Combine the sugar, pumpkin pie spice, eggs, evaporated milk and pumpkin in a bowl; mix well. Spoon into the unbaked pie shell.

▲ Bake for 30 minutes. Reduce the oven temperature to 350 degrees.

▲ Bake for 25 minutes longer or until a knife inserted in the pie comes out clean.

▲ Garnish with whipped topping.

▲ Fresh pumpkin may be peeled, cut into cubes, and cooked in water to cover in a saucepan over medium heat for 1 hour or until tender.

▲ Yield: 8 servings.

Approx Per Serving: Cal 403; Prot 9 g; Carbo 49 g; T Fat 20 g; 43% Calories from Fat; Chol 70 mg; Fiber 2 g; Sod 77 mg

Liz Henshaw, 1989 ABWA National President
1988 ABWA National Vice President, 1987 ABWA District Vice President
Director of Quality, Stewart Title
Houston, Texas

Sweet Potato Pie

   3   large sweet potatoes
 1/4   cup butter
 1/2   cup evaporated milk
   2   egg yolks
 2/3   cup sugar
 1/2   teaspoon salt
   1   teaspoon vanilla extract
   2   tablespoons brandy
 1/4   teaspoon nutmeg
   2   egg whites, stiffly beaten
   1   unbaked (9-inch) pie shell

▲ Place the sweet potatoes in a saucepan with water to cover. Cook over medium heat until tender; drain.

▲ Peel the sweet potatoes and mash in a bowl.

▲ Preheat the oven to 350 degrees.

▲ Combine the butter and evaporated milk in a saucepan. Heat over medium heat until the butter melts, stirring occasionally.

▲ Add to the sweet potatoes; mix well. Add the egg yolks, sugar, salt, vanilla, brandy and nutmeg; mix well.

▲ Fold the egg whites gently into the mixture. Spoon into the pie shell.

▲ Bake for 30 minutes or until a wooden pick inserted in the center comes out clean.

▲ Yield: 8 servings.

Approx Per Serving: Cal 359; Prot 5 g; Carbo 47 g; T Fat 16 g; 40% Calories
   from Fat; Chol 73 mg; Fiber 3 g; Sod 356 mg

Sharon Walker, Administrative Assistant
University of Michigan Medical Center
Ann Arbor, Michigan

Contributors

Barbara Adrian, 1993 Top Ten
    Business Woman of ABWA
Sue Alberti
Bernice Alexander
Connie Alexander, 1984 American
    Business Woman of ABWA
Lottie Allen
Pamela L. Allen
Darlene Anderson
Frances Anderson
Sharon K. Anderson
Darlene Andrews
Susan J. Bailey
Karen Bappe
Marsha Baskette
Roberta Baskette
Judith M. Bastian
Carolyn L. Beane
Ruth Beasley
Marvis M. Bedford
Diane M. Beedon
Janice Bell
Cydney Berry, 1993 National
    Vice President, 1992 District
    Vice President
Vicki S. Berry, 1980 National
    Secretary-Treasurer
Judith Bliss
Myra Blunt
Mildred Boner
Mazel Bradley
Pamela Bratton, 1985 National
    Secretary-Treasurer, 1984 District
    Vice President
Tracey Bright, 1993 Top Ten
    Business Woman of ABWA
Betty L. Brock
Darlene Brooks
Debbie Burger-Williams
Ednaearle Burney
Beulah Butler
Mary D. Butters
Grace T. Cadmus
Ollie Cameron
Adriana Cantelli
Celena H. Casseday
Carmen Castillo
Rosemary Catalani
Louise P. Ce Balt
Helen Chalut, 1970 District
    Vice President
Anna Chidester
Thelma M. Chisholm
I. "Chris" Christopherson

Vickie Chunn
Dorothy J. Cissel, 1980 Top Ten
    Business Woman of ABWA
Carolyn Clark
Marianne Cobarrubias
Betty Cole
Barbara Conklin, 1993 District
    Vice President
Sandra W. Conn
Sara Connor, 1995 American
    Business Woman of ABWA
Emily D. Copenhaver
Dawn Cramer
Karon Cramer
Rhonda Cramer
Kay P. Crocker
Julia Crozier, In memory of
Diane Cullen
Sara Ratliff Davis, 1990 Top
    Ten Business Woman
    of ABWA
Debi DeBenedetto
Judy Degginger
Beth Dehaemers
Jane W. Deibler, 1980 District
    Vice President
Merna J. Denmark
Beth Dettaemers
Marilyn Dial
Nellie E. Dorsey
Susie Dreiling
Susie M. Dye
Jean Dyer
Bobbi Economy, 1995 District
    Vice President
Carolyn Elman, ABWA Executive
    Director
Dianna Emerson
Becky Epley, 1993 Top Ten
    Business Woman of ABWA
Debbie Everman
Mary Agnes Fagg
Lou Mae Fangmann
Lucille Farrar
Bonnie Flickinger
Jean Foster
Phyllis Foster
Lois Francis, 1990 District Vice
    President
Meryl Frantz
Marie Fretz
Jean Fulkerson, 1967 District
    Vice President, 1962 Top Ten
    Business Woman of ABWA

Contributors

Vivian Gardner, 1978 Top Ten Business Woman of ABWA, 1973 National President, 1971 District Vice President
Judy Gatewood, 1994 District Vice President
Lori Gatewood-Murphy
Beverly Gellinger
Jeneva W. Gibson, 1972 National Secretary-Treasurer
Linda Gibson
Janet Given
Nita Gooch
Wanda Gooch
Mary Gordon
Lois Gowler
Carol Gunn
Donna Gustafson
Ethelyn Hall
Karen Hamilton
Christine Haner
Queen Hardin
Patricia Harding, 1975 Top Ten Business Woman of ABWA
Sue Harper
Betty Harris
Debbie Harvil
Sharen Hausmann
Jo Ann Hayes
Hallie M. Head
Peggy Hehr
Pat Helt
Liz Henshaw, 1989 National President, 1988 National Vice President, 1987 District Vice President
Janae Herman
Jana High
Shirley Hoffman
Sue C. Hopper
Judy Howe
Flo Hughes
Margaret B. Hughes
Nancy Hughston, 1992 Top Ten Business Woman of ABWA
Dorothy Huston
Evalyn K. S. Inn, 1976 Top Ten Business Woman of ABWA
Julia Jackson
Nina Fields Jackson
Beverly Jenkins
Mary Lou Jessup, 1977 Top Ten Business Woman of ABWA
Mildred D. Johnson

Margaret Keenan-Denniston
Mary Louise Kennedy
Augusta Kilcrease
Mary C. Knott, 1974 Top Ten Business Woman of ABWA
Myrleen Knott, 1992 National Secretary-Treasurer, 1991 District Vice President
Edith L. Kralik
Criss Kramer
Mary Kristensen
Fran Kudray
Carla S. Lallatin, 1978 Top Ten Business Woman of ABWA
Sue Lane
Mary Lee
Ruth Granley Locke
Connie Loesch-Cargin, 1989 Top Ten Business Woman of ABWA
Yvonne Long
Opal Lucas-Williams, 1968 National President, 1967 National Vice President, 1966 District Vice President
Nancy O. Lundy
Karen Maihofer
Gladys Makerewich, 1961 National Secretary-Treasurer
Adele Mariani
Gail Marsh
Judith A. Martin
Judy K. Martin
Lorrie Martin
Pam Martin, 1995 District Vice President
Melanie Mayberry
Marilyn McCauley, 1990 Top Ten Business Woman of ABWA, 1981 District Vice President
Carol L. McDonald, 1990 Top Ten Business Woman of ABWA
Mary Ann McElroy
Ruth McKamey, 1971 National President, 1970 National Vice President, 1969 District Vice President
Patti L. McLaughlin
Sharon Menne
Cindy A. Mims
Mary Lou Minton
Joleen Mitchell
Ellen M. Moore
Patricia L. Morse
Margaret-Haley S. Moya

Contributors

Caroline Moyer
Martha Murray
Wendy S. Myers, Editor in Chief,
  Women in Business®
Shirley Newman
Emogene Nichols
Jane M. Nichols
Lynne H. Nixon
Jessie Norton
Karen Paben
Karen M. Panko, 1996 Top
  Ten Business Woman
  of ABWA
Marilyn Pedersen, 1994 District
  Vice President
Janis C. Peterson
Barbara Pevoto, 1996 Top
  Ten Business Woman
  of ABWA
Bernice M. Piwowarczyk
Gina L. Plummer
Nelda Porter
Pam Powers
Phyllis Preston
Annie Price
Janet M. Priewe
Carol Lee Prosser
Sandy Reed
Janet Reinhart
Dora Mae Reither
Zaharo Dolores Revelos
Lois Revenaugh, 1995 District
  Vice President
Audrey L. Richardson
Jacqueline A. Roddy
Carolyn E. Rogers
Linda Rollings
Shirley L. Romberger
Sara Root
Maxine Budde Ross
Barbara H. Rowe
Mary Ann Rushton
Wanda M. Rutherford
Alisa C. Salmons, Intern,
  Women in Business®
Katheleen D. Sanford, 1995
  District Vice President, 1994
  American Business Woman
  of ABWA
Lillian Sharp
Joan Simmons
Mary Smith
Carole J. Smock
Barbara Snyderman

Louise Spicer, 1992 National
  President, 1991 National
  Vice President, 1990 District
  Vice President
Marilyn S. Stallard
Sandra Stanfield
Carol Stearns
Barbara Stephens
Dimple Stephens
Susan Stout
Joanne Streiffert
B. Joan Suddarth, 1980 National
  President, 1979 Top Ten
  Business Woman of ABWA, 1979
  National Vice President, 1978
  District Vice President
Pam Sultzman
Marilyn Swenson
Leslie J. Taylor, Intern,
  Women in Business®
Jeannie Teasley
Caroline Thomas
Linda Todd
Shari Todd
Cora Mae Trent
Beverly A. Trimble, 1992 District
  Vice President
Pat Trusley, In memory of
Kathryn A. Van Such, 1994 Top Ten
  Business Woman of ABWA, 1990
  National Secretary-Treasurer,
  1989 District Vice President
Constance M. Rhoad Via
Sharon Walker
Garnet Wall
Diane Walters, 1994 Top Ten
  Business Woman of ABWA
Erma L. Walters
Joan Warlick
Donna Rita Weeks
Rita Mary Weir
Maureen Welling
Kathy Wells
Linda Wentz
Bettie White
Meriam White
Susan E. Widelko
Jane Wilkin
Gladys Williams
Laura Wolf
Rilla Woodruff
Lila Wright
Sheila Zia-Gerschler

▲ Unsalted air-popped popcorn gets only 5% of its calories from fat and has only a trace of sodium. Even microwave popcorn (check labels) may derive as few as 9% of its calories from fat and have as few as 8 milligrams of sodium in a 3-cup serving.

▲ Vary dips by substituting yogurt for sour cream or Neufchâtel cheese for cream cheese. Cottage cheese processed in a blender until smooth and creamy can be substituted for either sour cream or yogurt to reduce calories.

▲ A mixture of equal parts of nonfat yogurt and ricotta cheese blended in a food processor makes a good base for dips.

▲ Replace the milk in your pancake recipe with club soda for the lightest pancakes ever. This batter must be used at once, however, as the soda goes flat.

▲ Make low-fat yogurt cheese by placing 1 pint of plain yogurt in a bowl or colander lined with a double thickness of cheesecloth or paper towels. Let drain in the refrigerator for 24 hours. Use as a spread on muffins, bagels, crackers and breads. It is lower in fat and calories than cream cheese, butter or margarine and can be mixed with your favorite fruit, vegetables or seasonings.

▲ It is better for your heart if you spread jelly on your bread rather than butter. Jelly has sugar, but no fat; butter is 99% fat.

▲ To reduce fat, cholesterol and calories in your favorite cake mix, substitute an equal amount of applesauce for the oil called for in the mix. For the average cake mix, you will reduce the calories by half and the fat by more than three quarters.

▲ Forget the frosting. You can make a quick and easy finish for a cake by placing a paper doily on the top and sprinkling it lightly with confectioners' sugar. Lift the doily carefully from the cake.

▲ Bake guilt-free brownies by replacing the 1/2 cup oil and 2 eggs called for in the brownie mix with 1/2 cup nonfat yogurt and about 4 tablespoons of unsweetened applesauce.

▲ A low-calorie substitute for sour cream is 1 cup low-fat cottage cheese mixed with a teaspoon of vinegar and 1/4 cup skim milk. Process the mixture in a blender or food processor until smooth.

▲ Use dairy products made from skim or low-fat milk to reduce fat and calories in the diet. Evaporated skim milk can be substituted for cream in many recipes.

▲ Use yogurt in your favorite recipes in place of other diary products in order to reduce fat. You can use it as a cooking ingredient if you protect against curdling and separating by blending 2 tablespoons flour or 1 tablespoon cornstarch into each cup of yogurt.

Saving Fat and Calories

▲ To reduce calories in your favorite trifle recipe, use sliced angel food cake sprinkled with unsweetened fruit juice instead of pound cake and sherry.

▲ Take advantage of the current popularity of fancy and flavored coffees and serve them instead of dessert. Add a selection of toppings such as shaved chocolate, grated orange rind, cinnamon sticks or grated nutmeg.

▲ Save calories by topping desserts with lightly sweetened nonfat sour cream instead of whipped cream.

▲ For your next quiche, line the pie plate with mashed cooked beans or cooked rice or noodles for a delicious, lower-fat alternative to pastry.

▲ If your family shies away from vegetables, purée vegetables such as zucchini and carrots and add them to a favorite spaghetti sauce. With a thick rich texture, meat will not be missed.

▲ Baked or roasted chicken has fewer calories than stewed chicken. Remove the skin to further reduce calories.

▲ Use lemon or vanilla yogurt as the dressing for fruit salads or coleslaw to reduce calories and cholesterol and add zing.

▲ For a tasty low-fat substitution, skip the mayonnaise and spread sandwiches with a mixure of nonfat yogurt, fresh horseradish and chopped chives.

▲ To reduce calories and cholesterol in pasta dishes, substitute chicken broth with 1 tablespoon of cream for the whole cream used to thicken sauces.

▲ A leaf of lettuce dropped into the soup will absorb the grease from the top of the soup. Discard the leaf immediately.

▲ Instead of sautéing vegetables in butter, margarine or oil, "sweat" them in a covered heavy saucepan over very low heat for 10 minutes or longer.

▲ Save time by purchasing cheeses already shredded, but save fat by using the finely shredded cheeses. It will require less to achieve satisfying color and flavor results.

Index

APPETIZERS. *See also* Dips; Snacks;
    Soups, Cold; Spreads
    Almond Ham Roll-Ups, 19
    Aunt Sherry's Hot Dogs, 28
    Cheese and Bacon Rolls, 20
    Crabbettes, 22
    Crab-Mushroom Canapés, 23
    Green Chile Cocktail Fingers, 24
    Hot Curried Cheese Appetizers, 21
    Pita Wedges, 25
    Pizza Burgers, 26
    Quick Nachos, 24
    Stuffed Hot Dogs, 28
    Stuffed Mushrooms, 27
    Taco Chicken Nuggets, 117
    Zucchini Balls, 27

BEEF. *See also* Ground Beef; Veal
    Beef Stew, 69
    Cheesy Beef Sandwiches, 70
    Chuck Roast and Potatoes, 67
    Grilled Beef Bundles, 71
    Holiday Roast, 67
    Hot Chipped Beef Dip, 12
    Quick Chimichangas, 71
    Savory Pepper Steak, 68
    Texas Corn Chip Pie, 88

BEVERAGES, COLD
    Champagne Sparkler, 31
    Cranberry Cordial, 32
    Fresh Peach Daiquiri, 32
    Guilt-Free Holiday Eggnog, 34
    Racy Red Punch, 33
    White Wine Sangria, 33
    Wine Sherbet, 34
    Yummy Irish Cream, 31

BEVERAGES, HOT
    Fireside Coffee, 30
    Spiced Tea, 30

BREADS
    Beer Bread, 189
    Corn Bread Cake, 189
    Fried Biscuits, 187
    Sour Cream Coffee Cake, 188
    Spoon Rolls, 190

BROCCOLI
    Baked Broccoli and Tuna, 140
    Broccoli Casserole, 163
    Broccoli Salad, 57
    Hominy Harmony, 182
    Impossible Chicken and Broccoli
        Pie, 126

Pasta con Broccoli, 154

CAKES
    Apple Cake, 213
    Applesauce Carrot Cake, 214
    Country Shortcake, 222
    Greek Cake, 218
    Hummingbird Cake, 219
    Lemonade Cake, 220
    Pineapple Torte, 221
    Sour Cream Coffee Cake, 188

CAKES, CHOCOLATE
    California Earthquake, 215
    Indian Chocolate Cake, 216
    Texas Devil Cake, 217

CANDY
    Buckeyes, 202
    Microwave Fudge, 202

CHICKEN. *See also* Turkey
    Best-Choice-Ever Baked Chicken
        Supreme, 109
    Buttermilk-Pecan Chicken, 111
    Chicken Aloha, 110
    Chicken and Linguini
        Stir-Fry, 124
    Chicken Breasts Diane, 112
    Chicken Breasts Oriental, 112
    Chicken Breasts Wellington, 113
    Chicken Cacciatore, 106
    Chicken Can-Can, 115
    Chicken Pizzaioli, 105
    Chicken Roll-Ups, 129
    Chicken Strata, 128
    Creamy Baked Chicken
        Breasts, 114
    Green Enchilada and Chicken
        Casserole, 125
    Impossible Chicken and Broccoli
        Pie, 126
    Leftover Chicken Pie, 127
    Microwave Chicken Breasts
        Cacciatore, 107
    Microwave Honey-Glazed
        Chicken, 117
    Orange Chicken, 116
    Oven Chicken and Linguini, 108
    Phony Abalone, 120
    Quick Chicken and Macaroni with
        Vegetables, 122
    Raspberry Chicken, 119
    Reuben Chicken, 121
    Rosemary Chicken, 120
    Santa Fe Chicken for One, 118

Index

Shake and Bake for Chicken, 130
Shrimp and Chicken Kabobs, 146
Sunshine Barbecued Chicken, 104
Taco Chicken Nuggets, 117
Thai Chicken Salad, 51
Tomato Lover's Chicken, 123
Tortilla Soup, 39

CHILI
15-Minute Chili, 130
Quick Chili, 37

COOKIES
Cake Mix Cookies, 203
Chocolate Raspberry Truffle
    Cookies, 205
408-Calorie Cookies, 204
Quick Pudding Cookies, 207
Texas Pecan Tassies, 208
Whole Grain Snack Cookies, 210

COOKIES, BAR
Chew Bread, 203
Lemon Angel Bars, 206
O'Henry Bars, 206
Pumpkin Cheesecake Bars, 209

CRAB MEAT
Crabbettes, 22
Crab Cakes, 144
Crab Meat Mousse, 16
Crab-Mushroom Canapés, 23
Sherried Hot Crab Meat, 14

DESSERTS. *See also* Cakes; Candy;
    Cookies; Pies; Salads, Dessert
Apricot Ice, 193
Chocopea Dip, 195
Easy Peach Cobbler, 196
Fat-Free Trifle, 199
Harvest Pumpkin Dessert, 197
Peach Crisp, 195
Pumpkin Ice Cream Dessert, 198
Shari's Cheesecake, 194
Strawberry Angel Food Delight, 200
Sugar-Free Banana Ice Cream, 193

DIPS
Artichoke Dip, 11
Chocopea Dip, 195
Clam Dip in Bread, 13
Hot Chipped Beef Dip, 12
Sherried Hot Crab Meat, 14
Shrimp Dip, 14
Spring Garden Dip, 11
Taco Dip, 15

EGG DISHES
Anytime Super Quiche, 148
Breakfast Tacos, 149
Cheesy Bacon and Egg Pie, 151
Chiles Rellenos Casserole, 152
Creamed Eggs on Toast, 152
Easy Eggs Benedict, 149
Garden Eggs, 150
Louisiana Puddin', 185
Pasta Frittata, 155

FISH. *See also* Tuna
Halibut and Sour Cream Bake, 135
Sweet Mustard-Sauced Fish, 134
Turbot with Grapefruit Butter, 136

FROSTINGS
Confectioners' Sugar Icing, 217
Cream Cheese Frosting, 218

GROUND BEEF
ABWA's Famous Beefburgers, 73
All-Purpose Coney Island Sauce, 72
Arizona Hash, 88
Beef and Rice Skillet Dinner, 76
Berry's Mexican Delight, 83
Cheeseburger Pie, 89
Chow Mein Casserole, 77
Enchilada Casserole, 82
Hamburgers on the Grill, 72
Mexican Jumbo, 86
Mexican-Style Spaghetti, 87
Microwave Lasagna, 80
Microwave Mexican Manicotti, 81
Mock Filet Mignon, 73
Mom's Goulash, 78
Olé Casserole, 84
Pizza Burgers, 26
Quick Chili, 37
Quick Nachos, 24
Quick Salisbury Steak, 74
Shepherd's Pie, 90
Spaghetti Lasagna, 79
Spaghetti Pie, 91
Sweet-and-Sour Ground Beef, 75
Taco Dip, 15
Taco Salad, 51
Tex-Mex Bake, 85
Upside-Down Pizza, 92
Wednesday-Night Special, 78

HAM
Almond Ham Roll-Ups, 19
Breakfast Tacos, 149
Cheesy Potato Soup, 38
Easy Eggs Benedict, 149

Index

Garden Eggs, 150
Microwave Macaroni and Ham
    Dish, 158

HOT DOGS
    Aunt Sherry's Hot Dogs, 28
    Stuffed Hot Dogs, 28

MACARONI
    Baked Macaroni and Cheese, 158
    Macaroni Relleno, 159
    Microwave Macaroni and Ham
        Dish, 158
    Quick Chicken and Macaroni with
        Vegetables, 122
    Yum-Yum Macaroni Salad, 53

MEATLESS MAIN DISHES
    Baked Macaroni and Cheese, 158
    Deli Veggie Sandwiches, 153
    Italian Veggie Pasta, 156
    Lemon Pasta, 157
    Macaroni Relleno, 159
    Pasta con Broccoli, 154
    Pasta Frittata, 155
    Tomato Garlic Pasta, 160

PASTA. *See also* Macaroni; Salads, Pasta
    Chicken and Linguini Stir-Fry, 124
    Garlic Oil for Pasta, 160
    Italian Veggie Pasta, 156
    Lemon Pasta, 157
    Mexican-Style Spaghetti, 87
    Microwave Lasagna, 80
    Oven Chicken and Linguini, 108
    Pasta con Broccoli, 154
    Pasta Frittata, 155
    Spaghetti Lasagna, 79
    Tomato Garlic Pasta, 160
    Tuna Noodle Casserole, 143
    Tuna Pasta Sauce, 142

PIES
    Impossible Coconut Pie, 224
    Minnie-Jean's Pecan Pie, 226
    Pecan Pie, 227
    Pumpkin Pie, 228
    Sweet Potato Pie, 229
    Toasty Coconut Pie, 225

PORK. *See also* Ham; Sausage
    Chinese Pork Pita Sandwiches, 98
    Chow Mein, 99
    City "Chicken," 101
    Easy Pork Chops with Stuffing, 96
    Grilled Butterflied Pork Chops, 94

On-a-Budget Pork Chops, 95
    Oriental Grilled Pork Chops, 95
    Peach-Glazed Pork Chops, 96
    Pork Chop Casserole, 93
    Quick-to-Fix Pork Chops and
        Apples, 97

POTATO. *See also* Sweet Potato
    Baked Potatoes and Toppings, 166
    Hash Brown Potato Bake, 169
    Potato Casserole Supreme, 168
    Quick Scalloped Potatoes, 167
    Vegetable Casserole, 171

RICE
    French Rice, 183
    Green Rice Casserole, 184
    Louisiana Puddin', 185
    Rice Casserole, 183

SALADS, DESSERT
    Apple Snicker Salad, 49
    Pretzel Salad, 49

SALADS, FRUIT
    Apple Snicker Salad, 49
    Cranberry Salad, 44
    Easy Fruit Salad, 45
    Easy Fruity Salad, 48
    Festive Fruit Salad, 45
    Finger Gelatin, 44
    Frozen Fruit Salad, 46
    Frozen Strawberry Salad, 50
    Low-Fat Frozen Fruit
        Salad, 47
    Orange Light Delight, 48
    Pretzel Salad, 49

SALADS, MAIN DISH
    Bean and Tuna Salad, 50
    Taco Salad, 51
    Thai Chicken Salad, 51

SALADS, PASTA
    Easy Linguini Salad, 52
    Pasta Salad, 54
    Yum-Yum Macaroni Salad, 53
    Zesty Pasta Salad, 55

SALADS, VEGETABLE
    Broccoli Salad, 57
    Cauliflower Salad, 59
    Easy Caesar Salad, 60
    Greek Salad, 61
    Green and White Salad, 59
    Marinated Bean Salad, 56

Index

Napa Salad, 58
Potato Salad, 63
Radicchio and Onion Salad, 63
Sweet Sauerkraut Salad, 64
Tropical Salad with Papaya Seed
    Dressing, 62

SANDWICHES
ABWA's Famous Beefburgers, 73
Cheesy Beef Sandwiches, 70
Chinese Pork Pita Sandwiches, 98
Deli Veggie Sandwiches, 153
Open-Face Tuna Sandwiches, 138
Tunaburgers, 137

SAUCES
Remoulade Sauce, 144

SAUSAGE
Stromboli, 100

SEAFOOD. *See also* Crab Meat; Fish
Basic Shrimp Creole, 145
Betty's Oven Seafood Spread, 17
Clam Dip in Bread, 13
Salmon Spread, 16
Shrimp and Chicken Kabobs, 146
Shrimp Dip, 14
Slang Jang, 42

SIDE DISHES. *See also* Rice
Best-Ever Microwave Pickles, 186
Dumplings, 181
Hominy Harmony, 182
Robert's Dressing, 180

SNACKS
Finger Gelatin, 44
Oyster Cracker Snacks, 25
Whole Grain Snack Cookies, 210

SOUPS. *See also* Chili
Cheesy Potato Soup, 38
Hodgepodge, 37
Paradise Soup, 38
Tortilla Soup, 39

SOUPS, COLD
Chilled Sweet Pepper Soup, 41
Cucumber Soup, 40
Gazpacho, 40
Slang Jang, 42
Sweet Strawberry Soup, 42

SPREADS
Betty's Oven Seafood Spread, 17

Crab Meat Mousse, 16
Garden Greek Appetizer, 20
Jezebel, 18
Roasted Garlic, 18
Salmon Spread, 16

SQUASH. *See also* Zucchini
Easy Cheesy Squash Casserole, 170
Squash or Zucchini on-the-Run, 171
Vegetable Casserole, 171

SWEET POTATO
Sweet Potato Casserole, 172
Sweet Potatoes au Gratin, 173
Sweet Potato Pie, 229

TUNA
Baked Broccoli and Tuna, 140
Bean and Tuna Salad, 50
Healthy Quickie, 143
Impossible Tuna Pie, 141
Open-Face Tuna Sandwiches, 138
Tunaburgers, 137
Tuna Casserole, 139
Tuna Noodle Casserole, 143
Tuna Pasta Sauce, 142

TURKEY
15-Minute Chili, 130
Grilled Turkey Breast, 131
Hodgepodge, 37
Presto Potpies, 132
Turkey Sautéed with Pears and
    Pecans, 131

VEAL
City "Chicken," 101
Veal Scallopini with Marsala, 102

VEGETABLES. *See also* Broccoli;
    Potato; Salads, Vegetable;
    Squash; Sweet Potato; Zucchini
Baked Corn Casserole, 164
Cheese-Scalloped Onions, 165
Scalloped Tomatoes, 174
Spinach Casserole, 169
Stir-Fry Cabbage, 163

ZUCCHINI
Fresh Zucchini Bake, 176
Squash or Zucchini on-the-Run, 171
Zucchini Balls, 27
Zucchini Boats, 178
Zucchini Casserole, 175
Zucchini Patties, 177

The Working Woman's Quick Cookbook

Order Form

Please send me _____ copies of *The Working Woman's Quick Cookbook* at $15.95 per book, which includes shipping and handling charges.

Name _____

Address _____

City _____ State _____ ZIP _____

Daytime Phone (_____) _____
In case we have questions about your order.

Amount Enclosed $ _____

❑ Check payable to ABWA
❑ MasterCard   ❑ Visa

Account No. _____ Expires_____

Signature _____
            (required for charges)

❑ Please send me information about joining the American Business Women's Association.

Send to:
The Working Woman's Quick Cookbook
American Business Women's Association
9100 Ward Parkway
P.O. Box 8728
Kansas City, MO 64114-0728
(816) 361-6621

Or fax your credit-card order to (816) 361-4991

AMERICAN BUSINESS WOMEN'S ASSOCIATION